Inside Football

Inside Football

Fundamentals, Strategy, and Tactics for Winning

George Allen

with Don Weiskopf

Allyn and Bacon, Inc.
Boston

Library of Congress Catalog Card Number: 70-102753

Cover photograph by Fred Kaplan

Printed in the United States of America

To my loving wife, ETTY, who has provided me
with appreciation in victory and support in defeat.

Without her support, consideration, and sacrifice,
success would have been impossible.

Contents

Foreword

George Allen, the man who I personally believe is the country's best qualified authority in building winning football teams, has put a great deal of work into this book. One must look at his overall career, not just his recent successes with the Rams, to begin to appreciate his command of the game.

INSIDE FOOTBALL represents a remarkable achievement in the comprehensive scope of its coverage—nothing is neglected. Chapter after chapter is devoted to every aspect of the fundamentals, strategy and tactics used by teams that are consistent in their winning records. Above all, it is a book about the demanding little details as well as the basics which go into organizing football players into a smooth working machine.

With its almost six hundred photographs, the book is particularly valuable to the high school coach, athlete and serious football fan, as well as college and professional coaches. By stressing fundamentals and the correct execution of football strategy, George Allen is putting improved football performance within reach of the team with average or even less than average player material. Moreover, his insights into player psychology and the techniques he has used to build positive attitudes among his teams is provided for the first time in book form.

In many instances, the sequences of photos presented in the book follow the flow of the action rather than a set left-to-right or top-to-bottom presentation. In teaching a football skill pattern, the athlete must be taught to visualize the complete movement pattern necessary for a particular play. By having each sequence series flow in "the direction of the play," the viewer can analyze the skill with vivid clarity.

Indeed, these sequence patterns illustrate the skill as it actually is. The pictures flow up the page when the player moves upfield away from the camera, while in the series that run down the page, the player is shown coming downfield toward the camera. And this brings us back to George Allen, the man. From his job as defensive coach for the Chicago Bears to his present position, George Allen's career has been capped with ever increasing success. In just a few short years, he has developed one of the steadiest offensive units and most devastating defensive teams in the game. He has built the Rams into one of the most respected teams in the NFL and brought them from years of second division finishes up into the thick of the championship fight.

A great planner and organizer, he loves organization and pre-planning. He is an extremely sensitive man who will accept nothing but the best. One of football's most dedicated coaches, George works 14 to 18 hours a day on football. George Allen is an alumnus of Alma College, Marquette University (where he played football in 1944) and the University of Michigan, where he handled some Junior Varsity coaching duties under Fritz Crisler.

George began his Pro coaching career with the Rams in 1957 after nine years of highly successful college coaching at Morningside (Iowa) and Whittier (California). Following the 1957 season, Allen left the Rams and joined the staff of the Chicago Bears as a defensive specialist under the great George Halas. Quickly, he became one of Halas' most valued assistants.

With the Bears, Allen was instrumental in molding some of the strongest defensive units in the National Football League. It was Allen who built the Bears' awesome defensive unit that led the league in 10 of 18 defensive categories, and finished second in seven others. His defensive unit devastated the highly-touted passing attack of Y.A. Tittle and the New York Giants in the 1963 NFL Championship game.

The spectacular rise of the Los Angeles Rams from also-ran to a title contender in only two years under Allen's tutelage earned George the coveted NFL "Coach of the Year" award by *The Sporting News.* When Rams' owner Daniel F. Reeves signed him in 1966, the Rams' record over the previous seven years was 65 defeats, 25 wins and four ties. Not since 1958 had they had a winning season or finished better than fifth. Under Allen in 1966, they moved up to third place with an 8–6–0 record. The following year, the Rams completed an 11–1–2 season and captured the Coastal Division Championship by beating the Green Bay Packers and the Baltimore Colts on consecutive weekends. In 1968, the Rams' record of 10–3–1, although impressive, could not overtake the Colts in a race that went down to the wire.

Although the Rams failed to make the play-offs, George again was selected to coach the West team in the annual Pro Bowl game in Los Angeles. The West team, paced by many of the Rams, defeated the East 10–7 in a rain-soaked defensive struggle in the Coliseum. Remarkably enough, Coach Allen received the game ball. In making the presentation, veteran Green Bay tackle, Forrest Gregg said: "Thirty-five players wanted this win, but one man wanted it more than the rest of us—George Allen."

The 1969 edition of the Rams proved to be another successful year in the brilliant career of Coach George Allen. In winning their first 11 league games, the Rams made a runaway of the Coastal Division race.

From the attendance standpoint, the Rams have established themselves as one of pro football's biggest gate attractions. They have already set an NFL record for the highest season attendance total, drawing 1,230,059 fans through the turnstiles in 22 games.

A soft-spoken, articulate man, Allen believes that his players are to be treated as men. His basic philosophy is that each of his players has the maturity and willingness to achieve the goals that he has set for him. And he sets high goals, both offensively and defensively.

One of the greatest competitors I have ever known, George believes there is only one thing to do and that is to win. He must win. However, if he loses, he does not blame anybody but himself. He does not stop there, but he sets out to do something about it. He prepares a new program, designed to bring victory next time.

George uses a simple, basic approach in building outstanding football teams. Defensive enthusiasm is the trademark of the clubs George coaches. He believes in fundamentals, physical conditioning and purposeful drilling.

In addition to his brisk year-round coaching schedule, George has had time to author five other books on football. They are *Encyclopedia of Football Drills, Complete Book of Winning Football Drills, How to Train a Quarterback, How to Scout Football* and *Pass Defense Drills.*

> BLANTON COLLIER
> Head Coach, Cleveland Browns

Acknowledgments

To the members of my coaching staff: Ted Marchibroda, Ray Prochaska, Howard Schnellenberger, Marion Campbell, Joe Sullivan, and Tom Catlin, for the valuable contributions they made in the writing of the book.

To my players on the Los Angeles Rams for their excellent demonstrations of the basic techniques of the game and their candid commentary on how they play their positions.

To Fritz Crisler of the University of Michigan and George S. Halas, owner and former head coach of the Chicago Bears, with whom I had a long association, and Daniel F. Reeves, President of the Los Angeles Rams.

To Dean Miller for his demonstrations of Exer-genie exercises which appear in sequence form in the chapter on Conditioning.

To John Griffith, publisher of Athletic Journal, for the use of his sequence-speed camera, and to contributing photographers Fred Kaplan and Vic Stein. Some of the game action photographs used in this book are reproduced by courtesy of the Addison-Wesley Publishing Company, *The Los Angeles Herald Examiner, The Los Angeles Times,* Wide World Photos, United Press International, and the Associated Press.

To Mrs. Annegrete Weiskopf, who typed the manuscript, and Melvin Davis, who printed many of the photos.

To the many coaches across the nation who made significant contributions to the chapter "High School and College Organization", particularly Vic Rowen, San Francisco State; John Ralston, Stanford University; and Ray Schultz, American River College.

And to my good friend Don Weiskopf of Sacramento for his able assistance in planning, writing, and editing this publication. Don is the author of many books and articles on sports and was responsible for taking the majority of the photos in this text.

Inside Football

The Quarterback

1

Fig. 1-1. (See reverse). The T-formation quarterback is the key man in today's pro-ball formations. He has the task of coordinating and directing the offense.

1

The T-formation quarterback is the key man in today's wide-open, pro-style formations. He has to be proficient at many things. He must be a passer, a general and, on occasion, a runner. Moreover, he has to be a clever ball handler, an expert faker, and he has the task of coordinating and directing the offense.

No other position in sports demands such rigid conformity to the basic fundamentals. From Pop Warner to Pro, the better he learns the fundamentals, the better the quarterback will perform. Therefore, a coach spends more time with his quarterback and his back-up man than he does with any of the other positions.

High school, as well as college coaches, are adopting professional tactics, and the end result has been a high scoring brand of football, filled with plenty of excitement and upsets. Tight formations are rarely seen anymore because every team is forcing the defenses to play man-for-man. The defensive backs have been cracking open many games with their interceptions and long returns. Improved defenses, combining great size with mobility, have placed increasing pressure on the quarterback.

An intelligent, hard working, effective quarterback is the greatest single asset that a football team can have. It is his responsibility to lead and direct his team toward the goal line (Fig. 1-1). This calls for the proper selection of plays, which demands a sound understanding of offensive football and—above all—defensive football. The signal caller must have the ability to detect defensive weaknesses and take advantage of what the opposition is doing.

Qualifications

First of all, the quarterback has to be a passer. He must be able to make long and short passes accurately and with a minimum of arm action. Some coaches place more stress on the running ability of the quarterback, believing it is easier to teach a boy how to pass a football than it is to teach him how to run.

I like a quarterback who can run just enough to keep the defense honest. In recent years, the quarterback's ability to run has gained more prominence. The very

A   B   C

Fig. 1-2. THE COMPLETE QUARTERBACK. The quarterback is a real asset to a ball club if he can pass well, run, and be a good ball handler. (Roman Gabriel and Milt Plum, center)

An intelligent, hard working, effective quarterback is the greatest single asset that a football team can have.

popular run-pass option play has been a prime factor in the success of many of the top collegiate elevens. I don't think a team can win with a quarterback who cannot be mobile to some degree.

The quarterback should have good size. The tall quarterback has a tremendous advantage, for example, a boy like Gabriel who is 6'4''. Roman is an example of the new dimensions for pro quarterbacks. He is able to see more things that take place, and he is much stronger than the other quarterbacks in the league. He's strong enough to break tackles behind the line,

and he's able to throw off his back foot. And I believe a championship football team has to have a quarterback who is disciplined to stay in the pocket and throw (Fig. 1-3). Maybe someday somebody will win with a scrambler, but what happens, they end up with a 2nd down and 20 situation, and they can't pick that up. So, I like our quarterback to stay in the pocket and execute from there. For one thing, it gives the lineman more confidence. They know where he is going to be.

The quarterback must be quick with his hands. He must release the football

Fig. 1-3. THE QUARTERBACK HAS TO BE A PASSER. He must be disciplined to stay in the pocket and throw. Below, Roman Gabriel (18) squares away to let loose a pass to Jack Snow for an 11 yard completion. Forming the pocket around Gabe are center Ken Iman (50), shown blocking Dallas Cowboys Chuck Howley (54), and Ram halfback Les Josephson (34).

quickly on both short and deep passes. Quick and sure hands are also used to advantage in handing off or faking to the remaining backs in the backfield.

But right along with his physical attributes, the quarterback has to be a strong leader. He should act the part. If he has confidence in himself, his teammates will very likely take their cue from him. For the signal caller to be a leader, it helps to be a high caliber individual, with good character.

One other quality that a top quarterback must possess is toughness. To be

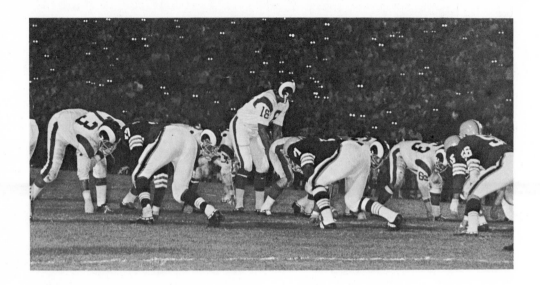

Fig. 1-4. DIRECTING THE ATTACK. The quarterback must be a leader. Roman Gabriel, above, exemplifies the feeling of confidence as he barks out the signals loud and clear.

successful, he has to be tough. He should be able to take some physical punishment, since he is going to get knocked down often.

I like to have a quarterback who is dedicated, because a coach lives or dies with his quarterback. The two have to get along and understand each other. And if they don't, their team is not going to win.

The quarterback must develop a mastery of mechanical details, such as the exchange from the center, various pivots, ball handling and fakes, and perfection of passing and running techniques. He must be able to keep the ball moving. Therefore, in order to lead his team effectively, he must learn to study the opposing defense. To call the correct play, he must use the knowledge of his team's strengths and the opponent's weaknesses. In short, he has to be a student of the game. He has to be able to work and study motion pictures, and if he doesn't, then he is not going to be prepared. *There is no easy way.*

The quarterback should have a clear, crisp voice. It gives a team needed self-confidence when the signal caller comes to the line of scrimmage and really belts out those signals—the letters, colors, and code words—loud and clear!

As he scans the defense, his head is up and his eyes shift from different players, up and down his own line. Besides checking things out, he can call his signals with the necessary authority.

By all means, the quarterback must establish a consistent method of calling cadence, so his team will become confident with it and will respond by firing off the line of scrimmage on that count.

The quarterback should follow the game

6

Fig. 1-5. AS HE SCANS the defense, the quarterback's head is up as his eyes shift from different players, up and down his own line.

plan. When he is getting in trouble with the game plan, because the defense is doing something differently, he will be able to read what the defense is doing to him and use that portion of the game plan to defeat a specific area of their defense.

"I try to think at least two plays ahead," said Gabriel, "when I call a first-down play. I've got to think what I'm going to come back to for a second and long situation, or second and short."

In choosing his plays intelligently, the quarterback must have a thorough knowledge of defensive football. Along with its strengths and weaknesses, he must know the theory of the defense. He must learn how to take advantage of defensive tactics, like audiblizing at the line of scrimmage to counter different alignments. This calls for a complete knowledge of the blocking assignments of every man on

every play, against every type of defense.

Therefore, the signal caller must be able to recognize quickly the various defensive formations which confront his team. So, the modern Pro quarterback must pass, run, and above all, *THINK!*

The correct play

The successful quarterback has the ability to call the correct play at the correct time. His offense simply will not work if the defense is ready for his play, no matter how well he can throw the ball or how well his backs carry the ball. It's very simple to evaluate a quarterback . . . the ability to "read" the defense and call an effective play is a prime asset of any outstanding quarterback at any level of competition. The test is whether there is one man on the squad who can do this, regardless of how he performs.

Fig. 1-6. The quarterback should follow the game plan. If the defense starts out to do something differently, he will anticipate and "read" what tactics the defense is attempting to execute.

On the right, Roman Gabriel goes to the sideline to discuss strategy with Coach Allen.

The successful quarterback has the ability to call the correct play at the correct time.

The weaknesses of the defense must be hit! Naturally, the specific game plan will change from one week to the next, according to the strengths and weaknesses of the opponents. Whether the quarterback passes or runs on a particular play may depend on the defense he "reads" when he approaches the line of scrimmage.

The signal caller must mix up his plays and use a varied attack. In setting up the defense for a long pass or run, the element of surprise is so very important. It takes generalship, as well as talent, to win a football game.

It is the quarterback's job to know what the situation is at all times. He should be busy thinking about what plays work against the team he is playing. He must consider what down it is, how much yardage he needs, what the score is, and the prevailing weather conditions.

Most of the NFL quarterbacks are "reactive thinkers." Their strategy is built on what they believe the opposition thinks he is going to do, and what they expect the defense to do. Therefore, they try to disrupt and confuse the defense.

A typical call

When the quarterback goes back in the huddle, he will call the formation. After the formation, he calls the ball carrier, then the whole number, the type of blocking, the style of play, and then he gives the snap count. For example, if he would call an end run, he would say: "Red right, 29 on 3."

Should the quarterback listen to suggestions from his teammates? Well, I think as time progresses, as the season progresses, the quarterback will get to know his players. While he has to listen to them, he has to be in control of the game, rather than let other individuals control him. Only sparingly would I recommend this type of information. For instance, his teammates can tell him what backs are coming up fast for the short passes, and what linemen can be trapped or "suckered."

Before he calls the signals, the quarterback must get into a comfortable position, so that he is able to take the ball properly. The play cannot start or be executed properly unless he gets the ball. First, we have the quarterback call the defense, by number; they might give an audible call or a dummy call, then a number following it. Then, they go into a normal cadence call. It might be, for example, "46–2–26, set, hut one, hut two."

Audibles

Modern football has been marked by shifting defenses, in which the offense is often faced with the possibility that the play it called in the huddle will run into a stone wall. Therefore, the signal caller tries to counter the defense and to come up with a better play. Thus, he goes to an audible. When they automatic, most of the teams will pass or go to quick hitting runs or trap-type plays. The quarterback should be positive that he has a good idea and

that it is going to work. He shouldn't be guessing.

Taking the Snap

The quarterback, as he takes the snap, must receive the ball comfortably and accurately. The placement of the hands is so vital in getting off a good snap. This is why the center and quarterback must spend a considerable amount of time perfecting the exchange (Fig. 1-7).

Stance

The quarterback's stance should be as natural as possible (Fig. 1-4). His feet should be spread approximately shoulder-width apart, with the toes parallel to the line. The weight is equally distributed over the feet with a little more weight on the toes (Fig. 1-9). The back is straight, the knees are bent slightly, and the hands are under the center to a point almost up to his wrist. There is a bend in the elbow so that he is able to give with the center's forward charge in the event that he has to.

We have our quarterbacks place their right foot forward a bit. When he takes the first step back with his right foot, it will bring him back a little farther, than if they were parallel. Some coaches like to employ the strictly parallel stance, though.

The right hand thrower puts his right hand under the buttocks of the center. The thumb of the other hand is placed in the groove of the right thumb; the thumbs are not parallel. This tends to keep the hands together more and also gives the

C   B   A

Fig. 1-7. TAKING THE SNAP   The quarterback and the center must spend a great amount of time perfecting the exchange so that it becomes automatic. (Roman Gabriel)

Fig. 1-8. POSITION OF HANDS. The quarterback places his right hand under the seat of the center. The fingers are spread slightly, the hands are in a relaxed position. (Roman Gabriel)

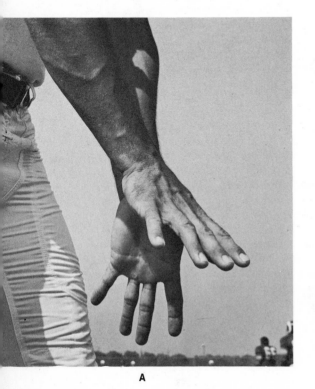

A   B

Fig. 1-9. STANCE. The feet should be spread approximately shoulder-width apart, with the toes parallel to the line. The back is straight, the knees are bent slightly. (Roman Gabriel)

quarterback a little more of the ball. He must make sure he exerts enough pressure to let the center feel his hands. This gives the center a target to shoot for. The fingers are spread slightly, the hands are in a relaxed position (Fig. 1-8). The type of cadence will determine the snap of the ball. A team might use a cadence in which the ball is snapped on the first, second, or third sound, for example, "hut one, hut two, hut three." In this case, the center might start the snap on the "hut" part of the count. The ball, as well as the line, are moving on the "hut" count.

Exchange

We have the center bring the ball up in a quarter snap or turn of the ball. We feel we are getting the ball as quickly as

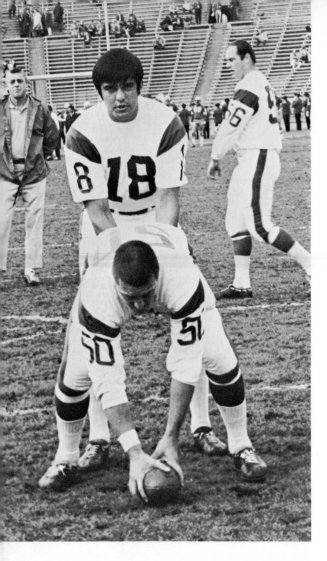

Fig. 1-10. The quarterback should be in a comfortable, relaxed position as he stands close behind the center. The weight is equally distributed over the feet, with a little more weight on the toes.

Notice that Roman Gabriel's right toe is slightly forward as he calls out the signals behind center Ken Iman.

we can from the center with this quarter turn. Also, by turning it a quarter, it allows the quarterback to get a good portion of the ball. If he allows the center to snap it naturally, the ball will make about a quarter of a turn, and it will fit perfectly into his hands (Fig. 1-11). It will hit his hand with the laces against his fingertips. It should hit his hand hard, with a good "pop." By coming straight up against his palm, if he dropped it, it would fall straight down.

Once he has control of the ball, the quarterback should bring it in to his stomach and work from his stomach, parallel to the ground. He keeps his hands on the ball at all times, prior to giving it to the back. The hand closest to the back should be removed, and the hand farthest away from the back should follow on through the direction the back is going.

The quarterback should get into the habit of riding with the center's motion. His hand has to go with him because he has to move forward and sometimes laterally as he snaps the ball. He doesn't want to be pulling away as the center moves forward.

A

B

C

D

Fig. 1-11. THE EXCHANGE. The center (Frank Marchlewski) brings the ball up in a quarter-snap or turn of the ball. The ball should hit the quarterback's hand hard, with a good "pop." In this series, Roman Gabriel pushes off hard with his left foot and moves to his right to complete the execution of a play action pass.

13

Pivots

In handing the ball off to a back, the quarterback must be able to execute the following pivots: Open pivot, inside, reverse, drop-back.

Open pivot

(Fig. 1-12). The open (or front) pivot is, perhaps, the most natural pivot and is easiest to teach and perform. We use it in conjunction with what we call the Dive series, when the halfback or fullback is hitting straight into the line. The quarterback comes down along the line of scrimmage and just hands the ball to the back hitting into the hole, very basic and fundamental, nothing to do but hand the ball off to him.

In Fig. 1-12, Gabriel is shown starting to lead-step toward Bass, the ball carrier, a short move, approximately one foot. His head immediately looks for the target. He has the ball in the area of his stomach, with his elbows in. Notice that his weight shifts to his right foot as he extends his arms and places the ball in the pocket. Observe that the distance is slightly less than an arm's length between the quarterback and the back. This helps our faking as well as the effectiveness of the hand-off and helps prevent fumbling caused by two players bumping into each other.

Inside pivot

(Fig. 1-13). This pivot is used on the inside power play and the fullback dive play, since it provides better deception. It enables the offense to have other backs lead the ball carrier.

In Fig. 1-13, Milt Plum, the quarterback, pivots on his left toe and swings his right leg through on the inside. He becomes balanced as his weight shifts to the left foot. The quarterback is now ready for the handoff. The right foot is parallel to the left.

The quarterback, by keeping his elbows in close to his body, will do a better job of concealing the ball. The ball carrier can do his part by providing a wide pocket. The close elbows are the secret to hiding the ball from the defense.

Reverse pivot

The reverse pivot is just the opposite from the open pivot. The quarterback, instead of opening up towards the back, opens up away from the back, more or less from the blind side. This is the pivot used basically for the power sweep or off-tackle play, where the quarterback flips the ball to a halfback (Fig. 1-15). The pivot also is effective for some fake off-tackle and roll-out passes.

The quarterback's hand will follow the center's movement forward, although the quarterback's body is starting backward. The weight shifts to the right toe, as the pivot is performed off that toe.

Next, the quarterback brings his elbows in to conceal the ball from the defense. The left leg follows naturally and ends up directly behind the right foot. The feet are approximately 18″ apart. The quarterback then naturally moves in the direction of the roll-out.

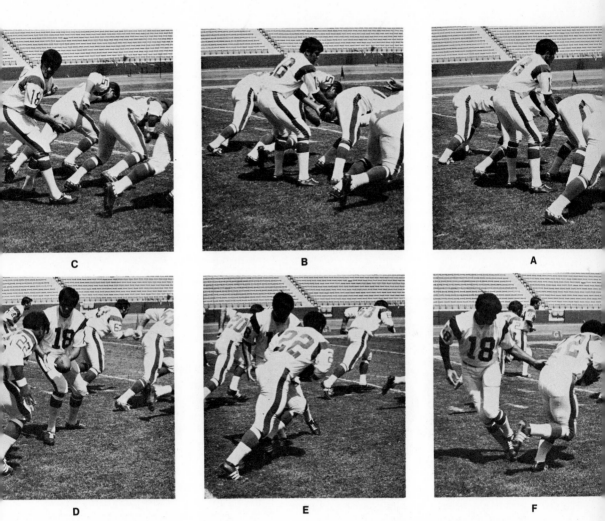

C   B   A

D   E   F

Fig. 1-12. OPEN PIVOT. This is a basic pivot in which the quarterback just hands the ball to the back hitting into the hole. We tell the quarterback to step first with the foot closest to the hole, parallel to the line of scrimmage. On the second step, he hands off the ball to the offensive back. The quarterback must open up towards the back, turn, and hand him the ball. For protection, he keeps both hands on the ball until he actually hands-off. (Roman Gabriel and Dick Bass)

C   B   A

D   E

Fig. 1-13. INSIDE PIVOT. The inside pivot provides better deception than the open pivot. Above, the quarterback pivots on his left toe and swings his right leg through on the inside. He becomes balanced as his weight shifts to the left foot. He then hands off to the running back. By keeping his elbows in close to his body, the quarterback can do a better job of hiding the ball. The runner does his part by providing a wide pocket. (Milt Plum and Willie Ellison)

Fig. 1-14. INSIDE PIVOT AFTER FAKE. Using an open pivot, quarterback Milt Plum moves to his right as if to hand-off to a runner. After making a good fake, he turns to his right and hands-off with his right hand to another back hitting off the left side of the offensive line. The initial fake must look as much like the hand-off as possible.

Fig. 1-15. REVERSE PIVOT AND PITCH-OUT. This pivot is just the opposite from the open pivot. Taking the snap, the quarterback's body moves forward on to his right toe. He then exe- cutes a reverse pivot off the left toe. Using both hands, he flips the ball to a halfback on the power sweep or off-tackle play. (Milt Plum)

Drop-back pivot

(Fig. 1-16). This action is used by most quarterbacks who throw from the Pro-type pocket. As he gets the snap, the quarterback lets his hands follow the center's move forward, but begins moving his body backward.

Perhaps the most important step is a hard push-off from the left foot. Actually, we tell our quarterbacks to spring off the left foot. The quarterback should sprint backward with his body facing that direction, but with his head turned toward the defense. Notice that his eyes never leave the defense, as the ball is brought up to the area of the shoulders with both hands holding it firmly.

Because of the time element, the quarterback moves backward as fast as possible in getting to the desired depth. We like our quarterbacks to take a little jump so he can get set off his back foot and be ready to deliver the pass. He must make sure he gets set on his back foot and is ready to step up into the pocket to throw the ball.

Hand-off

The first thing we tell the quarterback, upon receiving the ball from center, is to bring the ball into his stomach and work parallel with the line of scrimmage at all times. In handing off to the ball carrier he keeps both hands on the ball until he actually hands off. The responsibility of a good hand-off is primarily with the quarterback because the back must have his eyes on the hole in front of him (Fig. 1-18).

In Fig. 1-17, as Plum takes the ball from center, he immediately brings it close in to his body. His hands come quickly back toward his stomach, his elbows in close, his hands grasping the ball tightly.

The quarterback must always remember to keep his body between himself and the defender to conceal the play and protect the ball. As he moves with short, sliding steps, he should pick up the back and focus in on the target area he is going to hand it to.

He should place the ball into his pocket firmly, not necessarily hard. When he receives it, the back should have good control over it.

The moment that he places the ball in the pocket, the quarterback removes the hand closest to the ball carrier, as he follows through with the hand farthest away. After handing off, he must make sure he doesn't look at the ball carrier to tip off the play to where it is going.

If the hand-off is to the right, the quarterback gives with the left hand, his hand moving quickly from left to right into the stomach of the back.

There are a number of reasons for a fumble occurring on the hand-off. Occasionally, the quarterback won't work from his stomach. He may put the ball down a little too low, where it hits the runners knees. His legs are coming up, and they just kick it out of there. And sometimes, we find that the backs do not give the quarterback a proper target or pocket to place the ball into.

C   B   A

D   E   F

Fig. 1-16. DROP-BACK ACTION. As he receives the snap, the quarterback lets his hands follow the center's move forward, but he begins moving his body backward. The most important step is a hard push-off from the left foot. He sprints backward with his body facing in that direction. However, his head is turned toward the defense as he looks over his left shoulder. Meantime, the ball is brought up into throwing position. The quarterback must continually strive to improve his quickness in setting up. (Roman Gabriel)

C
D
B
A

Fig. 1-17. THE HAND-OFF. In handing off, the quarterback should keep both hands on the ball until he actually hands off. At this moment, he releases his hand closest to the back, then follows through with the remaining hand (right). The quarterback focuses in on the target area he intends to hand off. (Milt Plum and Willie Ellison)

Fig. 1-18. HAND-OFF. The running back receives the ball with the outside foot ahead of the inside foot. This gives a good pocket for the quarterback and helps prevent the possibility of a runner knocking the ball out of the quarterback's hands. The distance between the quarterback and the halfback is such that they are just brushing shoulders. (Tommy Mason and Roman Gabriel)

Faking

Faking plays an important part in a good hand-off and helps create more deception in the backfield (Fig. 1-19). The hand-off and fake to a running back is, perhaps, the most difficult skill for a quarterback to perfect. His chief concern is trying to fool the linebackers. He has to make the three linebackers think either pass or run.

We tell our quarterbacks to have actual contact with the back. For example, if he is faking to the fullback, we tell him to make sure that he is touching at least the stomach of the back and placing the ball there. The back tries to come in and fake like he is getting the ball and moving into the line.

Most faking should be done with both hands kept on the ball until the moment it is given to the back or pulled away and given to another back. Then the quarterback may employ a shoulder dip, keeping the ball tucked away and dipping with his shoulder as the faking back comes by.

The pivot man should put the ball in there and then take it out because at that instance a defensive lineman might have seen it go in. Then because he may have been obscured by an offensive lineman, he might not see the ball come out. So, the big thing here is making contact on any fake that he has.

A good fake at times can be done in dropping straight back, but it is a little harder when moving off to the side or a 45 degree angle. The quarterback should hide the ball even after the fake, in case he has to throw. In addition, the back to whom he is faking to also assumes a responsibility of faking and deceiving the opposition.

B

A

Fig. 1-19. FAKING. We like our quarterback to fake with both hands. He should place the ball in the back's stomach, and, then, if he is not the intended carrier, take it away again with both hands. (Milt Plum)

No quarterback can make a living if he doesn't have protection.

Fig. 1-20. SPRINT-OUT LEFT. As the quarterback starts his pivot, his left heel is off the ground, enabling the pivot to be executed quickly on the left toe. As he brings the ball into a throwing position, he starts to turn his shoulders square towards the target. He must push-off with his right foot as he steps to his left. We prefer him to reverse his feet and set quickly before throwing. (Roman Gabriel)

C

B

A

Running

All our Ram quarterbacks go through exactly the same running drills as our backs do. This running practice is designated to improve their running skill even though they are primarily throwers.

The roll-out pass is when the passer rolls out to the same side as the intended receiver with the idea of placing pressure on the defense. This maneuver forces the defender either to drop-back and cover the receiver or move up to rush the passer. The result is that one or the other is left open.

One of the biggest offensive threats in football is the quarterback who can smoothly execute the roll-out option run or pass. More than any other play, this one play pressures the defense. If the defender pressures him the quarterback must throw, usually on the run. If the opponent loosens up, the quarterback should run, quickly and deceptively. Speed is the key. How quickly can he get to the option run or pass area? Then he must execute this pivot in flawless fashion.

Roll-out right

At the snap, the quarterback's weight shifts from both feet to the right toe. He spins on the right toe and then springs off his right toe. This enables him to get away quickly. While he rolls-out he is bringing the ball up to the throwing position and keeps both hands on the ball until ready to throw. It is important that he keeps his eyes continuously on the defensive area to his right.

When the defense starts to exert pressure on him, he must prepare to throw the ball. We remind our quarterbacks to turn their shoulders square to the target. After cocking the ball, he is ready to throw, raising his throwing arm overhead and throwing with a direct over-the-head motion.

Roll-out left

This pivot and pass is very difficult for a right-handed quarterback. As the quarterback starts his pivot, his left heel is off the ground, enabling the pivot to be executed quickly on the left toe. As he rolls out to his left, his eyes are focused on the defensive man to his outside, and he starts to turn his shoulders square towards the target as he brings the ball into a throwing position.

The right-handed quarterback must throw with a sidearm motion when running to his left, which is a difficult maneuver. The elbow is straight out and the ball is held away from the body.

On the roll-out, we tell our quarterback to take off to an assigned depth, so that the proper blocking can take place up front. As he rolls out to this depth, he wants to key his defender, one way or the other. This is the way we use the option. Once he has keyed the defender, then he must make up his mind, either to throw the ball or run it.

The quarterback sneak

The sneak is a surprise maneuver employed by the quarterback. It is one of the safest ways of picking up a yard or so, especially if the quarterback is big and strong. With the offensive line wedging in toward the center, he can go straight ahead behind this wedge.

The quarterback draw

This play is nothing more than a typical draw play, with the quarterback doing the running. The quarterback goes back as if to pass, but instead of throwing, he moves forward, keying his blockers and runs into a lane opened up by his blockers, similar to a draw play executed by a fullback or a halfback.

Successful execution of the draw play demands a big, strong type of runner, one capable of breaking an arm tackle, or two. Most quarterbacks like to take the time to make a pump before starting forward. Bill Wade was effective on this type of play.

The bootleg

The bootleg play can be a powerful weapon for the quarterback who is a running threat. A big part of the success of a bootleg depends on the acting ability of the other backs. Therefore, we tell our backs to hit in there just as if they had the ball.

On the bootleg, the quarterback tries to get outside of the defensive end, while he is working against the offensive blocker. After he gets outside the end, he hides the ball on his hip from the linebackers and the halfbacks. Then he can decide whether to throw or to run by the manner in which they react to the situation.

Since it is easier for a right-handed passer to throw while running to his right, most bootlegs go to the right.

The Pitch-Out

We like to have our quarterbacks execute a pitch-out by keeping both hands on the ball. If they call for the pitch-out, we want them to take the ball away from the back hitting into the line, pull it into their stomach, then throw it with both hands out to the receiver. With two hands, the quarterback has a good grip on the ball and good control.

The back who will receive the pitch-out is instructed to run with his hands in a natural running position, then take the ball with both hands at hip level. Again, the quarterback should use two hands to prevent a lineman from coming through and hitting him when he has one hand on the ball, not to mention a good tackle.

By keeping his rear low on the spin, the quarterback can hide the ball better from the defense.

Drills

The key to success of the T-formation is the quarterback! For success, the quarterback therefore has to spend many hours learning to handle the ball and learning to fake. He literally has to live with a football. He must learn how to take the ball from center until it becomes automatic. He should practice doing it on the count. In addition, a full-length mirror comes in handy when practicing faking and pivoting.

We use a daily technique period for our quarterbacks. This session is devoted to basic fundamentals, such as setting up quickly to pass, throwing, follow-through, looking-off, and all the other things which are sometimes overlooked. They also work on reading the defense and having a key in each defense they throw against. In addition, our quarterbacks spend considerable time studying films and utilize the self-improvement chart.

Passing ²

The best passers in the NFL have a strong arm, the quick release, and the deadly accuracy over a full season.

2

To win, a team must have an effective passing attack.

A strong passing attack keeps the defense from bunching up. Therefore, the passing attack should feature a variety of name pass patterns, and individual pass cuts to keep the defensive unit off balance and out of position. The running game must be established first, then, it will be much easier to get the passing game rolling. In addition, the play-action passing game must be co-ordinated with the offense.

The Pro's, of course, have emphasized the passing game for years. The college game now has more passing. This emphasis on passing has been going over to the high schools, as well, and I believe it will increase.

I favor a precision type of passing, in which the receiver goes to a prescribed depth and then breaks. The ball must be thrown *before* the man makes his break. Then, the defense doesn't have as much chance to break it up. We have a stop watch at every practice. When the timing is off, it is someone's fault and we want to know why.

Perfection in the passing game is a matter of timing and practice. There is no substitute for hard work and practice, and timing will only come through practice. It can't be done on a blackboard but requires hours of drilling against a defense, such as our 7-on-7 period provides. Too much emphasis is put on blackboard passing.

We call it 7-on-7 because seven offensive players are matched against seven defenders. For 25 to 30 minutes each day—even more if necessary—we move up and down the field and try to create tactical situations so the players will get used to playing the hash marks. We do everything we can to make our passing game realistic.

Basic Qualities

Ability is the No. 1 point in becoming a top-notch passer. A passer has to have ability to throw the football. The best passers have a strong arm, the quick release, and the deadly accuracy over a full season.

Secondly, he has to be physically strong, because the quarterback takes quite a beating from those huge defensive linemen. In addition, they are all superbly coordinated athletes.

All outstanding passers have good depth perception. They are able to pick out their receivers, even in heavy traffic and when they have to go to an alternate receiver. *This is the big test.*

Fig. 2-2. TIME TO SET. If a quarterback has time to throw, any defense is in trouble. Here, Rams' quarterback Roman Gabriel is given good protection by the Rams offensive line. Guard Joe Scibelli moves in to take out Willie Davis of the Packers. Facing the target, Gabe's feet are comfortably spread, with his weight basically on his back foot.

Setting Up The Pass

The passer must get back to the pocket as quickly as possible. This is one of the most important points in successful passing. The sooner the quarterback can get back, the more time he has to set up to throw the ball. The defense can go after opposing passers who do not get back quickly enough. We work almost every day in training camp on increasing our speed in setting up the pass. As a yardstick, for the seven-step drop-back, we have our quarterbacks strive for 1.75 seconds in getting back. For the five-step, it is 1.3 seconds.

Our quarterbacks have a specific amount of steps for a certain pattern, and this is the way we operate our passing game throughout the season. However, when a breakdown occurs, the quarterback must be ready to unload the ball, when and if this is necessary. There can be a great deal of false steps in quarterbacking, in dropping back for the pass. You will find that a boy often takes a step forward upon receiving the snap from center. To eliminate this, have him take his first step backward on the right foot; you want him back as quickly as possible. He should not work from a parallel stance: have him place his right foot slightly ahead of the left, prior to the snap.

The quarterback *must execute quickness in going back.* Although his hands remain in contact with the center, the quarterback's body is just starting to leave right before the snap. This gives him a little edge in getting back quicker.

If the right foot is slightly forward on the initial stance, the first backward step of the quarterback will give him an additional 6 to 8 inches. The quarterback's feet should point toward the goal line so that his hips are free to move.

As he drops back, the QB is glancing over his shoulder, looking downfield as much as he can. He takes short, quick, jabbing steps as he goes backward. He is actually working hard to set up quickly. He is running in "modified" form. He looks directly at the intended receiver, but sees the entire field with his peripheral vision. He hits his maximum depth and then readies himself on his last two

Fig. 2-3. HEIGHT AND HIGH RELEASE ARE VERY VALUABLE QUALITIES. In this photo the Rams' Quarterback Roman Gabriel throws over Ordell Braase of the Colts. Roman fired three touchdown passes and led the Rams to a 34-10 victory over the Colts to win the 1967 NFL Coastal Division Championship.

The passer should stay in the pocket protected by his blockers in front. A tall quarterback like Gabriel has the advantage of throwing over his men up front and over the hands of the rushers.

Fig. 2-4. PASSING FROM THE POCKET. Quarterback Roman Gabriel, behind a well-formed pocket, delivers a long one against the San Francisco 49ers. Observe tackle Charlie Cowan (73) doing his pass protection job with excellent results. In all pocket passing, it is wise to have a prescribed depth for the quarterback to throw from, even though he may be forced to release the ball earlier. Roman is concentrating on his receiver and is not concerned with the rush, a characteristic of a good, courageous quarterback. Note the good follow-through.

steps. The quarterback should throw with his weight on his back foot. Many quarterbacks take a little jump after a set action. The important thing is for him to get set on his back foot and be ready to step up into the pocket to deliver the ball.

Balance is the key to the drop-back action. Many inaccurate passes are caused as a result of the quarterback being off-balance at the deepest point. Usually, this occurs when the quarterback overstrides when taking his jump step. This ends in a poorly thrown pass.

Of course, if the passer can throw off-balance—and occasionally he has to—he will have that much better chance of making good.

Again, we like the QB to work out of the pocket. While the scrambling quarterback is an exciting quarterback, we don't like to get in situations where it is 2nd and 19, or 3rd and 18. Basically we want him to drop back, stay in that pocket, and execute from there. Unless the QB is forced out of the pocket, he should stay

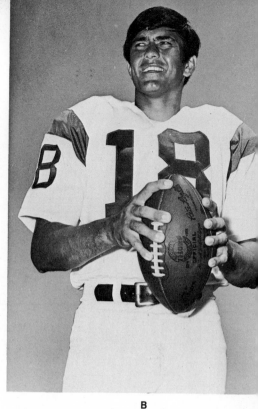

A   B

there. Teams have not become great using quarterbacks who try to prove they can run.

Passing Technique

The actual passing delivery is a smooth overhand motion with a good follow-through. During our workouts, we place considerable emphasis on the proper follow-through which we feel is essential for better direction and distance.

The short passes are thrown with a snap of the wrist and often hard and right at the receiver. The long pass is usually a "soft" throw and should lead the receiver. The passer aims the ball so the receiver will just reach it while running at full speed.

Once the passer is back in the pocket and decides to throw, he should use the minimum amount of motion in throwing the ball. Long arm action delivery is

Fig. 2-5. GRIP ON BALL. The passer should use a firm, comfortable grip. Roman Gabriel likes to grip the ball with the thumb underneath the three fingers on the lacing, well spread out and slightly behind the center of the ball. Looking over the field, he holds the ball in a cocked position at shoulder level, allowing for a quick release. The passer should grip the ball firmly, since palming it tends to inhibit a smooth passing delivery. The fingertips should feel the pebble grain of the football. The passer should always have both hands on the ball prior to the release.

undesirable; it destroys timing and assists the defense.

Grip

The passer must first have a good grip on the ball. This means a grip which enables him to be comfortable when throwing. Some individuals stress seeing daylight between the ball and the palm.

A   B

Others who palm it have been equally successful.

Our passers grip the ball with the thumb underneath and the fingers on the lacing, well spread out and slightly behind the center of the ball. We tell them not to squeeze the ball, but have a firm enough grasp to keep the ball from slipping.

Stance

The passer should assume a stance that is natural for him when he arrives back in the pocket. His feet are spread, and his body is balanced as he faces the target. His weight rests on the ball of each foot so that he can shift quickly in any direction.

When he first gets back in the pocket, his weight basically is resting on the back foot. This is the foot which is dug in, ready to push off for the start of the throw. The other foot is planted in the direction he intends to throw the ball.

Fig. 2-6. BALL GRIP. The fingers of the passer are comfortably spread and relaxed. In illustration A, Milt Plum's throwing hand is turned slightly so the little finger is on the opposite side of the laces from the other three fingers. He has two fingers across the laces, rather than three which Roman Gabriel uses (see Fig. 2-5).

In illustration B, Billy Anderson employs a very common grip, with all fingers placed across the strings. Whatever grip is used, the grip must be maintained in practice until mastered. All three passers have both hands on the ball. In addition, none of the passers is palming the football.

The quarterback should hold the ball at shoulder level or a little above. The ball should be held with both hands. I have noticed that some young passers hold the ball too low. This can cause fumbling because the defense can slap the ball away.

The delivery

In delivering the football, the passer should step with his lead foot directly

Fig. 2-7. THE DELIVERY. The passing delivery requires the coordination of the shoulders, arm, and feet. Using the wrist primarily, the short, quick pass is thrown more overhand past the ear. The ball is cocked; the wrist motion is the same as that used to crack a whip, assuring proper timing, and thereby increasing the speed of delivery. The arm is extended almost straight up as the delivery nears completion. A good follow-through assures accuracy and the necessary velocity. On all quick passes, the ball should be held at shoulder height to eliminate unnecessary movement of the ball.

35

A   B   C

at the receiver. It is essential that a quarter-back have "quick hands," to get rid of the ball in a hurry. However, he should never turn his wrist. He should use an inward and downward pull of the fingers and hand on the ball. The elbow should lead the way, followed by a smooth, "loose arm" motion, which whips the ball toward the receiver. The speed of the arm and hand action is in proportion to the velocity and distance the ball will travel.

As for the correct arm angle on the pass, the three-quarter to overhand delivery seems the most effective. Roman Gabriel has that, although sometimes he throws directly behind the ear. I think it depends upon the man himself.

Fig. 2-8. PASSING TECHNIQUE. Pushing off the back foot, the passer steps directly at the receiver with his lead foot. Cocking the ball, he executes a smooth arm motion, with the elbow leading the way. For most passers, I recommend using a three-quarter to overhand delivery. Using an inward and downward pull of the fingers

Otto Graham preferred the half-and-half arm motion, which forced the nose of the football to point up as it was released. This action resulted in a softer and an easier pass to catch. Throwing past the ear generally causes the nose

D

E

F

and hand on the ball, Roman Gabriel, above, employs strong wrist action in whipping the ball straight and quickly to his receiver. He executes a complete follow-through; this helps improve his accuracy. Passers must be careful of overstriding: it destroys timing and accuracy.

of the ball to point down, making it heavy and more difficult to catch. This motion is not so successful today because of the height of the linemen.

It is advantageous for a passer to be able to adjust his arm angle for a particular type of throw. In the case of a short, quick, bullet pass, the ball would be thrown more overhand past the ear. The passer must lift his arm a little for this type of pass.

On the long pass, he may lower the arm angle and use a little more three-quarter motion to help soften up the ball. We refer to this as a "nose up ball." In throwing the "long bomb," some passers like to exaggerate throwing the elbow out in front of the body, so that the point of the ball will stay up. This long arm action causes the ball to carry farther.

The three-quarter arm motion is often the most natural delivery for most passers. However, the overhand motion enables the passer to throw over the heads and arms of opposing players.

Release

At the time of release, the shoulders of the passer should be square to the receiver. In releasing the ball, he should draw the fingers and the hand inward and downward. This tends to give the ball the spiral flight so necessary for a properly thrown pass.

When the delivery nears completion, the arm should be extended straight out. The palm of the throwing arm should be facing the ground. The index finger is the control finger, and it should be the last finger to leave the ball. It should point in the direction of the target. The throwing hand comes across the body, and the thumb of the passer is pointed down.

The weight has transferred from the QB's rear foot forward onto the front foot. *Above all, he must not throw across his front leg or throw from a flatfooted position.* This is a common error. To assure good "zip" on the ball, the passer must step directly toward the target.

The actual release of the ball generally requires moving forward a step or two from the initial position within the pocket.

Follow-through

A good follow-through is essential for accuracy and distance. Upon releasing the ball, the throwing hand should come across the body. It should not be hurried. The weight should be on the front foot at the time of the release.

During practice, our quarterback coach, Ted Marchibroda, urges our passers to exaggerate their follow-through movement and to make sure their thumb points toward the ground.

Types of Passes

To keep the defense off-balance, a variety of passes and pass patterns should be at the disposal of the offense. Actually, to be effective, the offense doesn't need many pass patterns; just a few basic ones and some counter key passes will do. *It is the manner in which they are executed that is all-important.*

Passes fall into the following three major areas: 1) the pocket pass; 2) the roll-out pass; and 3) the play pattern pass.

Passing from the pocket

In setting from the pocket, the passer must make certain that he receives the exchange from the center so that the "fat" of the ball is well seated in the palm of his passing hand. The footwork involves turning and sprinting three steps, then setting. Quickly, it's "1-2-3 and set." This "1-2-3 and set" will place him at a depth of 6 or 7 yards. He should be in a "stand tall" position, ready to step in the direction he will throw the ball.

When passing from the pocket, the passer must remember to stay in the pocket or step up. The linemen cannot block effectively if he leaves the pocket. This is very difficult for young passers to realize and learn and must be stressed during each practice session.

Turn-out or Turn-in pass

This pass is so named because the receiver goes in a turn-in or-out pattern. It is a medium pass for which the quarterback has to really rifle the ball, usually head high. This can vary, depending upon where the defender is positioned. Sometimes it is better to throw lower. The pass is usually thrown to a flanker or spread end who goes downfield 10 yards, then stops or comes back a couple of steps.

Timing is an important factor as far as the turn-in or turn-out pass is concerned. The moment the receiver turns around the ball should already be on its way. Again, this pass has to be fired very hard and must be accurate.

Swing or flare pass

This is a relatively short pass with a slight lead which permits the flaring halfback or fullback to run into the path of the ball. The passer should have a slight loft on the ball so that the receiver will be able to take the ball in stride. It's a much softer pass than the turn-in or turn-out pass. This type of pass is hard to master.

Long pass

The long pass is more difficult to complete and is not thrown more than a few times during a game. This is because on almost every play two deep defensive backs will cover any receiver the offense sends. The passer has to really reach back and let it go. The trajectory of the "long bomb," is much higher than with

other passes. The timing of the "lead" to the receiver requires a great deal of practice between the passer and the receiver.

The passer should be cautioned not to throw the ball too hard when executing the long pass. He should develop a rhythm in his delivery. It is very important to get the ball to him quickly as he breaks open so that the receiver doesn't have to break stride. Let him run under the ball. In delivering the ball, he must not "cross" the line the receiver is running. If the ball is under thrown out on a line, the receiver can adjust; in fact, he is more difficult to cover because of this.

Jump pass

This is a quick short pass to an end or flanker cutting diagonally across the field. It is sometimes called a "look-in" because the end takes about two or three steps, looks up, and he has the ball. The reason for the jump is to get above the charging linemen for a better view of the receiver. Although the Rams have pretty much gotten away from the jump pass, some teams use it to some success.

Screen pass

The screen pass is a fine weapon. This play often works against a team's putting a strong rush on the passer. We often call it when we need long yardage, and the defense is spread out for a long pass.

Of course, faking by the quarterback and his teammates in the backfield is the key to a successful screen pass. The

D

C

B

A

Fig. 2-9. THE RELEASE. The passing delivery is a smooth overhand motion with a good follow-through. A proper follow-through provides better direction and distance as well. The left foot steps in the direction of the target. The throwing hand should come across the body. The passer must be careful to step in the direction of the throw, especially when throwing to his left.

Fig. 2-10. PASSING MOTION. Back in the pocket, the passer digs in with his rear foot and steps in the direction he intends to throw the ball. He should use an easy, relaxed throwing touch as he lets his throwing arm follow through naturally. On the long pass, he may lower the arm angle and throw it a little more three-quarters to help soften up the ball with a nose-up release.

C   B   A

D   E   F

Above, Milt Plum exaggerates throwing the elbow out in front of the body, enabling the point of the ball to stay up. The young quarterback should attempt to reach out and shake hands with his receiver to assure the proper follow-through. The passer should remember to keep two hands on the ball and not wind up. The ball must be kept up next to the ear. Note that in these pictures the ball is held too low.

41

A   B   C

halfback or the fullback fakes a block moving to one side or the other, but stays in the backfield. In the meantime, the offensive linemen at the defense sift through. Then, they move over in front of the receiver.

We tell our quarterback to take his normal drop-back, as he would in throwing a pass. At this point, he takes a good "hesitation," and then as he drops back further, he flips a short pass before the onrushing defensemen. It has to be a soft pass which we like for the receiver to catch on the run.

The Roll-out pass

The roll-out, or running, pass is usually a short pass—five or six yards—and can be "thrown" into the flat easily. It is usually a true option run-pass which helps offset a strong pass rush from the inside. Although it doesn't take a great passer to execute this play, the roll-out pass does require a considerable amount of time and practice to perfect.

The quarterback sprints out at controlled speed, while holding the ball in a "ready position." He looks immediately to the area he is running toward, usually the flat.

When using the option on the linebacker, the quarterback keeps his eyes on him constantly. If the defender "pops" across the line of scrimmage, he will unload the ball softly to the receiver in the flat. But if he drops out to play pass defense, the quarterback will continue running at top speed.

The running pass has been a valuable weapon for us and we put a lot of emphasis on it. We feel it can make the big play for us—a score. In addition, if we show the running pass, we know the defenders are going to be a little concerned. Therefore, if they know we have the ability to throw it, it helps our running game. The majority of our play action passes are in conjunction with our running game.

The important point for the passer to remember is to try *to set himself* as he releases the ball. *He should avoid throwing the ball when off-balance.* So, have him find a solid footing when he decides to make his throw.

The play pattern pass

This type of pass involves faking a running play—usually one of your most successful plays—then setting to throw. The most important point is for the quarterback and the rest of his team to really fake a running play. This pass should look exactly like a run, in which the receiver tries to make the defensive secondary believe he is blocking or just loafing downfield.

Then, the quarterback pulls the ball from the back that he is faking to and either sets in the pocket or continues to roll-out. For the most part, play pattern passes include both the short pass and the long ball which could be a "post" or a corner pass. The short one over the middle or out to the sideline are both highly effective. But, again, the quarterback should really fake a running play. He shouldn't give the pass away until he is ready to throw!

Correct Mental Attitude

The successful passer realizes that occasionally he is going to be knocked on his back, even after he has thrown the ball. He must be able to concentrate on his target, no matter how many defenders he has around him. He must not let this pressure upset him.

The great passers have the COURAGE to hold on to the football until the last split-second before throwing it. They are able to stand back in the pocket and take some occasional punishment. Unitas and Starr have been superb at this for years. They know how to relax and go limp when hit. And if they try to fight some of those big rushmen, they are going to get hurt.

Toughness, in my estimation, is one of the biggest factors in becoming a successful passer. Over the years, Unitas has been the best quarterback in the league, and one reason is because he has been the toughest. While there are others

Fig. 2-12. TOUCHDOWN PASS! Having rolled out to the right, QB Roman Gabriel sets up and unleashes a deadly strike into the end zone. His weight has moved forward on his front foot. Notice the excellent—highly essential—protection by the offensive linemen. Observe that Gabriel throws off his left toe, rather than flat-footed. Flat-footed passers are often injured.

equal to Johnny in passing ability, there aren't as many throwers who are as tough.

A passer must remember not to let interceptions bother him. If he makes a mistake, he must be mentally tough enough to learn from it, to stay loose and be even more determined to succeed the next play. The interception is history, so forget it!

Split Vision—Looking Over the Field

The passer must develop split vision as much as he possibly can. He has to pick out his receivers and then deliver the ball

to them. Most truly great passers are gifted with uncanny perception, along with their judgement and superb delivery.

However, hard work and preparation can help improve the passer's perception. Working every day with the same receivers is a big advantage. Every time he throws a pass, he is prepared for any situation that may arise. If a particular pattern is called, he will know instinctively how to successfully get the ball to a receiver.

Peripheral vision, to a degree, is something that can be developed by preparation —knowing the defense and what he is trying to do. The passer develops a mental

A   B   C

Fig. 2-13. HITTING THE RECEIVER ON THE QUICK PASS. The passer must be capable of picking out his receivers and then delivering the ball at the proper time. Roman Gabriel dem-onstrates how to hit the receiver before he breaks his stride. The passer must hit the receiver at the *exact* moment he is open.

picture of where this area will be. This is why he must keep his head turned toward the defense as he drops back to the pocket.

Use as many receivers as you can. Try not to limit it to two. Even though the quarterback has an initial receiver, this doesn't mean he shouldn't hit any one of three other men on a particular pass pattern. For example, if the passer finds that the split-end is covered on an intended short pass, he might go to the halfback or flanker on some deeper pattern. After seeing the split-end is not open, the passer moves his vision back to the left and picks up the tight end or the flanker. If everyone is covered, he will either have to "eat the ball" or make sure he throws it away from the defenders.

Above all, he must never throw the ball into a crowd of defenders. If there is any question in his mind that a defender might intercept the ball, he should not throw it. He might throw it into the ground toward the feet of the receiver, so no one can get it. However, *he must never throw the ball up for grabs.* In some situations, he might decide to dump the ball off to the fullback out in the flat.

In addition to locating his receiver, the passer might have to move around in the pocket. If his primary receiver is covered, he will have to move around, shuffle his feet, and be ready to locate another receiver. The quarterback who is light and nimble on his feet certainly has an advantage in staying out of the hands of the defensive linemen.

Faking

Eye and arm faking can prove to be very helpful to the passer. Looking one way and throwing in another direction can be quite deceptive to the defense. By moving

ball and thus simulate a throw. As he starts his forward motion of his arm, he just pumps the ball and brings his arm to a stop quickly about halfway through his delivery. This often causes the defender to freeze, allowing the receiver to gain a much needed extra step.

The bootleg play is another method used to fool the defense. The quarterback will fake a hand-off and then, keeping the ball hidden behind his leg, will slip out into the flat.

Drills

If he expects to play well, the quarterback must also practice well. This certainly applies to throwing a football. A young, aspiring passer can even practice by himself. The old tire drill is still a good one. An old tire hung up in the backyard can provide a good target. At first, he should stay close enough, then gradually move back. Later, he may practice throwing the ball through the tire while running to his right, then to his left.

One-knee drill

An effective method used for warming up is to get down on one knee. The passer brings the ball with both hands to a "ready position" which is about numeral high. Then he raises the ball in a "cocked position," which is around the area of the ear. With the elbow extended out slightly, he snaps the ball with his wrist, throwing only 7 to 8 yards for this warm-up procedure. As he delivers the ball,

Fig. 2-14. WARMING UP ON ONE KNEE. Milt Plum engages in this effective drill, snapping the ball with his wrist. Throwing only seven to ten yards, he concentrates on having his passing hand finish with his palm down and out. He throws as many as 10 to 12 passes in this kneeling position daily. This allows him to throw with his arm and eliminates body motion. This is an excellent drill for young passers who need to learn to throw a spiral. A weighted ball is used in this drill.

his head or eyes just slightly, he may cause a defender to be pulled out of position, particularly the linebackers. However, I do feel that too much has been made of this in the past.

Another way for the quarterback to deceive the defense is by faking with his passing arm. The passer will pump the

he should concentrate on having his passing hand finish with his palm down and out.

After he has thrown 10 to 12 passes in this kneeling position, then he stands up and passes 10 to 12 yards from a straight standing still position. He should concentrate on stepping in the direction he is passing. This is most important for balance and control.

Footwork drill

After practicing ten or twelve passes from this position, the quarterback can begin practicing his footwork, with the emphasis on dropping straight back and setting himself in the pocket. Here, he practices his footwork at top speed, without throwing the ball. Then, the last step is to practice the footwork and deliver the ball to the receiver at the specific distance the play is designated. This calls for a precision type of passing. The receiver goes to a prescribed depth and break, and the ball is thrown before the man makes his break.

The passer should practice throwing all types of passes, long and short, running and standing still. Many times he will be the last player to leave the field. He will usually stay as long as any receiver will keep running.

Pass Receiving 3

No matter how well designed and executed, a pass pattern is no better than the protection given the passer and the accuracy of the pass.

3

Speed is, in my opinion, the prime requisite of a good pass receiver. An offensive receiver simply has to have the speed to beat those defensive backs because the defensive backs today can run like race horses.

An outstanding pass receiver, however, has more than just exceptional speed. Besides running a 4.6 or 4.7 forty yard dash, he has tremendous hands and is capable of making the great catch. He is able to dive for the ball and come up with it. He can catch it over his shoulder. He can turn in the air, twist, and catch the football. Then, after he catches it, he knows how to run with the ball.

If a receiver doesn't have great speed, he will have to work very hard, particularly on his timing and precision work, to be able to perform his pass cuts near perfect. When the other players have left the field, he is the one who must stay to work on stops, starts, pass cuts, catching the ball, anything to make up for this lack of outstanding speed. Actually, anyone who wants to work hard can become a fine receiver and be able to fit into the pass offense.

Secondly, a pass receiver must have great faking ability—maneuverability to get open, because even though he may have speed, it won't be enough to get open.

| A | B | C |

Fig. 3-2. GOOD HEIGHT is a major asset in catching passes. Bill Truax, above, stands 6'5''. He is also blessed with sure hands. Notice that Billy has his eyes glued directly on the ball. As he "looks the ball into his hands," his fingers are relaxed and well-spread. His elbows are in close to his body, so if the ball slips through his hands, he can cradle it against his body.

A pass receiver must have a strong desire to want to catch that football—no matter where it is thrown. It takes real courage for a receiver to stick his head in there and catch the football when he is covered by one or two defenders. There is no substitute for hustle. The more hustle, the more spirited, the more dedicated the receiver is, the better he is going to be.

An outstanding receiver needs height. Most of the real good receivers are over six feet tall. Casey at 6'4'' and Billy Truax at 6'5'' have provided Roman Gabriel with big post targets. There are very few Johnny Morrises and Tommy McDonalds anymore at 5'9'' or 5'10''. I think the ideal

Fig. 3-3. CATCHING IN THE CROWD. Willie Ellison (33), although surrounded by the Pittsburgh defensive secondary, hangs on to a forward pass thrown by Roman Gabriel. He quickly tucks away the pigskin. Notice that Willie has his finger over the nose of the football. The complete receiver must be able to catch the ball in heavy traffic.

receiver is one who is about 6'3''. Of course, if a receiver is too big, he isn't maneuverable enough, and conversely, if he is too small, he will make a difficult target for the passer.

Stance

We use a three-point stance for our outside receivers. There are two reasons for this. First, we want the outside receiver to feel as though he belongs to the team. Secondly, we feel he will have more explosion from the line of scrimmage. He must get into the secondary as quickly as he can. If he stands, he is not going to take that first full step.

53

A   B

Fig. 3-4. THE THREE-POINT STANCE provides the receiver with more explosion from the initial stance. Flanker back Bernie Casey, above, executes a comfortable stance with his weight distributed evenly over the three points. This stance also eliminates body lean and sway. These pictures show Casey with his head up and his eyes focused directly downfield. He has a comfortable staggered stance with a little weight on his forward hand: this allows for a quick push-off.

The upright stance, often used by spread ends, enables the potential receiver to read the defense better, and they can maneuver better in case a linebacker tries to hold them up. On the upright stance, the offensive player should use a jab step and drop his right foot back a little to get extra drive in the first step. With the upright stance, it is very easy to get caught leaning and in motion.

We ask our tight ends to take a right- or left-hand stance, whichever is natural. Most of them are right-handed. The tight end should employ a stance which will allow him to take off the quickest. Since nothing usually happens for 5–7 yards, we have the ends take a track stance, with their buttocks not as high as those of a sprinter on the track. They place one foot back where they can dig in, so they can

Fig. 3-5. STANCE. The split end can get into the secondary more quickly by using a three-point stance. If he stands, he is not going to take that first full step. In many stadiums, it is difficult to hear the quarterback's cadence. Notice Jack Snow is looking directly into the football. This way he will not move too soon or too late.

really come out of the blocks. The right toe is in line with the instep of the left foot.

Mental Attitude

In lining up and readying himself to move into his pass pattern, there are three things on which the receiver should concentrate. First, he has to understand from the films he has been watching, what general type of defense he is playing. Then he has to think, as he looks into the defensive secondary, what will they be doing on this down. Third, he has to consider what he has done before and how the defense reacted to what he did.

A

B

Fig. 3-6. THE TIGHT END'S STANCE. The right arm, forming a tripod with the feet, should be straight and under the right shoulder. The hips are slightly lower than the shoulders. The right foot is staggered back several inches. The left arm rests above the left knee in a position to explode. The end's head is up, his eyes are open; he looks directly down field so as not to tip off his intentions. His feet are slightly wider than the width of his shoulders, providing the necessary balance to drive forward or move laterally. If his feet are too close or too wide, the receiver will lack good maneuverability. Billy Truax, above, demonstrates the proper stance.

These are the points he has to think about to help him run an intelligent route.

Whatever route he runs, he will have run it countless times in practice. He has run it so well in practice, that he knows that if he runs an intelligent route, it has a good chance of being successful in the game. He thinks to himself that he has done this so much that he has an almost sure completion here. In short, confidence —intelligent confidence—that comes from experience, best explains the proper mental attitude we like to see in all our receivers.

56

Releases

A receiver must avoid being held up by the defense, since this throws the passer's timing off. Whichever release is used, it must be done with speed. Actually, when the receiver releases slowly there are not many patterns that are effective. He has to release with speed, and then he goes into a glide. This is where he has to drive them off with some more speed, and then he will go into his final move.

I don't believe a pass receiver needs a lot of releases. He does need an inside and outside release. Tight ends, for instance, have to be able to step inside as well as outside. Furthermore, they must learn the correct faking techniques.

We spend a lot of time on releases in our fundamental periods, prior to the passing game. We have the receiver fake a block or to "blast" . . . to come off as if he was trying to engage the linebacker and slip him and come on out.

We also use what we call the single head and step fake, in which the end fakes with the head and a step to the outside and then releases inside. Conversely, he can head and step fake to the inside and release outside. Another release would be the double fake, where he fakes to the outside, fakes to the inside, and then comes back to the outside.

Our tight ends also have used to good success a release whereby they actually fake as if they are going to hook the linebacker. The end simply starts out as if he is going to hook the linebacker who

is responsible for containment. When the linebacker starts to defend himself, trying not to be hooked, the tight end is able to slip through on the inside.

The *low* release has proven a quick and effective way to release. The receiver should drop to all fours, scramble along the ground, get up and then resume his pattern.

The *inside arm* swing is another successful release which our offensive coach, Howard Schnellenberger, teaches our ends. As the tight end drives, either to his inside or his outside of the linebacker, he takes his inside arm and makes a great sweeping motion over the top. As the linebackers try to grab hold, the end has a terrific lever which rips their hands off him.

There are other releases that the boys just pick up individually, but these are the basic ones.

Holding Up Receivers

Most defenses are continually using stunts or tactics in an effort to hold up the receivers. The biggest thing they try to do is to disguise the direction in which they are going to force him. Of course, if he knows which way they are going to force him, he can normally make an intelligent decision how to get out.

The receivers will split his outside avenue, making it difficult for him to go to the outside. So, now, he decides to take an inside release, but all the time, they are thinking inside. Now, they try to force

Fig. 3-7. BLASTING OFF. Tight end Dave Pivec, coming off the line of scrimmage, sets up the linebacker with an imaginary block which helps the timing of the play-action pass. He steps into the linebacker (Dean Halverson) with his left shoulder, forearm and foot, warding off the hold-up as he slips through into the secondary.

A B C

D E

Fig. 3-8. HEAD AND STEP FAKE. The tight end (Dave Pivec) fakes with his head and left foot to draw the strong side linebacker outside (Dean Halverson). Then the tight end must release as quickly as possible after his preliminary fake. Many tight ends do not work enough on this technique.

Allowing himself to be held up is one of the worst mistakes a tight end can make. However, it is very difficult to hold up a receiver if he executes a proper release.

Fig. 3-9. RUNNING AN INTELLIGENT ROUTE. The receiver (here, Jack Snow) must understand the type of defender and the kind of defense he is playing and how he plans to outmaneuver. He must be able to "read" and understand the total defense. This is an absolute must.

him to go in one direction, because mentally, they are alert for that direction.

The defenders who do the best job of holding up the receivers are those who can use their hands effectively. Some players try to hold with their forearms—the forearm lift—and they can deliver good punishment. By the same token, their holding or restricting surface is small, and their range of motion is small, so if the receiver is quick, he can normally elude these people.

Most linebackers have strong wrists and forearms and can extend their arms at least two feet in either direction—forward, sideways—and if they have good power, the receiver might find some difficulty.

Normally, the linebackers try to get one hand on the potential receiver's helmet or at least one hand on his shoulder pads. A typical hold would be one hand on his helmet and one hand on his shoulder pad. Others may use two hands on the shoulder pads. They hold on pretty tight. The defense also employs what we used to call the "Take Down," where they would grab the receiver's shoulder pads and pull him forward. This is bordering on a very ticklish officiating point, but it is rarely called. Once the defenders get hold of a receiver, he is usually off-balance and ends up on the ground.

Getting Open

The most important thing in running a pattern is to drive off the defender. If a receiver cannot drive off the defender, faking isn't going to help. If the receiver does a good job of driving off the defender, faking won't be necessary. However, the defender has to respect a receiver's ability to go deep before he can drive him off.

The threat of beating a man deep, of really exploding off the line of scrimmage, is the thing which causes most patterns to be open. With more and more speed, there seems to be less and less faking. Faking is still a big part of pass receiving, but with so much speed, the fake is really the drive to the goal line, the threat of beating a man deep.

If the defensive back can just backpedal the way he wants to, he is going to cover most everything the receiver does. As a result, somehow the receiver has to provoke his movement. He must cause the defender to turn in one direction, losing his balance. With good speed and with explosion off the line, the receiver can provoke him or make him conscious that he is going to go deep on him. Next he will find himself moving backwards faster than he can and then he will get turned in or out. This is exactly what his defense coach does not want to happen. "Don't let them get you turned and throw a touchdown pass!" So, this is where we start, and I think it is most important in our passing attack.

We might start out with a head and shoulder fake, in a particular direction, trying to freeze a man in that direction and then breaking out. This is about the simplest thing he can do. The next simplest move would be a head fake in the direction he is going to end up, coming back with a head fake to the direction which he is NOT going to go . . . and then coming back in his original direction.

And from there, the pass receiver can go into a variety of things. He may go into a two-step, which is actually a crossover, a plant in the direction away from where he is going to go, plant, and break in that direction. Or, he could go to a three-step maneuver, the same type of thing.

Our receivers often use a zigzag run, a weave type run after the defensive back —just watching his feet. Once we get him turned in the direction which we are not going to go, we will break in the direction which we intended on going.

Another thing we do is simply run. Let us say we are going to run an "out." We just run at the inside shoulder of the defensive man and continue to run until we force him to turn in that direction and cross his feet. Then we break out.

There is a real fine thing that Casey did—and this is good only for a tall, long-legged receiver: as he comes off the line of scrimmage to start into his pattern, he will start his stride at the right shoulder; on just one stride he will be at the defender's left shoulder, his left step will bring him to the defender's right shoulder. What it amounts to is a straddle-legged

B

C

D

A

run, but the defensive man doesn't know if he is going to continue in that direction or not. The defender begins to saunter back and forth and now Bernie has got him moving—thinking about something he shouldn't be thinking about, and at the right time, Casey will break into the pattern.

Fig. 3-10. SIDELINE PATTERN. Proper timing is most essential on the sideline pattern. The receiver should make a sharp sideline cut. Bernie Casey runs directly at the defender and tries to drive him straight back. He fakes to the center of the field, then breaks to the sideline. He drives off the outside foot by crossing over to make the break quick and sharp. This is one of the Rams' most effective maneuvers.

<table>
<tr><td>E</td><td>F</td><td>G</td></tr>
</table>

Running Under Control

We put a great deal of emphasis on running under control, a controlled stride. Coming off the line of scrimmage, we believe, is the most important thing. There has to be an explosion! "You can't come off the line of scrimmage fast enough."

Our young receivers are told: "We want you to go as fast as you can go . . . and still be under control."

On the other hand, Snow looks as if he is a race horse . . . and he is still under control. So this is very important. Jack has to be under control. He has to be able to make a controlled move where he wants to. After that, when he comes out of his controlled move, he is coming off his break, and then, it is an all-out thing, an all-out effort. It becomes a break to the ball, and even though we say all-out, we still like for them to have that little extra if they have to go get it—they can pull something from somewhere.

When running under control, the receiver has the ability to cut and angle away from the defender. Saving a burst of speed will help him run away from the man covering him. But when he makes his break, he must really explode! He must use all his speed to get the ball.

Pass Patterns

The Los Angeles Rams try to employ a precision type passing attack. We don't depend on trying to fool or out-finesse the defense. Precision passing is what we strive for. The receiver is instructed to go almost to a prescribed depth, then break . . . and Gabe knows where he will be. Gabriel can anticipate their break and throw the ball to them. That's the basic thing we try to do.

First, I must say that a pass pattern, no matter how well designed and executed, is no better than the protection given the passer and the accuracy of the pass. Furthermore, the success of the play rests in part on the hustle and deception of the decoy.

Perhaps the two patterns we do best are the "Sideline" and "Corner" patterns. The sideline is about 12 to 14 yards deep, and again, this is where the receiver uses that straddle-legged run, getting the man turned to the inside and he breaks sharply to the outside. He merely fakes to the center of the field, then breaks to the sideline.

Using the corner pattern, which he developed late in the 1967 season, Casey scored three touchdowns in the last two games on this same thing. Bernie's best pattern at San Francisco was an 8-yard "Slant in," so he was using his reputation with that "slant in," using it as a basis for his "Corner" patterns. And the defensive man had to respect it. Bernie would start in on his "Slant," take 3 to 5 steps and break to the corner.

Although he does not possess terrific speed, Truax is a great "Hook and Slide" man. He is great going inside and finding open areas. Here he has done a terrific job. Billy runs right at the defensive back until he gives ground, then he likes to spin, crouch, catch and spin on away. Against the teams that go to a zone defense, Bill is usually going to be a big receiver. Of course, Gabriel is strong enough to wait for him to find them before trying to hit him, providing, of course, he and his quarterback have their timing down pat. Six to ten patterns are all the split end needs to beat any

defense. He should have a couple of sidelines, two deep patterns, and two or three inside routes.

Snow has been either a short receiver or a deep receiver. One of Jack's best patterns is a "Short out," a five yard out. On this route, he simply sprints down five yards, plants and breaks out. Gabe throws out there to him in 1.5 seconds.

The "Up" pattern is the other thing Jack has done. He does it by using a very slight fake, not a hard fake at all, just a slight fake out or in, or a Curl, that doesn't slow him down very much, just enough to make the defensive man hesitate. Then Snow takes off! The defender seems to lose Jack after the ball is in the air. They seem to have him covered pretty well until Gabe releases it, and then he beats them to the ball.

On the "Stop and Go," we like to have one of our outside receivers make the man defending him believe he is going to run what we call a "Curl" or a "Strike" pattern. Let us say Jack comes down, and as he turns in on his "Curl," if the man has really taken it or is playing him close, Snow doesn't have to do very much. All he has to do is kind of hesitate and throw his head around, and that will be enough to freeze the defensive man, to make him stop going backwards. Jack hasn't lost much speed in doing that, and then, he can sprint right on by him.

Now we come up against a man who is playing loose and isn't as concerned about coming up and intercepting or breaking it up. Now, Jack will have to come down and will have to make a hard "Curl"

Fig. 3-11. SLANT PATTERN. One of Bernie Casey's best patterns is an eight yard "slant in," which he uses along with his corner patterns. Cutting off the outside foot, the receiver makes the break quick and sharp. He avoids making a circle out of the pattern. He runs at top speed through the entire maneuver, driving the defender back. Again, timing is essential in this pattern, since the receiver is only open for a fraction of a second.

A

B   C   D

in there. He will have to come to a complete stop and face Gabe. Gabe might have to pump at him. And when Jack sees the pump, he plants or continues his whirl and goes up. So, it depends on how the defensive man is playing whether or not the pattern will go.

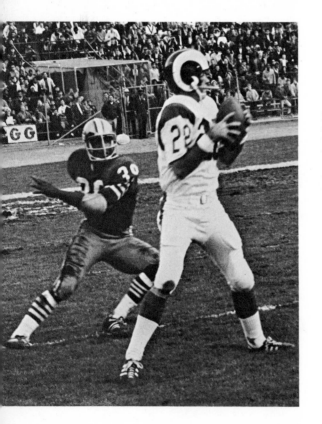

Fig. 3-12. THE CURL OR STRIKE PATTERN is one of the three most difficult passes to defense. Flanker Pat Studstill comes down hard, turns in on his curl and receives a bullet pass. Defending is Kermit Alexander of the San Francisco 49ers. It is essential that the receiver be on balance as he runs the strike.

D   C   B

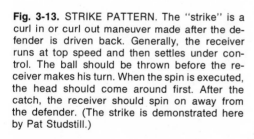

The pass receiver must follow the ball right into his hands.

Fig. 3-13. STRIKE PATTERN. The "strike" is a curl in or curl out maneuver made after the defender is driven back. Generally, the receiver runs at top speed and then settles under control. The ball should be thrown before the receiver makes his turn. When the spin is executed, the head should come around first. After the catch, the receiver should spin on away from the defender. (The strike is demonstrated here by Pat Studstill.)

A

67

A

Fig. 3-14. STOP AND GO. Flanker back Bernie Casey sprints down quickly and turns in on his familiar curl pattern. After hesitating and throwing his head around, causing the defender to hesitate, Casey explodes right on by him with short, choppy steps to accelerate. A common fault is to make too pronounced a preliminary fake.

B

E   D   C

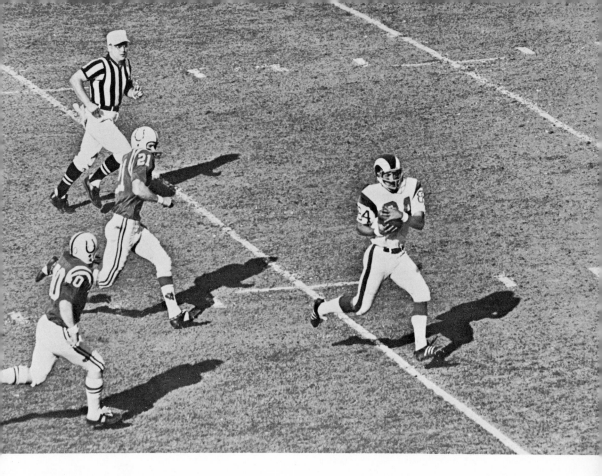

Fig. 3-15. THE LONG BOMB. When a receiver gets open like this, and he has the speed of Jack Snow, the defense is in trouble. Above, Jack scores on a long aerial from Gabriel against the Baltimore Colts.

There are actually three basic types of pass patterns:

1. *One-on-One (Individual).* The receiver isolates the defensive back and tries to outmaneuver him. The most common—and hardest—pattern to defend against is the outside or sideline break.

2. *Combination pattern.* Here, two or more receivers work together. A decoy clears a zone for the primary receiver. The decoy must make the defender stay with him in a certain zone. He sprints full speed at the defender and drives him back so that the primary receiver can break into the open zone.

3. *Play pass pattern.* This pattern evolves off a backfield action that looks like a run. This action holds the defenders and gives the receiver a slight advantage in getting open. The receiver should try to get into the open as fast as possible.

The Long Bomb

On the long over-the-shoulder catch, the passer will throw the receiver a long lead pass over the head. It is important for the receiver to learn to run with his arms in a normal running position. He should never run many yards with his arms extended. He waits until the ball is ready to settle into his hands and then extends his arms and catches the ball. This is one pass where the ball definitely must be "looked into the hands." In pointing his thumbs out, the receiver "forms a basket" with his hands.

By controlling his stride, the receiver is able to slow down a bit if the pass doesn't lead him enough, or he can make that extra effort forward to catch the ball if the passer leads him a little too much. It is very important for the passer to get the ball to him quickly as he breaks open, so that the receiver won't have to break stride. Since a receiver has the speed to cover a lot of ground, the passer tries to let him run under the ball.

Fig. 3-16. THE LONG PASS. When a receiver runs a deep pattern, the passer should get the ball to him as he breaks open. The receiver should not have to break his stride. It is effective for him to run under the ball. The ball should not cross the line the receiver is running. In this series, split end Jack Snow gives an excellent demonstration of following the ball in flight and then "looking the ball into the hands." Perfecting the timing for the Long Pass takes considerable practice.

The Goal Line Pass

A goal line situation is anything inside the 8 yard line, where the offense finds the depth very restricted. If they are on the 6 yard line, let's say, they only have 16 yards in which to operate. Because the defense plays so much different in this area, we have to practice a completely separate component of our passing game, rather than combining the two.

The defense normally jumps very close to us and very tight. They play man-to-man, and they take an inside position on the receivers—real tough. Here, all we have to do is catch the ball. We don't have to run with it when we get down there, so they have got to prevent the catch. Of course, by taking the inside position, this takes all our inside cuts away, forcing us to throw the outs. This is very difficult to do in this restricted area because their men are playing so close to our receivers.

So, when we get down to the goal line, it becomes a battle, man-on-man, like the one-on-one situation in basketball. Every move our receivers make, the defenders are going to make, and it is a real tight competitive thing. The receiver must try to use any fake or move to get that man out of position . . . just one step . . . and then he should break in there. Gabe will have the ball waiting for him.

A

B

C

D

Fig. 3-17. THE GOAL LINE PASS involves tight competition between the receivers and the pass defender. Tight end Billy Truax, above, breaks into the clear and receives a touchdown pass from quarterback Roman Gabriel against the 49ers at Kezar Stadium.

Primary Receivers

As for the number of primary receivers, we go two ways on this point. First, we give our two outside receivers identical assignments, and they both become primary receivers. Now, Gabe has a certain defensive man he keys, telling him which man to go to. We do this after the snap of the ball, and it is a very quick thing. Regardless of what defense they have called, whether they are trying to double up, we have a good pattern on the side, away from the double up.

In teaching this, we say there is but one primary receiver because after he makes his decision of who to go to, there is one guy.

The other way involves flooding a zone, in which we run either two or three people into a zone, with certain varying routes. We give a linebacker or defensive back the option of who he wants to come up with, actually, a "two on one" situation. When we do this, Gabe keys the defender we are trying to put "two on one." He doesn't key our receivers. He keys the defensive man. Now, we just let the defensive man pick out whichever man he wants to cover, and we throw to the other one. So, now, we have two basic primary receivers. We don't do quite as much with that alternate or outside receiver that a lot of teams do. Maybe we will next year.

Adjusting a Pattern

Quite often, a receiver has to adjust his pattern into a different area. For example,

72

A

B

D

C

if he is to run an 8 yard "Slant" and a linebacker has come right into the area, he may have to adjust his pattern into a different area, maybe 3 or 4 yards farther. These are things that the quarterback and the receiver have been able to work on during practice. Gabe will look for the receiver to adjust his pattern, and he knows how the various receivers like to adjust their routes. He knows where to look for them. Of course, if Gabe thinks there is no possibility of having the adjustment working, he will go to another receiver.

Fig. 3-18. FLY PATTERN. This "up" pattern involves a very slight one-step by the flanker back, just a slight move outside or inside that doesn't slow him down. Then he accelerates downfield. The passer gives him a good lead and the receiver strives to beat his defender to the ball. On this pass play, the passer must "read" both the defender and the receiver. (Bernie Casey demonstrates the pattern here.)

73

A   B   C

Catching the Ball

The success or failure of any pass pattern, of course, depends upon the receiver catching the ball. Even the best of patterns is worthless unless the ball is caught.

I don't believe in changing any habits a receiver has if he has had success catching the football. If the player is experiencing some difficulty, then we go back to the basics and try to find where his trouble is.

Look the ball into the hands

We like for our receivers to make any catch with both hands . . . and in their hands. They must follow the ball right into their hands. One of the key factors

Fig. 3-19. LOOK THE BALL INTO THE HANDS. The outstanding pass catchers will follow the ball into their hands with their eyes. The head should "pop down" and look right into the fingers. Many passes are dropped because the receivers fail to look the ball in. (Bernie Casey is shown here.)

in making a catch is the head and the eyes. We spend considerable time on the field emphasizing the movement of the head and the eyes.

Many receivers do not follow the ball the last six inches into their hands with their eyes. They follow the ball to a point about 6 to 8 inches from their body. Then, there comes a place on every catch, where he has to move his head in order to keep the eyes on the ball. This is the place

74

Fig. 3-20. THE HIGH BALL. On the hook or curl patterns, the receiver normally will want his thumbs together, giving him more strength.

As a rule, the receiver will take any pass that is above his waist with his thumbs in. This hand position also provides the passer with a good target. The receiver must put the ball away quickly on this type of pass. (Bill Truax demonstrates hand position here.)

where many receivers will not turn their head. The head remains in the position where they were looking back at the passer, and consequently, they do not follow the last six inches into their hands with their eyes. They think they are looking the ball into their hands, but they cannot see the ball the last six inches.

We have a little drill where we watch the head "*pop down.*" If the head snaps right down and looks into the hands, we know they are watching the ball. That's one reason why they drop a pass—the head hasn't snapped down right into the fingers.

Another basic point that should be remembered concerning the head is when a receiver makes his cut, his head should precede his body in the turn. For example, when he makes a sideline cut,

he turns into the boundary. Now, the natural tendency is for the receiver to come down, plant and turn, turning his body as he plants into the boundary. What we want him to do is to come down, plant his feet and throw his head around. He can turn his head much quicker than his body. Naturally, his shoulders and body will follow his head around. What this does, it lets him pick up the ball several yards farther from him because the ball will be in flight by the time he sees it.

Run from the waist down

We ask our receivers to run from the waist down. We don't want his upper body, his shoulders and arms, to get involved in his running motion. We want it to be a fluid motion and to run from

75

Fig. 3-21. THE LOW BALL. The thumbs of the receiver are out for any pass below his waist.

Tight end Billy Truax, left, forms the basket with his hands as he bends over for the pass.

His thumbs are out as his relaxed hands "give" with the throw. He must keep his eyes on the ball all the way.

On the low pass, the receiver must flex his knees and bend from the waist.

the waist down. When he runs, he should not over-exaggerate and elongate his steps, unless he is in a real footrace with the man going deep. If he can take short or normal steps, his head will be on a more even plane. In other words, the longer steps he takes the more rise and fall he will have with his head. As a result, the harder it is for him to keep his eyes on the ball.

Turning the hands

One other point we stress is: which way does the receiver turn his hands to make the catch? There is really no hard and fast rule on it, but there is a rule that most receivers use. As the pass receiver is running away from the ball, say he is running a "Corner," a "Flag," or an "Up" pattern, he normally turns his thumbs out—his hands will be in a basket fashion. By the same token, any ball that he is going to catch, like a "Slant" or "Hook," he normally will want his thumbs together. As a rule, any pass that is above his waist, he will take it with his thumbs in. Any pass below his waist, the thumbs are out.

Changing shoulders

In catching the ball, our receivers are taught to change from one shoulder to the other. Occasionally when the quarterback is rushed, he puts the ball on a different side than was expected. On this situation, we have the receiver take his eye off the ball and swing from one shoulder back across to the other. This is something he cannot do unless he practices it a lot, and we work on it every day. In several cases last year, it paid off when Jack made some big catches.

In our system, we swing from side to side, depending upon the formation so our receivers must be adept at catching the ball over either shoulder. Casey, who played the right side for the 49ers for years, is a good example. When we find a receiver like this, all we do is put him on the other side and give him 90 percent of the work over there and 10 percent from the side he is used to. However, some receivers do have a side they prefer, where they have played the most, but we find they make the adjustment very easily once they get practice at it. Once they get time to work on it, they can play both sides with equal ability.

Give with the hands

The receiver should relax and not fight the ball. Stiffness of the fingers will cause more dropped passes than anything. So, he shouldn't grab or stab for the ball. As the catch is made, the hands should "give" with the ball, like an outfielder catching a fly ball. This "give" adds to the smoothness of the catch.

Above all, he must remember to catch and have control of the ball before starting to run with it. He concentrates on the ball from the time he sees it leave the passer's hand until he sees it in his hands. He must "look the ball into your hands!" He watches it all the way, even after he has made the catch.

Putting the Ball Away

Once he catches the ball, the receiver must tuck the ball away as soon as possible, so as to prevent anyone from knocking the ball out of his grasp. We give our receivers practice running with the ball. We want them to practice running like a back as soon as they catch the ball.

On all our pass drills, we ask the receiver to tuck the ball away, put it away, and drop his outside shoulder. As soon as he catches the ball, we want him to put it under his arm with a good proper hold on it and drop his outside shoulder. This is generally the direction the defender will come from, and 98 percent of the time when the receiver catches the ball, a split instant after he has it, the tackler will be there. So we want the receiver to be ready for the blow. He must know it is going to come and to drop his shoulder to protect the ball so he doesn't fumble. He must put the ball away, quickly and securely. Next, the receiver should be instructed to turn and drive directly upfield as quickly as possible. He can then check the situation and run accordingly.

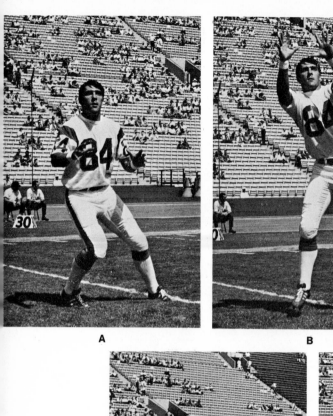

A

B

C

E

D

Fig. 3-22. GOING HIGH FOR PASS. Outside receiver Jack Snow reaches high for a quick throw. His thumbs are pointed in for the high ball. After catching the ball, he quickly tucks the ball away and drops his outside shoulder to protect the ball. This prevents the ball from being jarred loose. He then turns quickly and drives directly upfield.

A   B   C

Fig. 3-23. CATCHING BALL IN STOMACH. On the curl or strike pattern, receiver Pat Studstill catches the ball in his mid-section. The throw is low enough for him to turn his thumbs out, in basket fashion. Catching the ball against the body is vital in pro football because of the tightness of the defense. All receivers should practice catching the ball against the body.

We are real proud of the fact that in 1967, our receivers had but one fumble, and from reviewing the film, I don't think there was any way we could have prevented it. The defender came up and made a beautiful tackle. He put his head right smack on the football, and it came squirting out.

Fig. 3-24. CATCHING DRILL. Offensive end Coach Howard Schnellenberger drills the offensive receivers on their pass catching technique. Each man receives as many as 10 or 12 throws in front of the net.

Drills

There is nothing that can take the place of team drill. The ends and backs, all potential receivers, should spend most of their time as a team so that the passer can learn the position of every man on every pattern. In our 7 on 7 period, almost daily, they go against the linebackers and deep backs, working on their various patterns. Playing against a top defensive unit like we have helps.

Playing end is a series of wind sprints —short, fast runs, so he must do a lot of running. He should practice short, fast sprints of 10 to 15 yards. He should run in a straight line, then cut sharply to the left or right. When he cuts to the left, he must make sure he shoves off from right foot. When he cuts to the right, he should shove off from his left foot. In other words, he should never cross one leg over the other when he makes his cut.

Centering

4

The T-formation center should be just as effective a blocker as the other offensive linemen.

4

The center is a key man on any football team. No other player on the field has more responsibility than the center. If he doesn't perform his job of getting the play started by snapping the ball back to the quarterback, the offensive team cannot function.

The center controls the timing of his team, and proper timing is the essence of any offense. If he doesn't execute the exchange properly, the center can cause his team to bog down due to fumbles, miscues, and poorly-timed plays. Typically, the center will snap the ball back to his quarterback about 60 to 65 times per game. Therefore, the exchange has to be fast, hard, accurate, and automatic.

Poise and coolness under fire is a must for every center because of the punishment that is sure to come his way. In the NFL, the even defense has helped all centers considerably. He should be a strong tough athlete who likes to mix it! He has to enjoy making hard contact with the opposition. If he doesn't explode into a defender with aggressive quickness and power, the defense will surely come to him.

In addition, the center must be able to make the long pass to the punter in punt formation, and to the holder's hands on the placement and field goal attempts. Ken Iman has done an excellent job for the Rams since 1965.

I can assure all center candidates that they will see plenty of action, and that they will be playing an important role in the success of their team. Playing center will put them into the thick of every play. Not enough players consider playing center, but usually there is less competition at this position. Football centers—like catchers in baseball—are always in demand.

In selecting their offensive line, some coaches, unfortunately, fill every other position, then take the leftovers and make them centers. However, we don't believe that "almost any boy" can play offensive center on a football team. The center's position involves considerable responsibility, and by all means should not get the leftovers.

I always like to have at least four centers in training camp. This man is the key to proper organization. I want to carry a center on the taxi squad every year, besides having another player on our 40-man squad who has played center.

Qualifications

The center, like the quarterback, should be a leader. He must be intelligent enough to know the blocking and what is taking place in the backfield. He not only forms the huddle, but he is the first one up to the line, too. He has to know the snap count, to get the ball back to the quarterback quickly. Therefore, he must know the situation as far as the last possible movement by the defense. By making the necessary calls and adjustments, he aids the rest of his teammates on the line. In fact, he makes as many adjustments at the line as the quarterback.

Above all, the center should be quick. Quickness is more important than size. We call it short speed, speed within a radius of five yards. I prefer to have a center around 6'3" or 6'4", and weigh 245—that's big enough. Yet, there have

been some excellent ones like Jim Ringo who at one time played at 234 or 235.

A large player at the center position provides greater protection for the quarterback. Moreover, a tall center enables the quarterback to stand higher, giving him a better view of the field and the defense. Another important asset of the center is hustle, providing he has the necessary size, of course. Generally speaking, if the center hustles, his team likewise will hustle. The center sets the pace for the entire offensive line.

To be a pivotal man, a player must have strength to successfully perform his blocking responsibilities. The center should be a punishing blocker who really blasts the middle linebacker when he fires out at him. He has to be able to cut the big tackles, fellows who will be 25 to 35 pounds bigger than he will be. His blocks often will determine whether or not the ball carrier will be able to run the shortest line to the goal line—and that's straight ahead!

Therefore, the center has to have the strength to turn the tackles and the quickness to get to the middle linebacker. And, too, when they start playing an odd defense, he has to have the ability to ward off individuals. So, we are asking for a tremendous football player.

Stance

The stance of the center is slightly wider than that of the normal offensive lineman, as widely apart as the ability to move

Fig. 4-2. ASSUME A GOOD BASE TO SNAP THE BALL. The feet are slightly staggered, toe to instep. We have our center sit back on his haunches. The ball is placed right in front of his nose. The Rams' centers keep the seams straight up, the way our passers like it. (Ken Iman)

Fig. 4-3. TAKE A COMFORTABLE STANCE. The center should use an even stance, one from which he can move in any direction. While some centers keep the left hand on the knee, we have our center put both hands on the ball. However, everything is done with the right hand.

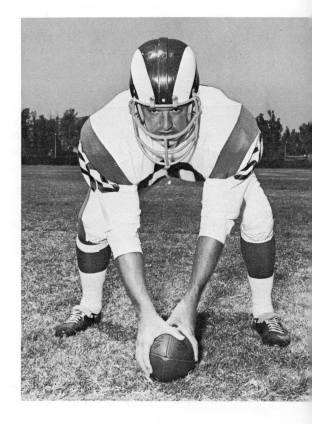

in any direction will permit without lowering the buttocks. This provides the necessary base to snap the ball back to the quarterback. The important thing is to establish a stance which is comfortable and what the players do best. By starting with a comfortable stance, the center can effectively carry out his duties of charging and blocking, after executing a successful snapback.

We like our centers to use a staggered stance. By placing the right foot back slightly, the righthanded center finds he has more freedom to make his snapback. The feet are parallel to each other, pointing straight ahead and are slightly wider than the width of the shoulders. Some coaches advocate a square stance with the feet even and parallel.

The center should be leaning well forward over the ball so that his head is almost up to the front part. The head is up so that his eyes can focus on a point about five yards downfield. The shoulders are square, and the back is straight with the hips high enough to allow the quarterback to stand almost erect. His weight should be distributed evenly between the football and the balls of his feet.

"Make sure your knees are pointing straight ahead, rather than kneeing inward," says offensive line coach Ray Prochaska. "This allows ample space to bring the ball up to the quarterback."

It is up to the quarterback to apply enough pressure to the center's crotch with the back of his hands. Therefore, the center will know exactly where his hands

are, and this will serve as a target as he brings the ball up.

Delivery

The Rams employ the two-hand snapback to the quarterback. The two-hand method is more secure, because the center can bring the ball back a little faster and harder than with the one-hand technique. The one-arm snap does have one advantage in that it has the free hand and arm that can be used to club away at the man playing on his nose. But, with the two-hand snap, centers have better control. They seem to be a little more efficient in getting the job done.

Grip

Coming up to the line, the center grabs the ball and positions it the way he wants it. Normally, the laces on the ball are turned halfway down on the right side. The right hand is placed well up on the front half of the ball, similar to the position taken when throwing a forward pass. The fingers are well spread, and the thumb extends over to the left side of the ball.

The left hand which supports most of the center's weight is placed on the rear end of the ball. The fingers are together with the thumb extended over the top of the ball. His weight is supported by the upper part of the palm at the base of the index finger. He should tilt the ball forward so that the rear end of the ball points at about the level of his knees. He must be

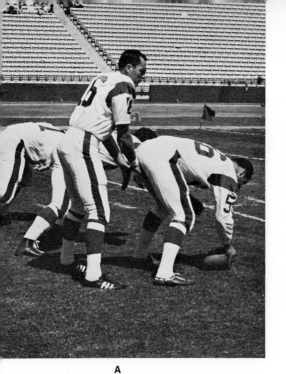

A

B

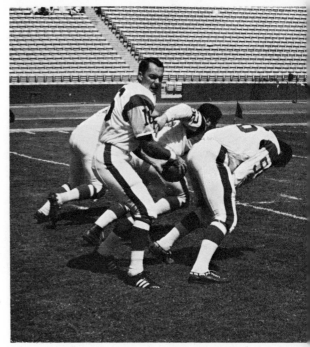

C

Fig. 4-4. THE ONE-HAND SNAPBACK is another method of snapping the ball. Using his right hand only, the center makes a normal quarter turn, putting the ball between his legs. The left hand, which had been resting on the left knee, moves into blocking position.

careful, however, not to tilt the ball too far forward because the rules state that the ball may not be at a greater angle than 45 degrees from the ground.

Unless he lines up the ball properly and correctly every time, the center cannot be consistent on the exchange. The center should keep his body in the same plane throughout the exchange.

87

A

Fig. 4-6. BALL EXCHANGE. The center keeps his arms stiff on the snap. From a slightly staggered stance, he brings the ball straight up like a swinging pendulum. This action enables the center to get the ball to the quarterback at a quarter turn. As the center drives the ball back and up, his body weight starts forward. As contact with the quarterback's hands is made, the center takes his first step forward. The ball is placed with the laces up into the fingertips of the quarterback. (Ken Iman)

Fig. 4-5. CLOSE-UP OF THE GRIP. The right hand is placed well up on the front half of the ball. The fingers are well spread, and the thumb extends over to the left side of the ball. The left hand is placed on the rear end of the ball rather than on the knee.

The left hand is there to balance off the weight. Used as a guide, it comes up as a blocking lever immediately on the snap. The snap is made solely with the right hand.

B

C

Ball Exchange

The ball exchange from the center to the quarterback must become automatic. Therefore, these two players must practice together countless hours so they have complete confidence in each other.

Although the center has both hands on the ball, it is lifted by the right hand only and should be brought up with all the speed and force possible. The delivery arm hand should swing like a pendulum. The quarterback wants it horizontal so when the center snaps it, he has to turn it. He does it with one motion—real quick!! It is a natural twist of the wrist. As it comes up, the ball should be turned over so that the side of the ball that was on the ground will contact the hands of the quarterback exactly in the middle of the center's crotch.

The snapback is simply a normal turn, a quarter turn to put the ball between the legs. Nothing real hard about it, just a natural way of turning the arm. The quarter-turn is faster than the full wrist turn. He just uses the other hand as a guide as he comes up.

Since the laces will still be on the right side, the quarterback receives the ball with the laces across the fingertips of his right hand so that he can pass or hand-off immediately without having to juggle or adjust the ball in his hands. It is easier for the quarterback to grasp the ball if the center turns the ball slightly to his left as he brings it up. The ball is then at a 45-degree angle from the line of scrimmage when it reaches the quarterback's hands.

The quarterback places his hands so that the thumbs of each hand are on top pressing against the crotch of the center.

A

B

C

E

D

Fig. 4-7. EXACT TIMING. This is the secret to a good exchange. Where the laces end up is highly important. As he brings the ball back and up with force, the center rotates his wrist by turning his fingers to the left as he lifts the ball with him on his first step. The exchange should occur before the step. (Center Ken Iman demonstrates here.)

With the throwing hand on top, the fingers of each hand point downward and outward and press against the inside of his thighs. This keeps the quarterback from having one of his fingers jammed by the ball and will enable his hands to completely surround the fat part of the ball as it comes up to him.

THIS IS A MUST:—the center must deliver the ball to the same spot in his crotch every time. Any inconsistency may cause fumbles.

The secret to a good exchange is where the laces wind up. The quarterback wants these laces right under the fingertips of his top hand. Then, he is all set to hand-off, pass, or whatever he wants to do.

As he delivers the ball, usually the center's buttock's go up, his head goes down, and his back bows. It is very important then that the quarterback's hands ride with the ball and that the center keep his body in the same place throughout the exchange. As the center moves forward, the quarterback must maintain pressure with his hands on the center's buttocks by extending his arms until the ball is exchanged cleanly. Otherwise, a fumble will likely occur.

The Charge

The charge of the center depends on the type of block assigned to him. The important thing is to move on the snap. He should start his charge and snap the ball at the same time. He should not bring the ball up and then start to move. He must move on the snap.

The charge is started by driving hard off both feet. The center must make sure that he "fires out" and snaps the ball exactly on the starting count. When the ball is snapped, the center's body is going forward; he has to catch up with it with his feet. If he is going to block to either side, the movement then must be lateral rather than straight.

A   B

As contact with the quarterback's hands is made, the center takes his first step forward, usually with his right foot, followed by the second step, which should be a short, hard driving step. On a pass play, there should be a slight movement ahead, but very slight, though, because the center has to go back for pass protection.

Sometimes, the center will anticipate the signal and center the ball before his linemen have heard the starting count. This has happened many times without being corrected and the other offensive linemen are blamed for not getting their blocks. The defense now will be able to move on the ball and beat the offensive line to the charge. Thus, the offense loses its biggest advantage—knowing the starting count. So, this timing must be watched carefully every day.

Each center and each quarterback are different in their techniques. When fumbles occur on the exchange, the movement of the center should be checked. Quite often, he is guilty of carrying the ball with him on his first step. Or, his snapping action may cause the ball to arrive too low for the quarterback.

The center must be able to cope with the defender who sets himself right up in front of his nose and tries to give the center a rough time. The center can cut him down to his knees by his quickness. He can shoot right out after him and try to drive him back if he is big and strong

C

Fig. 4-8. THE CHARGE. As contact with the quarterback's hands is made, the center takes his first step forward, followed by the second step, which should be a short, hard driving step. The feet are well spread so that he has good stability to move into a block. He must drive with explosive power. (Ken Iman)

enough. Of course, if he is blocking "a Butkus," and if he isn't as big or strong, he is in trouble. But, still, the head and shoulder block and a good forearm might prove effective. Usually, a quick block to try to cut him down at his knees is effective against the big middle backer.

Blocking

To a large extent, blocking is desire and determination on the part of the player to beat his man and get the job done. If a man is blocked out of the play, normally, the center's work has been successful.

Aggressive blocking is what it takes to perform at the center position. We like to

see our center snap the ball, go after his man and aggressively block him. He has to "Run him down"!

Blocking the middle linebacker is usually a matter of harassment. It is seldom a crisp block. The center just gets in the middle linebacker's belly and keeps him occupied as long as he can.

Blocking on the draw takes plenty of timing. The center drops his head and drives his shoulder into the linebacker's gut with everything he has. Timing and speed is what makes good blocking for the draw.

With increasing emphasis being placed on the passing game, pass blocking has become an important responsibility for the center. His first job is to pick up the middle linebacker. After that, he is an

A

B

E

C

D

Fig. 4-9. AGGRESSIVE BLOCKING Is A Must. With a man on his nose, the center must establish a good base and keep his feet moving. In protecting the passer in the cup, the center must step out aggressively into the defender and sting him. Then, he steps back, making the rusher show his charge: at this point he can "rooster fight" him. (George Burman)

option blocker, picking up any leakage through the line, helping out the four interior linemen, whoever misses.

With his knees slightly bent, the center leans forward from the waist, his elbows high and parallel to the ground. The fists are clenched in front of his chest, thumbs in. We like our centers to drop back about four yards, approximately three yards in front of the quarterback. At first, the center had better look or else he will end up with his rear in the passer's face. But after a while, he can sense this position. Good pass protection demands that all penetration be stopped at this point, about four yards behind the line of scrimmage.

All in all, the T-formation center should be just as effective a blocker as the other linemen. The fact that he shares with the quarterback the important responsibility of ball exchange should not diminish his effectiveness as a blocker. This is the one big advantage over a single wing center.

On a running play going to the right, he will block with his left shoulder. As he snaps the ball with his right hand, he will drive his left shoulder at his opponent, bring his left hand up to his chest for a broader blocking surface. He should aim his head directly at the man's mid-section and slip it by the right side only at the last moment.

The first step with his left foot should be straight forward in a short quick jab. The second step comes just after he makes contact, and then he brings his right foot up under him very quickly at the side of the defensive man. As it hits

the ground, he drives off the right foot and lifts him in an attempt to turn the man to the left.

From then on, he continues to drive after his opponent with quick, choppy powerful steps, always working to keep himself between the play and the man he is blocking. If he completes his first block, he should go downfield after another man.

Forming the Huddle

The center should take pride in forming a good huddle. One of his responsibilities after each play is to hustle back and establish a point where his teammates will form the huddle for the next play. A point 7 to 7½ yards behind the line of scrimmage is sufficient, where the quarterback can give his signals without the defense interfering or reading what will happen.

A sloppy huddle is the fault of the center, usually a sloppy center. The center should be told to go back to the point and hold up his hand so that the rest of the team can form the huddle and then go straight up to the line for the next play.

We are real concerned with our huddle, the reaction that we have, and the manner in which we come out. Linemen are always looking for a possible tip-off, such as an expression by the quarterback or certain mannerisms by ball carriers or pass receivers. We hope that we are not giving anything away. In fact, during practice, we want our defensive linemen to tell us what they see. After all, what they see, the opponents have got to see.

As he breaks quickly out of the huddle and comes up over the ball, the center should be thinking of his blocking assignment and the technique he will use in carrying out his assignment. The prime concern of the center is the snap count and the importance of delivering the ball at the exact time.

Centering to the Kicker

The quickest way to lose a ball game is to have a kick blocked and usually the fault is traced to a slow or inaccurate pass from the center. I may be wrong, because I don't have statistics to prove this point, but it appears as though good centers are getting scarce. I'm referring to their ability to make the precise snap to the holder or kicker. This is why a man who desires to become a good center must practice the long spiral pass every opportunity he gets.

When a team lines up in placekick or punt formation, it becomes the important responsibility of the center to fire the ball back low, quick, and accurately in a perfect spiral.

When the center places his hands on the football, it will be approximately at arm's length directly in line with his nose and the middle of his body. His weight should be distributed evenly on his feet with good balance. In fact, he should spread his legs a bit wider than he would in exchanging the ball.

Centering the ball to the holder on the placekick isn't really hard. It is more or less a quick lob. The holder who is only seven yards behind the center doesn't want the football coming at him like a bullet. He likes a nice, crisp lob with a steady spiral about two or three feet above the ground. The ball should come back where the punter wants it, usually between the hips and the knees. The important point here is that it should always be the same speed. The ball has to come back at the same speed every time. Otherwise, the center can destroy the kicker's timing.

On punts, the center does the same thing, but he gets more of his arms into play: his whole body works. In a lot of cases the punter is very far back, but he still wants the same kind of pass. The ball must be centered accurately with a firm spiral, and he wants something on the ball. We want speed. This is why the center must put his entire body into this one.

Above all, the center must not watch the ball all the way into the punter's hand. As soon as the ball is passed, he had better get himself into blocking position. The ball should be aimed directly at the kicker's hands, in front of the belt buckle.

Centering with a Direct Snap

The spiral pass is also used almost entirely by teams that still run from the single-wing or short-punt formations. Therefore, a good center must know how to snap the ball back to one of the deep

A   B   C

backs with accuracy and with the proper speed. When I was coaching in college, the first two players I attempted to recruit were a center and a tailback. The reason was because we employed a multiple offense and shifted to the single wing.

A nice crisp lob is needed, with a good spiral. The center uses both hands on the ball when he passes. The left hand helps with the spin and the speed. Both arms do the job.

The feet of a single-wing center should be spread wider than in a normal stance. Most centers stagger their feet. If the right-handed center will place his right foot slightly back, he will give his passing hand a larger arch to pass through. The

knees are flexed for comfort and extra power. The ball should be at a comfortable arm's length in front of the center as he takes his position.

With the laces facing the ground, the right hand should be placed under the forward point of the ball with the fingertips gripping the laces. The fingers of the passing hand should be well spread. Actually, the grip and passing motion is almost the same as that used in throwing a forward pass. The only difference is now the center is throwing the ball back between his legs.

The left hand is placed lightly along the top of the ball with the fingers almost parallel to the seams of the ball. The left

D   E   F

hand is used only as a guide hand since the power in snapping the ball back is supplied by his right hand.

The center should be looking back through his legs and should be able to see at least the lower part of the legs of the man he is centering the ball to. The spiral is made by rolling the ball off the fingertips of the right hand, while the left or guide hand helps to direct the ball to the right point.

On most of the plays in the single-wing, the snap should be a soft spiral with a light touch, so not much follow-through is needed, and the center can quickly bring his head up as he starts to block.

Fig. 4-10. CENTERING FOR FIELD GOAL. The ball should be at a comfortable arm's length in front of the center. In this series, center Ken Iman has the laces down on the left side. His right hand is under the forward point of the ball. The power in snapping the ball back is supplied by the right hand, with the left hand serving as the guide hand. The spiral is made by rolling the ball off the fingertips of the right hand, while the left hand helps to direct the ball. The center must fire the ball back low, fast and accurately in a perfect spiral. His target is the holder's (Eddie Meador's) hands. Note the excellent follow-through with both hands. This is one fundamental which is often neglected. Another fault of present-day centers is that they have to pick the ball up before snapping it.

A

B

Fig. 4-11. DRILLS FOR THE CENTER. These are two drills which the Rams perform daily, before or after practice. The ball exchange, left, requires hours and hours of drill until it becomes almost automatic. The long spiral pass must be practiced at every opportunity.

Drills

The center, in his practice drills, must cover all of the situations a center is likely to encounter in a game. As for the ball exchange to the quarterback, this requires hours and hours of drill until it becomes almost automatic. Daily drill is required if the center is to stay sharp. Even a fraction of a second can make the difference. Every day before regular practice begins, the quarterbacks and centers spend 15 minutes working on the ball exchange.

The long spiral pass to a kicker must be practiced at every opportunity. Some centers find it helpful to practice first each day by standing up and throwing a two-hand spiral from directly overhead for a few minutes before turning around and throwing the ball through their legs using the same motion. The weighted training ball is helpful here.

Coach Prochaska runs all of our offensive linemen through the same drills. Our centers and guards can play either spot equally well. For example, everyone drills on pulling. They all go through this drill 100 percent true to form.

The only thing we ask the centers to do differently is to get out of the line of scrimmage faster. And here, they work individually with the quarterbacks.

Pass protection is probably the most difficult technique for the center, as it is for all linemen. It is perhaps more difficult for the center because he has to make adjustments, such as on the running plays. He has to effectively block nose-to-nose, so that he will not be defeated. No football team likes the defense to take advantage of a weak center. So, we drill on this by having a defensive man line up against him.

When the center snaps the ball, he must make an effective block on a defensive man. A center should never snap the ball without this forward motion. He might have the defensive man hold a blocking dummy.

He has to have the ability to come on out without being caught by the defensive lineman. We drill him so that he has to step equally well with either foot.

The center candidate should strive to build up his strength and stamina at every opportunity, but the best time for strength and endurance development is prior to the start of formal practice.

Offensive Line

Fully 90 percent of all offensive action is in blocking.

5

No football offense can succeed without a strong line up front, which can open up the holes and keep the rushmen away from the passer.

Blocking is the first principle in offensive line play. *Fully 90 percent of all offensive action is blocking. It is the essence of good offensive football.* Therefore, it is the first rudiment which a lineman must master, and the line coach cannot stress this fundamental enough.

Successful blocking must be taught in the first three weeks of the season and during spring practice. In order to teach players how to block, drills are necessary to perfect endurance and technique. A considerable portion of the practice program should be devoted to the teaching of these fundamentals since blocking is the backbone of all good football teams. Care must be taken to make this part of the practice program as productive and interesting as possible.

Many coaches fail to keep a record of the time devoted to drills and techniques used to teach fundamental blocks. A record of the time spent on each block should be kept on the Time Study Chart on blocking (see next page).

In this chapter, emphasis is placed on the following blocks:

1. Shoulder block
2. Reverse shoulder block
3. Trap block
4. Position step block
5. Cross-body block
6. Reverse cross-body block
7. Crab block
8. Double Team block
9. Pass block
10. Screen block
11. Downfield block
12. Blocking for kicks

All other blocks are secondary or relative to these twelve and originate from different situations that arise on a football field.

The fact that at least 90 percent of all action and energy in offensive football is used in blocking explains why greater supervision should be devoted to the techniques and drills used in teaching the blocking game.

TIME STUDY CHART ON BLOCKING

Number of minutes for each drill

	1st Week	2nd Week	3rd Week	Total
Date				
Shoulder Block				
Reverse Shoulder Block				
Trap Block				
Position Step Block				
Cross-Body Block				
Reverse Cross-Body Block				
Crab Block				
Two-On-One Drill				
Pass Block				
Screen Block				
Downfield Block				
Field Goal Block				
Punt Block				
Skeleton Backs				
Red Dog Blocking With Backs				

Fig. 5-2. THE OFFENSIVE LINE must be able to open up holes, like the one shown above giving Willie Ellison (33) some good running room.

Qualifications

In selecting offensive linemen, we look for the big, strong boy who is quick, agile, tough and has a great desire to play football. We like them to have what we call short quickness. That is, we are not looking for 100 yard speed but more like 10, 15, or 20 yards. The ability to move quickly over a short distance is the greatest asset of the lineman. Quick feet and leg power are very important.

Guards and centers are selected for size and agility combined. We will often sacrifice size to obtain that agility and toughness. Of course, the size of the guard should depend on the offense used. If he has to pull out of the line and lead interference, a team must sacrifice size for speed.

The guard has to be one of the toughest men on the field. Along with the center, he is involved in hard contact on every play. On running plays, he must block at the line of scrimmage or pull out and block

on outside end sweeps. On pass plays, he has to drop back to protect the quarterback.

A good strong man must be at the center position. He starts every play and is usually in the middle of the action. He must snap the ball to the quarterback with automatic consistency and be a durable blocker.

The tackles are usually the biggest men on the offensive line field. They must be strong, explosive, and have the quickness to block the defensive end. He is usually blocking the biggest man on the defensive line. This assignment determines to a great extent the merit of the offensive tackle.

Regardless of all of their physical attributes, offensive linemen have to be sold on playing in the line. Their dedication, or lack of it, will often determine the success of a football team. In short, they must like to hit!

Fig. 5-3. OFFENSIVE LINEMEN should not only be big and strong but quick—short quickness is a must! (Charlie Cowan, Joe Scibelli, Ken Iman, Tom Mack, and ex-Ram Joe Carollo are shown here).

Stance

Fundamental to all good blocking movements is a perfect stance. Without a good, balanced stance, it is difficult to start with speed or drive with power after making the initial movements. Most linemen use a balanced three-point stance giving them a solid base to move into their block. From it, they can explode ahead quickly, pull out or hold against a pass rush.

The Rams vary the stance, in terms of what is referred to as a balanced stance. We put a little more weight forward, and the stagger is a little greater than others. The stagger should depend on the build of the individual. We like them to line up with their right foot back, although not farther back than the heel of the opposite foot. The feet are placed about shoulder-width apart. Since the position of the lineman's feet may tip off the direction he is going, the guard may suddenly shift his rear foot as the play begins.

The lineman's head is up, the neck is firm, the eyes are looking straight down the field. His shoulders are parallel to the ground with his feet well up under him. The back is level and parallel to the ground.

The weight is evenly distributed over the hand and the feet. Although we put weight on the front hand, we are not as

Fig. 5-4. OFFENSIVE LINE SPACING has increased the effectiveness of offensive football by spreading the defensive linemen. Using man-for-man blocking, the chief task of the offensive line is to keep the hole open (Joe Scibelli, Ken Iman, Tom Mack, and Roman Gabriel).

rocked forward as those in the split-T. If a boy shows good ability to move forward, sideward, and can pull, and still have that real good "pop," we leave him alone.

The right arm on the ground should be in line with the right knee and perpendicular to the ground. When pulling out, this hand isn't as far in front of the shoulder, and very little weight is placed on it. The wrist of the free arm is placed slightly above the knee, with the hand clenched ready for use in blocking.

109

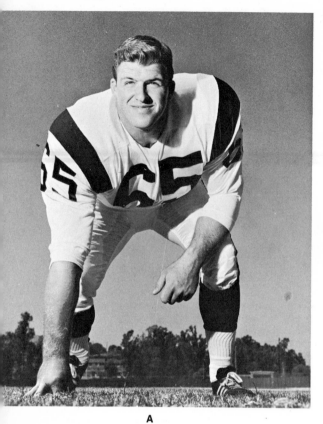

A

B

Fig. 5-5. A BALANCED THREE-POINT STANCE provides a solid base for moving into the block. The stance should be comfortable and give the lineman good maneuverability. The lineman's head is up, his weight evenly distributed over the hands and feet. Demonstrating the lineman's stance above are Tom Mack (A) and Joe Scibelli (B).

Fig. 5-6. THE CHARGE. The feet of the linemen should be well spread and should be advanced in short, digging, piston-stroke steps. Balance and control are highly essential. The head should be up, the eyes open. One of the common errors in the charge is to lower the head too soon. Above, the left guard has lowered his head.

This is the stance which will put the blocker in the most advantageous position to be ready to spring out quickly into his opponent when he hears the starting count.

Starting Count

Although there are many kinds of starting counts a team can use, the important thing is to keep the count simple. The offensive linemen have a big advantage over the defense in that they know when the ball is going to be snapped. Therefore, they must take full advantage of this factor.

The Charge

The offensive charge is the quick uncoiling of the line as a unit. Our entire running offense depends on the quickness and power with which our men drive off that line. Since the defense are bigger and can use their hands, the offensive line must depend on maximum momentum and surprise in opening up holes for the ball carriers.

Two types of line charges are used in football today: the Step charge and the Lunge charge. The type of charge or approach a lineman takes will depend on the particular play.

Step charge

This charge used against a waiting defensive tackle is executed by driving forward off the front foot while taking a step forward with the back foot. The lineman usually makes contact with the opponent as the rear foot completes its forward movement.

The biggest factor in the initial charge is "two quick steps." He must take short steps to keep both feet under him and give his body the necessary momentum to go forward. So, he must get off his marks fast, as fast as he can, and keep on balance. He must keep his legs driving!

The "Step" action only begins the block—to develop a driving force. After the forward momentum gets underway, the specific type of block will determine further movement.

Lunge charge

With an opponent playing head-on, the blocker doesn't need any position steps after his lunge. The lunge charge used against hard charging opponents is executed by driving with considerable force off both feet at the same time. The lineman comes into contact just as or just before full extension of the knees takes place. Once the feet are in their forward position, he takes short powerful steps in a churning driving action. The lunge charge is primarily used with shoulder blocks.

Lunging requires nothing more than straightening of the legs, without movement of the legs. A blocker must never rock back and forth before he makes his lunge. He must explode straight forward without first raising his body. To keep his head up, the blocker's eyes should be kept skyward.

Balance and control are the important things on the charge. He might "sting" somebody, but if he doesn't have balance after the hit, he'll fall to the ground.

Pulling Out

The fundamental technique of pulling and trapping linemen is often neglected by football teams. The Rams spend considerable time working on this action. This is the sweep type pull that can pick up the easiest yardage we can get. If we can get a back outside with a lineman in front, we can get away from all those huge people inside, and we can score points out there. We cannot get such easy yardage running up the middle.

There is no deception on the Power Sweep. The two guards simply lead the ball carrier around end. At the snap of the ball, both guards pull out of the line and clear a path for the runner. The blocking back will usually take out the defensive end or corner linebacker.

The guards are the keys to the success of the play. They must move out quickly, get out of the way of the runner and clear the path.

The Rams employ three basic methods in pulling out of the line: (1) Jump pivot; (2) Lead step; (3) Cross-step. We like the lead step technique (also called the pivot and step) because it enables the pulling

A   B   C

D   E   F

Fig. 5-7. PULLING OUT WITH JUMP PIVOT. In pulling to the left, the right guard pivots sharply on the toe of his outside foot (the right), spinning his body in a quarter turn. The first step of approximately six to twelve inches is made with his left foot. This places the pivot foot in a coiled position, and gives the guard the power to move quickly. The guard should stay low and pump his arm (demonstrated above by Joe Scibelli).

lineman to step directly into the hole much faster than does the cross-step.

Jump pivot

This maneuver is quicker than the cross-over in pulling out of the line. In going to his left, the right guard should pivot sharply on the toe of his outside right foot and spin his body in a quarter turn. First, he steps approximately 6 to 12 inches with his lead left foot. This places his pivot foot in a coiled position, providing the power to move quickly. The pulling guard must stay low and pump his arm vigorously.

Lead step

In pulling right, the lineman pivots sharply on the toe of his inside or left foot, spinning his body in a quarter turn. When he pivots, his outside or right arm thrusts back sharply, turning his shoulders and hips in the desired direction.

The first step of six to twelve inches with the right or lead foot will place the pivot foot (or left leg) in a coiled position, giving him the power to move quickly. A longer first step would disturb body balance and prevent a proper rear leg push-off.

In pulling out, it is most essential for the lineman to pivot first on the back foot. He doesn't pick it up at all. He pivots in a 45 degree angle on the ball of his rear foot, and he should keep the right knee locked in the stance position. The outside guard will pivot on a 45 degree angle any time he pulls for any kind of a sweep. The reason for the 45 degree angle is to make clearance with the offensive back going forward to block a lineman on the line of scrimmage. If the back hasn't cleared yet, the guard may deviate to a higher angle. The locked knee will keep him down, to the point that he can make the first step relatively short, about a foot and a half beyond the pivot foot. He doesn't want a long step of three or four feet!

A

Fig. 5-8. CROSS-OVER STEP. The lineman pivots on the left or near foot in the direction he is going. Then, he crosses-over with his right foot. He places his weight on his pivoting foot, but when the cross-over step hits the ground, the weight returns to both feet. When performed correctly, it is a one-motion pivot and drive off the rear foot.

Charlie Cowan and Joe Carollo are shown here pulling under a training bar to keep them low.

Cross step

From the basic stance, the lineman pushes off the fingertips of the down hand and pivots on the right or near foot in the direction he is going. Then he does a cross-over with his left foot. The weight of the player's body should be placed on his pivoting right foot and returned to both feet when the cross-over step hits the ground. Some linemen throw their arm

B

C

D

E

vigorously, to help them pivot quicker. Coach Prochaska stresses, however, a normal swing of the arm.

The pulling lineman should take his first few running strides in a low position and gradually he rises. When he crosses the line of scrimmage, he then will be in good blocking position and have good body balance. As he nears the defensive player who is being blocked, he will widen his legs to acquire a better blocking base.

Fig. 5-9. BLOCKING AGAINST DUMMY SLED. This type of sled work is needed every day in training camp and three times weekly during the season. The lineman first concentrates on the shoulder block, making quick hard contact and drives through the sled. He keeps his feet moving at all times.

In pulling out to block the defensive end, it's a one-on-one block. Although he knows which way he hopes to take the man, he will run straight at him. He doesn't know whether he will try to take him in or out. So, therefore, he goes straight at him, and at the last moment, he goes into the block he wants, a right shoulder or left shoulder block. What he is coping with here is knowing what the defensive man is looking for.

Blocking

The job of the offensive lineman is to defeat the man in front of him. The more battles he wins in the line, the more battles his team will win in games.

At first blocking fundamentals are taught against a single dummy. The linemen concentrates on the shoulder block, striving to make quick, hard contact and drive through the dummy. Later, he should work on the traps, cut-off, reverse, and other blocks. We cannot emphasize too much the necessity of daily repetition, along with proper coaching, to teach, polish, and perfect these blocks.

Next comes the one-on-one blocking against a "live" defender. This is necessary to acquire toughness and improve the technique. Later, the linemen progress to team blocking, first on the dummies and later in a scrimmage drill.

Shoulder block

The basic block in football is a straight shoulder block. This is the one-on-one. The running attack will succeed or fail depending on how well the linemen execute this block. In teaching blocking to his linemen, however, Coach Prochaska doesn't talk in terms of a right shoulder or a left shoulder block. He has our linemen thinking more of hitting their man with their forehead, then sliding off. The drive block is a favorite among NFL linemen, to drive a defender back. Exploding at the defender, the lineman jab-steps with his left foot, "thuds" his helmet into the stomach and drives him straight back.

"I tell my men to hit that target in the middle," said Prochaska, "hit the middle with your helmet. This prevents a deviation in his charge. The defender doesn't know what the blocker will do, and the blocker must not give away his intentions as well. As he charges, he will decide what shoulder should be used in the final block. We want him to get as close and tight to his man as he can, and then at the last pos-

sible moment, he will slip to the shoulder." Actually, on the up-the-middle plays, the blocking is optional for the offensive lineman. They must drive their opponents whichever way the rushmen first go.

Approach By taking short, choppy steps in the approach, the lineman will have his feet up under him, giving him more blocking power. When he gets close to his opponent, he should muster up all of his strength and explode into his opponent. If the defender is playing on his nose, he should take a short step with his back foot first. This first short backward step will enable him to follow quickly with a step forward.

Contact The blocker should hit right in the middle of the man with his head, and as he makes the block, he slides his head by him and hits sharply with his shoulder and upper arm. The arm is bent at the elbow, and the fist is on the chest, providing a wide blocking surface.

"The pop of the shoulder, the explosion of the blow is what makes a good block," says Prochaska, "explosiveness in a short distance. You have to have enough drive to stymie the defensive man, and then, it becomes balance and control."

Follow-through After making contact and stopping his charge, the offensive lineman must follow through with short driving steps. After he "pops" him, he has to keep up after him. The defensive man certainly is not going to stand there. So, when he starts moving, he has to keep

A

B

after him. This is where he has to go for him with his shoulder. Good shoulder and head contact is maintained by a well extended forearm and neck pressure. The movement of the defender will determine the follow-through foot action."

Hints on the shoulder block:

1. INSIDE foot, OUTSIDE shoulder is a good rule for this type of block.
2. Concentrate on the initial charge.
3. Work the bag laterally with the neck and head.
4. If the player is just working on the charge, he should take the bag straight back, using first one shoulder and then the other.
5. Stress keeping the head up in order to see the target and have him keep the back straight.
6. Aim the head right at the middle of the bag and just as contact is made, slide the head to the side. Let the shoulders do the work.
7. Work for a good lift with the upper arm, keeping the elbow even with the shoulder to provide more blocking surface.
8. The boys that come up with "strawberries" on their cheeks are usually doing it correctly.

Reverse shoulder block

This block is used on the line of scrimmage against defensive linemen who are reacting to the head of the offensive man on the straight shoulder block. The blocker tries to mislead his opponent by putting the head on the opposite side from where the play is going. It must be said, however, that this is a real tough block to execute. In teaching this block, the coach should insist on the players' getting their heads across quickly.

The blocker will move out from his stance with a driving step with the foot opposite the shoulder with which he is blocking. The approach is made just as though a shoulder block is about to be thrown, but when the blocker gets close enough to hit the man, he reverses the head and shoulders, contacting the defender in the mid-section with his shoulder, neck, and side of the head. The offensive man, actually, will help the opposing lineman take himself out of the play.

Trap block

A trap block is actually a one-on-one straight shoulder block applied from a different position. Everyone along the line must help out on this play, to open up

c

the gates so the trap block can be made. This is because the trapper has to have an opportunity to trap from inside out.

The trap block is used against the opposing lineman who is charging hard deep into the backfield. He is usually two or three spaces from the blocking guard. In order to reach him, the guard has to pull out of the line, behind his own line. In order to pull quickly, he should step with his near foot in a short jab fashion and then step in the direction he wants to go with the far foot.

During the trap block drill, the coach should concentrate on:

1. Proper pulling method.
2. Proper trap block with the guard's head behind the trapped tackle (if the guard is pulling to his right, he should hit the trapped man with his right shoulder).
3. Watching for pointing or pulling out too soon.

Position step block

A position step block is often used by our offensive linemen. Our ends also use this block frequently before going into their pass pattern. In referring to the position step, it all depends upon what it

Fig. 5-10. SHOULDER BLOCK. The one-on-one block involves hitting the target at the belt buckle. At the last moment, the lineman slips to the shoulder. He jab-steps with his left foot, thrusts his helmet into the "stomach" and drives the dummy straight back. He keeps his feet driving at all times. There is no substitute for quickness.

takes to block the man in order to prevent him from getting into the play. As a result, the blocker wants to momentarily delay the forward movement of the defensive man. In other words, a blocker shouldn't waste himself with a man unless he has to, particularly when the play goes to the other side of the line. After the initial impact is made with the shoulder, he immediately releases his block. Why knock a man down if turning him aside will accomplish the task?

The proper position the lineman has on the defensive man is much more important than the hard contact. If the position step block is applied correctly the offensive man is actually helping the opposing lineman to take himself out of the play.

Fig. 5-11. CROSS-BODY BLOCK. The lineman must begin this block from "handshake distance." After making contact, the blocker will pivot and whip his body across the belt line of the defender. The blocker should not leave his feet too soon and go to the ground. He should concentrate on "running right through" the defender. His target should be the nip of the defensive man. If he does this, he will not block the ground. He pushes off with his right foot and hits with his rear shoulder.

The proper way to teach the fundamentals of cross-body blocking is by practicing with a dummy.

In these pictures, the blocker takes off one step too far from his man. The block will have more power if he takes off from his inside foot, (Tom Mack demonstrates).

Cross-body block

Another block the lineman needs is the cross-body block, sometimes called the cut-off block. The body block is used on the line of scrimmage, on linebackers, and downfield on the defensive secondary.

In executing this block, we like our men to begin the block from what we call "handshake distance." The biggest problem most players have with it is that they want to start throwing the block a "mile away" from their target. After making contact, the blocker will pivot and whip his body across the defender's belt line. Usually, the cross-body is used when a normal pass block fails.

At first, it looks just like a shoulder block, but from there, the blocker slips his shoulder right by and exposes the side of his body. Most players will leave their feet, but when they hit the ground, we like them to roll through them. They should work their body around the defender's legs so he cannot get to the ball carrier. They should try to make him come out the back door.

The best way to teach the cross-body block is as follows:

1. Pair off two men. One man holds the bag and one is lined up in front of the bag in a three-point stance.

2. The men rotate after a right-side and left-side block.

3. The blocker starts the raise as if he were going to make a shoulder block.

4. If blocking to the right side, the blocker would:
   a. Shoot the right hand across the bag, about chin level,
   b. Contact the bag with the right hip, and
   c. Drive against the bag, using a crab-like motion.

5. Insist the men work on speed, power, and follow-through.

6. This block may be executed from a stationary or running position.

7. Errors to watch for in the cross-body block:
   a. Leaving the feet too soon.
   b. Keeping arms too close to body.
   c. Making contact too low.
   d. Hesitating before making contact.

A

B

C

D

Reverse cross-body block

The blocker begins his motion as if he were going to make a cross-body block. If the blocker is to the right of the bag, he will:

1. Make contact with the right hip.

2. Whip the legs around to the rear of the bag.
3. Keep his body between the bag and the ball carrier, using a crab-like motion.
4. Have reversed the position of the feet and head.

D

C

In drilling for the reverse cross-body block, the lineman should pair off, with one man holding the bag and one lined up on either side of the bag. The dummy drill will help build confidence before going against live competition.

Crab block

The crab block, also known as the single leg block, is effective against a strong opponent who knows how to use his hands, particularly the big defensive ends and linebackers in our league. The blocker tries to drive his knee up between the legs of the defensive man. He immediately "crabs" around his opponent, digging with his outside leg but keeping his inside foot stationary. He goes down on all fours and keeps after his man on all fours.

Double team block

The double team block matches two offensive linemen against the defensive player. We have found it is an effective play to give the attack some needed power. Perhaps the most common situation involves a double team by the tackle and end on the opposing tackle. In this case, the tackle is the Post man and the end is the Lead man. It's a good weapon to use against a defensive man who is bigger than his own lineman.

The Lead takes a short step with his inside foot and aims for the opponent's hip, just hard enough to break his charge. The Post man swings his shoulders and buttocks around in close contact with those of the Lead making sure there is no space for the defender to squeeze

B   A

through. The Post man uses a straight shoulder block, making sure he keeps contact with the opponent. When the team has made contact, they try to keep close together and not let the defender split between them.

In drilling for the two-on-one situation, the players are located in a line facing the coach and are then numbered off by threes. No. 1 faces Nos. 2 and 3, stays low; on the command to charge he braces against 2 and 3 to provide resistance. Then they practice double-teaming with short driving steps.

The man on defense does not try to break through but he does try to hold the two offensive men so that they will have to put real drive into their charge. It is a good idea to rotate the men after every three charges.

Fig. 5-12. DOUBLE TEAM BLOCKING. The post man breaks the charge of the defender, keeping him from penetrating. (He cannot out-charge the lead man; if he does so the block will fail.) The lead blocker steps with his right foot and makes contact with a straight shoulder block by pushing off from his left foot. His target should be his opponent's hip.

We are interested in moving the man later-ally, rather than backward, to create a larger opening. The post blocker's responsibility is to keep the defender from splitting the seam.

Fig. 5-13. CRACK-BACK BLOCK. This block is often used by the tight end on the middle linebacker. Since he has a five-yard running start, the blocker can get a good shot at him. His head must be in front of the defender. He should aim belt high so the defender cannot jump over him. He should keep his eyes on the target and hit him with a good "pop."

C

B

Fig. 5-14. PROTECTING THE PASSER. A fraction of a second is vital to the quarterback. The blocker wants to delay the rushman long enough—usually three to four seconds—for the passer to get the ball away.

The lineman's technique is to hit and fall back. He doesn't try to knock his man down. The more movement the better, so long as he keeps his balance. He maintains his balance by keeping his feet moving. He never gives up on a defender.

The offensive tackle is in a "four-second business." The only time that makes any difference to an offensive tackle is the first four seconds after the center snaps the ball. If he can hold his man out that long, the QB can get the ball away. In pass protection, quickness means more than weight or strength.

A

Pass Protection

The Los Angeles Rams put a great deal of stress on pass protection. Any football team has to. In the modern game of football, it's pass offense versus pass defense.

That's the name of the game in Pro football. If a team cannot stop the pass, they are going to be in trouble, and if they cannot throw it, they will be in trouble, too.

Pass protection comes from constant drilling. In our league, if a team cannot protect the passer, then they are going

Fig. 5-15. WORKING FROM THE CUP. Quarterback Roman Gabriel receives strong protection from such blockers as Charlie Cowan (73), Willie Ellison (33), and Joe Carollo (63). This is the type of protection which makes pass defenses suffer.

to be in trouble because all the defensive linemen are good pass rushers. In college and high school ball, a team very seldom has four pass rushers. It may have one man who can rush the passer, but he can be stopped. But in our league, everyone is skilled at this job, so protection is vital. No quarterback can make a living if he doesn't have protection.

We want our linemen to move everything they can in protecting the passer. We want them to keep loose and moving, not to be sitting ducks. The lineman must not let the defensive man latch on to him and grab him. The more movement the better we like it, just so he keeps his balance.

After making contact with the rusher, the lineman retreats, sets, and then uncoils again at his opponent. He does this time after time until the quarterback has gotten rid of the ball. "Keep your arms and legs pumping," explained Prochaska, "or else the rusher will grab you and slip by. You have to be able to hit on the run, just keep pecking away at the defensive man to keep him off balance."

Screen Block

The screen pass is an effective move by the offense when the defense is applying undue pressure on the passer. The linemen up front who must do a good job of being "con" men are the key to the success of the offense. After first sustaining the block, they allow their man to think he is about to smear the quarterback, only to learn he's been fooled. However, they shouldn't make it look too easy for the defenders or else they will sense something on the "phony" side.

The screen pass can be a deadly offensive weapon if the linemen properly execute their assignments. First, they must brush-block the defensive front four. Then they have to pull out and form a screen along the sideline for the runner.

The screen block is essentially a straight shoulder block. The blocker drives his forearms up toward the head of the opponent, forcing the defensive man to stand up straight. After making contact, he maneuvers his body between the defender and the hole where the ball carrier is to run.

Screen plays require much practice to perfect, but when used properly, they can certainly firm up a sputtering offense.

Downfield Blocking

Breakaway plays for touchdowns are the result of good downfield blocking. Therefore, all of the linemen should be adept at throwing an effective block downfield. The downfield block is actually 90% desire.

As he approaches the man he wants to block, the lineman gathers himself and then throws his body into him, making sure he is close enough to him before he takes off. He will have more blocking surface if he can get his body into the air lengthwise. So, at the moment of contact, he should extend his arm, body and legs to their fullest.

Downfield blocking is one of the most difficult phases of football to teach. It demands a terrific selling job from the coach. Dummy drills can provide the needed practice for the linemen in downfield blocking. The linemen have assigned dummies to contact and follow a predesigned course.

In drilling pulling linemen, defensive players, either holding dummies or being "live" as the case may be, are lined up in the three defensive positions representing: 1. Defensive end, 2. Defensive halfback, and 3. Defensive linebacker.

Blocking for Kicks

Knowing they can give no ground, the offense lines up with their feet widely spaced, set to dig in for the kick try. They should half straighten on the snap, with knees flexed, their heads and fists clenched. All down the line, they have their forearms poised to stop the defender's charge.

Blocking by the Receivers

Most of the blocking by our outside receivers involves the downfield body block. An outside receiver either blocks the

Fig. 5-16. DOWNFIELD BLOCKING makes the long runs possible. The most important point is to be aggressive and throw a block at the defender. Above, a downfield body block gives LeRoy Kelly of the Browns the opportunity to pick up a gain.

inside safety or the corner back on his side. "Quite a few outside receivers in pro ball have a tendency of going down and just pushing," said Coach Schnellenberger, "not really doing very much. The best way to get them out of this habit is to get them accustomed to the ground, get them used to rolling on the ground, so that the ground becomes part of the game, and we ask them to do this."

With our tight ends, Billy Truax has a variety of blocks he has to execute. The "tailor" block is a block we use on our sweep. He splits out three or four yards, and he has to stand up in the face of the linebacker, hold him on the line of scrimmage for about two counts and then let him go in the direction he wants to go and then shield him on out.

The "M" block is one of the more unique blocks we have. We call it a "Man" block. We ask Truax, our tight end, to

come off where we call a "Drive" block, to knock the linebacker straight back, keep his feet, and try to knock him back, and then turn him in any direction that he wants to go because our ball carrier has the option of running the hole that seems more open.

We have a "hook" block for our quick tosses to the strong side. On this, Bill simply hooks or jumps out and tries to get the strong linebacker or blocks the end. When we throw to the weak side, he has to pass protect like the guards and tackles.

Draw Play

This type of play is a running play that is made to look like a pass play. The linemen should let their men come in as though they were pass-blocking; then they push

128

A   B   C

Fig. 5-17. "BIG MONA" PASS BLOCKING DRILL. The lineman keeps his arms inside, chest high. Observe the wide base of offensive guard Tom Mack. Using short choppy steps, he hits with a heavy shoulder. He must keep his feet moving and stay in front of the bag.

the rushmen aside, and the ball carrier moves through the hole. The guard must ride his man whichever way he wants to go.

Drills

Since linemen are bigger and heavier than backs, they usually have poorer agility and movement. Therefore, the coach must use agility drills for the team as well as individual drills to improve each man's capabilities.

We use the board drill a great deal, driving the dummy with short, powerful steps, quicker movement, working on balance. The drills help the player execute the job he has to perform in the game, which is against one man. If he does that, we are going to win!

An offensive lineman has to have good position and body control. All of those little drills we have might look foolish, getting caught offbalance and whipping up off the ground and jumping around in a grass drill. But all of these drills are situations whereby the player is trying to condition his body so that no matter where it is, or what position it is in, he knows exactly where he is at all times.

129

Offensive Backfield 6

We want an offense which is very, very simple which excels in execution and ball control.

6

Through the years, there have been many illustrious ball carriers on the Rams' roster. None has performed more brilliantly and has combined so many of the qualifications of an all-round back than Dick Bass, a 5'10'' 195 pounder, the most productive rusher in Ram history.

Qualifications

A back has to have enough speed to be a pass receiver. He is a potential receiver on most pass plays. In college or high school ball, perhaps, most teams can get by with a back who cannot receive a ball because they don't throw the ball that much. But even then, it is going to hurt them.

Whatever his assignment may be—carrying the ball, running a good pass pattern, or blocking for his teammate—speed plays an important role. If a player cannot run with speed, he will be ineffective as an offensive back.

Toughness is essential. To become an outstanding back a ball carrier has to have courage and toughness, because he will have to take a beating.

An important characteristic of an offensive back is maneuverability. He has to make people miss occasionally, because if he doesn't, he is not going to stay healthy very long. Running with the ball involves good field vision, the ability to accurately judge distances, the balance to remain on his feet. The back must make quick decisions as to where he will run, while using his interference along the way. A ball carrier must develop the ability to change direction, change his pace, side-step, pivot, straight-arm, and slip opposing tacklers. As the old saying goes: Lunge, plunge, twist, turn, but keep going!

George McAfee, an all-time great with the Chicago Bears in the forties, had that famous cross-legged stride, but even McAfee couldn't change directions and turn on the speed like Gale Sayers. Gale is the fastest back in the league at getting

A   B   C

Fig. 6-2. FAST DRIVING RUNNERS can give needed punch to any offensive backfield (shown above, Tommy Mason and Dick Bass). In addition, an offensive back is a potential receiver on most pass plays.

to the sideline and fastest at turning the corner. He is able to keep his speed under control because he has outstanding balance, too.

Blocking ability is another quality of an all-round back. An offensive back cannot always carry the ball: he has to be able to block. A determined and sustained effort should be made by every back on every play to block his man, to successfully execute his blocking assignment. If every man in the backfield puts forth the same effort that the man with the ball does, few plays will prove unsuccessful.

The ability to start quickly is as important for a running back as it is for a charging offensive lineman. There are some backs who are never going to be great because they cannot start quickly. The only time they get going is after they are 10 yards down the field, and they can be stopped before they get going.

Ram fans will always remember the "Elephant Backfield" of the 1950's, featuring Tank Younger and Dan Towler. Even though both were huge in size, they possessed unusual quickness for big men.

To play halfback, an individual must have outstanding speed, good balance, and he must be able to move in all directions.

The good fullback must consistently get those two yards on third down, even when the defense knows he will be coming. Since he is the power runner in the backfield, he must be big enough to make the tough yardage. He should be a good blocker. He will be called on to explode through the line between the tackles, in

134

Fig. 6-3. DICK BASS, the most productive ground gainer in Ram history, gains valuable yardage against the 49ers in the mud at Kezar Stadium. Dick is the best "pick-a-hole" runner in football. He is capable of finding the right hole when the hole is closed.

addition to blocking for the quarterback and halfbacks. Furthermore he must have good enough hands to go out on pass routes.

The flanker back does not confine his efforts to merely catching passes. He must also be an able blocker.

The halfback normally lines up approximately three and one-half yards deep. He straddles the inside leg of his offensive tackle. The fullback's position is the same depth but is located directly behind the center and the quarterback.

Mental Aggressiveness

To become an outstanding runner, a player must have the desire to play the game, a winning attitude, and confidence. An offensive back has to have plenty of desire. Football is a rough, tough, bruising game, and if a boy doesn't like body contact and being knocked down, he shouldn't get into it.

An outstanding back has more than speed and size. He has *desire* and dedi-

Fig. 6-4. HARD RUNNING Les Josephson uses his blocking to go for a long gain against San Francisco. The key block was thrown by Joe Scibelli (71) on ground.

cation. Les Josephson is an excellent example. He must want that yard or two so badly that he will smash, twist, or squirm to get them.

Hard running by those in the backfield is often the difference between victory and defeat. A fast driving back makes the blocking in the line more effective because a block doesn't have to be held very long for a fast runner.

Many games have been lost because a back failed to give his best effort and a first down was missed by a few inches. A back might ask himself: "Could I have given a little more effort and made those three or four inches?"

Stance

The first fundamental of backfield play is the stance. Regardless of his speed, the back cannot make a good getaway without a proper stance. An offensive back must have one stance for all plays, whether he is going left, right, or straight ahead. Basically, he must assume the same stance, a well-balanced three-point stance which all ball clubs now use.

"The feet should be approximately shoulder-width apart, or slightly wider," said Bass. "If you are right-handed, you might drop your right foot back just a

A

B

Fig. 6-5. STANCE. An offensive back (Les Josephson shown above) should assume a comfortable, well-balanced stance and be ready to move in any direction. His head is up, back straight, with the weight evenly distributed on both feet. He looks straight ahead. This type of stance does not "tip" his intentions (Les Josephson).

shade, maybe halfway past the left foot. Your shoulder should be straight, and the neck and head should be up, so that you can see where you are going. Your back is level."

Generally, we like our backs to place a quarter of their weight on their hands. We don't want too much weight forward because our backs have to make more lateral moves than straight ahead movements. Sometimes this makes it a little awkward if the back is running a dive straight ahead, but in order to move laterally, we have to have it like this. Much of

the weight is distributed evenly on the balls of the feet. The inside hand rests comfortably on the ground, while the outside hand should rest on the outside leg.

Take-Off

An explosive take-off from the three-point stance is essential. "Always start fast and hard," suggested Bass. "Working with my quarterback, I get it down to a science, just like a sprinter would in a hundred-yard dash. I listen for the quarterback, and

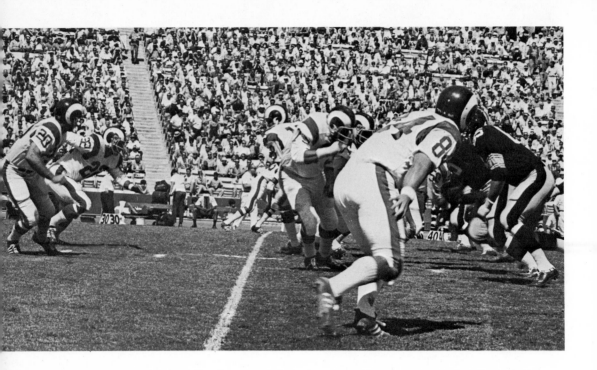

Fig. 6-6. AN EXPLOSIVE TAKE-OFF from the three-point stance is essential and is a skill which can always be improved upon. Always start fast and hard.

I find out exactly which way he calls it, 'hut one, hut two!' And I time it to this, so that I can explode on the right count. Maybe it is just a half count just before the snap, but it sounds like the same count. Paying attention and being alert is the number one thing,'' according to Bass.

"Track has done more for me in helping my start than anything else,'' remarked Mason, one of the most outstanding backs in the NFL. ''When I start, I always try to use my arms as much as I can because this kind of propels me. I'll start with short steps and run with my knees high. My feet are wide with my weight forward. I have my head and eyes up looking for the hole to open.''

If a team employs a rhythmical count, the back has to anticipate. On the non-rhythmical count, he has to concentrate even more on the sound of the quarterback, and just move as fast as he can.

In taking-off, an offensive back can use one of two types of starts: the Direct step or a Cross-over step. On the Direct step, he starts with the foot nearest the direction he intends to run. For instance, if he intends to run forward, he will take a short step with his starting foot, driving off full speed on his second step. He should take short, choppy steps until he reaches top speed.

On the Cross-over step, he will cross one leg over the other in the direction he intends to run; with the same motion, he will pivot on the ball of the other foot. In starting to his right, he will cross the left leg over the right leg, pivoting on the right foot and placing the left foot in the direction he wants to run.

Fig. 6-7. HAND POSITION. This picture shows the importance of the far arm, which serves as a back board to prevent the ball from slipping through. Quarterback Roman Gabriel's eyes are directly on target, while ball carrier Tommy Mason is looking ahead for the hole.

Above all, in starting, an offensive back must never lean or point. To prevent this from happening, he should keep his weight evenly balanced on the balls of the feet.

In short, backfield men must start quickly and be able to run with their bodies under control. "Don't waste your time dancing and dodging behind the line of scrimmage," suggested Bass. "Get moving forward fast and pick up all the yardage you can."

Receiving the Hand-Off

In receiving the ball, an offensive back should not be watching the quarterback or the ball. He has his head up. His eyes are looking in the direction he is going and toward the hole he hopes to go through.

"The way the Rams carry the ball," said Bass, "the inside arm is always up, giving a large pocket. The outside arm, the arm farthest away from the quarterback, is down. The elbow is close to the body. The inside arm should be parallel with the ground, about chin level. So, they just come together. I just put out my hands and feel for the ball. I never look at the quarterback. I always look for a hole because it's his job to get me the ball."

"I don't worry about this," remarked Mason. "The quarterback will hit me right there. When I do it enough, my hands go automatically to the right width as soon as I feel the ball. Some coaches teach their backs to hold the inside elbow up, but for me, this hurts my start. I

A

B

Fig. 6-8. RECEIVING HAND-OFF. The inside arm is always up, giving a large pocket. The outside hand is down, preventing the ball from slipping through. The ball carrier (Willie Ellison, here) puts out his hands and the quarterback (Milt Plum) places the ball in his gut. The ball carrier and the quarterback should brush shoulders to aid in deception.

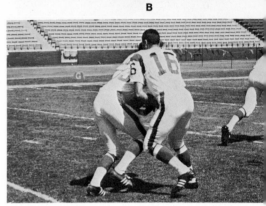

C

couldn't use my arms as well, as I would just grab the ball.''

Once he receives the hand-off, the ball carrier should put it immediately in the old pocket. "I tuck the corner of the ball up under my arm," explained Mason, "and I cover the other point of the ball with my hand. If I have the point covered, it's very hard to dislodge it."

"A quick hand-off is what we call a dive," said Bass. "We execute it from a halfback position straight ahead. I move as fast as I can go, three steps, and it's up to the quarterback to find me. On the third step, my arm automatically comes up and enables the quarterback to set it inside the pocket."

In taking off, the ball carrier should not waste a step. He pushes off his outside leg and steps forward with the inside leg. By doing this, he will get the ball in an open stance, with the outside foot ahead of the inside foot. This provides a good pocket for the quarterback and eliminates the possibility of a runner knocking the ball out of the quarterback's hands.

"Put the ball away immediately!" stated Mason. "Don't try to shift the ball until you are through the line of scrimmage. Always run with the ball away from the pressure. For example, when running to your right, you want the ball in your right arm with the hand over the point of the ball."

A   B   C

Fig. 6-9. RUNNING BACK Dick Bass provides a large pocket, and it is the job of the quarterback Roman Gabriel to give him the ball. Bass has the inside elbow up, and Gabe places the ball directly over the belt buckle. In illustration C, Bass has placed both hands on the ball and has the ball under good control.

After receiving the hand-off, the ball carrier should put it immediately in "the pocket." This is important because a ball carrier is often hit upon receiving the hand-off. He should tuck the corner of the ball under his arm.

Faking

Since football is a team game, faking is as important to the offense as carrying the ball. The successful execution of every play is dependent on the manner in which those without the ball carry out their fakes. They must convince the defense that they have the ball. A fake should never be considered an optional chore; it is a definite assignment for all members in the backfield.

"Faking has to be just as natural as running," suggested Mason. "If you exaggerate it, I think pretty soon, after they study it awhile, they will detect this. You wouldn't go real low, nor would you turn your back on anything to hide the ball, when you have the ball. You want to look directly toward the hole."

"Hold your hands the same way you would if you would take a hand-off," continued Mason, "and then continue running up into the hole. You should make it look as if you are actually carrying the ball."

Actually, the best fake a back can give is merely to run hard. He must use the same action for faking as when he receives the ball. It has been said that if a back isn't tackled on a fake, he isn't doing a good enough job of faking. When he goes through with his fake, caution should be taken not to bump the quarterback.

In running in the open field, an offensive back must learn to fake with his head and body. In fact, the head-and-shoulder fake is used to set up the Cross-over step.

141

Fig. 6-10. PROTECTING THE BALL. Les Josephson protects the ball with both hands as he bulls his way into the San Francisco defense for two yards. Clark Miller (74) is one of several 49ers trying unsuccessfully to jar the football away from Josie. Anytime a ball carrier is in a crowd, he should hold the ball with both hands. When running, his fingers should cover the nose of the ball. This prevents fumbling. He should keep the ball close to his body.

This fake is executed by dropping the shoulder and head to one side, drawing the defender out of position. This fake also sets up the Side step, which is executed by driving off the lead foot and trying to get as much lateral movement with the trail leg as possible.

The same fake should not be used each time. A player should vary his fakes to keep his opponent guessing. For example, he may run straight at the tackler, fake to the right with his head and body motion, then cut sharply to the left. Or, he may come to a sudden stop before he changes directions.

Faking can be vital in making an offense successful. A good fake will often freeze the linebackers and deep backs, increasing the ball carrier's chances of breaking away.

Blocking

In present day football, with the wide assortment of defenses, blocking is a key responsibility of every member of the backfield. The blocking chores are not merely left to the linemen up front. What with all the stunting and stack defenses, each back must be ready to contribute to the overall blocking pattern.

Without effective blocking, no offense can succeed. The passer will be forced to throw quickly or not at all. And those who carry the ball will find their holes have been sealed up. So, it becomes a matter of making up his mind to get the job done. When the play calls for a block, a back has to block!

An offensive back should become pro-

C   B   A

Fig. 6-11. BLOCKING TECHNIQUE. Dick Bass uses a running shoulder block in hitting the dummy fast and hard. He must get to the defender as quickly as possible. His head is up, his eyes are open and focused on the target.

Don't worry about getting position. Just hit 'em and keep driving! By setting a point one yard behind his opponent, the blocker can explode through the defensive man.

ficient in executing the following types of blocks:

Bob block

This is the most frequent type of block performed by a back. The fullback uses a "bob" block in handling the end with an inside-out approach. He will use a straight shoulder block and hit him hard at the numbers of his jersey. The halfback who must be able to block in the secondary, uses a drive shoulder to cross-body style of blocking. The quarterback, in leading the sweep, must be able to clean a hole and crack-back on the pursuit with an effective drive-shoulder block.

Fill block

With the return to power football and the pulling guards, the "fill" block has become a major block for offensive backs. The term "fill" is what the word implies. The back must fill the gap left by a pulling lineman.

The fullback normally does most of the fill-blocking and does it after faking.

Actually, a good faker usually doesn't have to block because he will be tackled.

Pass block

In protecting the passer, the back must be able to ward off rushers to his outside and still be aware of the "red-dogger." After firing into the rusher, he recovers back, keeping a wide base and maintaining good hitting position. In handling the hard-charging linemen, he often will fake to the numbers, then get to the defender's legs as quickly as possible.

One of the flanker's most important blocks is a crack-back on the outside linebacker on sweeps. Because of the size of the linebacker, he has to hit 'em low. In blocking the safety, the flanker has to screen him until the back gets up to him. He shuffles along in front of the safety until the ball carrier can cut off him. Then the flanker leaves his feet and tries to cut the safety down, or he tries to drive through him.

"For my size, the toughest block for me to make," confided Bass, "is to block a

143

Fig. 6-12. PROTECTING THE PASSER is a prime responsibility of an offensive back. Willie Ellison (33), keeping a wide base, combines with the tackles to form a protective pocket around Roman Gabriel.

defensive end on an end sweep. The secret here is to get there first and fast. I always set a point one yard in back of my opponent, and I try to reach this spot. By doing this, it enables me to explode through the defensive man. If I don't, then, I will fall short, and being much stronger than I, he'll just knock me to the ground."

Pass Patterns

An offensive back should spend a great deal of time on running pass patterns. They may look and sound simple, but for pin-point accuracy by the passer, a pass pattern takes considerable practice.

Among the pass routes used by the Rams' backs are the Flag or Corner, Flare, Sky, Shoot, Angle, and Circle in. There are many more. On the Flare, the back drives to the outside with a slight belly. After driving five yards, he looks back for the ball and continues on his route. The Flag or Corner involves running a circle, and after coming to a point 8 to 10 yards downfield, he drives to the outside at a 45-degree angle, looking for the ball over the outside shoulder on the break.

On the Sky pattern, the back starts directly toward a point three yards outside the strong side linebacker. Heading upfield, he looks for the ball over his inside shoulder upon crossing the line of scrimmage.

The Shoot route has the back driving at the outside shoulder of the linebacker to a point two or three yards downfield, then he breaks parallel to the line at full speed. He looks for the ball over his outside shoulder on the break.

In running an Angle pattern, the offensive back drives to a point four yards outside of the linebacker and continues

144

A   B

Fig. 6-13. RUNNING TECHNIQUE. A great runner, like Dick Bass, has exceptional field vision. For good balance, Dick runs with his feet apart with high knee action. Pumping his arms like pistons, he leans forward with the weight on his toes. He is under control and always ready to change direction.

upfield to a point where he can cut back inside the linebacker covering him. When he cuts back, he drives hard to the inside almost parallel to the line of scrimmage, looking for the ball on the break.

The Circle involves a back running a circle, then continuing upfield about 10 yards where he curls to the inside.

If flat passes have proven successful, a fast man can often free himself deep by first moving to the flat. Then he looks for the ball as the passer fakes a pass to the flat, followed by a burst of speed as he sprints deep to outrun the deep back who has moved up.

There are various ways for an offensive back to delay before going downfield for a pass. He may block momentarily, then break quickly to the outside for a pass.

Running Technique

A great runner has exceptional vision of the field. His judgment of distances is brilliant. His decisiveness enables him to make the right moves and to use his interference to the best advantage. In addition to speed, a ball carrier must develop the ability to change direction, change-of-pace, sidestep, pivot and straight-arm.

On a scrimmage play, the ball carrier has to think about the pattern he's running. Then, when he comes up to the hole and it is closed, he has to think about what his alternative move will be. He usually starts with short quick-steps and runs with his knees high. He wants to keep his feet wide, head and eyes up. His weight is

145

D   C   B

forward. When he is about to be tackled, he lowers his shoulders and drives forward for an extra yard or two.

"I always try to put the pressure on the defensive tackler," said Bass. "I run at him as long as he is there, and I make him declare first. If I can make a defensive man lean forward, then I can give him a left or right step and go around him.

"So I try to put pressure on him," continued Dick. "I run at him until he makes his move, rather than do it 10 yards from the player. With the defensive tackler just standing there, faking him will do no good. He'll just wait until you are finished faking. So, you run at him until you can make him declare."

Once a ball carrier gets past the line of scrimmage, he must use his individual ability to elude tacklers. Along with dipping a shoulder, he might try to change directions at the last minute. He might catch the defender with his head down and get away from him. "I don't like to plan my footwork," remarked Mason. "It doesn't work as well when I just react to the defender. I try to make him commit himself and then react on him."

The head and shoulder fake, side step, cross-over step, cutback, limp leg, and zig-zag are all open-field fundamentals. Former great runners with the Rams such as Tom Harmon, Glenn Davis, and Jon

Arnett had the uncanny ability to shift gears suddenly and move quickly into high.

The fullback should be effective at swinging away from a filled hole and into daylight. He might find it effective to give the defender a shoulder or a leg, then bag it through him.

The line plunge is a power play in which the runner hits the line with the ball buried in his stomach. His head is down, his knees high, and he unleashes all the drive he can. "Many times, I can pick up more yardage by spinning or twisting," said Mason, "because the tackler has no momentum to knock me off my feet. I like to pivot on the foot away from the tackler, and unless he has a good grasp on me, the force of the pivot should get me through."

A weaving run is made in the open field by swinging the hips and drawing them away from the tackler. The feet of the ball carrier should be well spread when approaching a tackler so that one leg may be thrown forward and outward from him.

Using his blockers

Knowing how to use his blockers is an important quality of a top running back. A runner should do everything he can to set up the lineman's block. By cutting and veering, he can bring the defender's inter-

146

A

cept line across the path of the blocker. The outstanding backs know when to stay with the blockers and when to leave them. Jim Brown was one of the greatest on this technique.

An offensive back must learn how to break off the blocks of his teammates. He not only knows where the blocks are coming from, but which way his blockers will take their man.

"When I have the room, I try to stay with my blockers as long as possible," said Mason. "But, when the blockers are being handled by the defenders, I will turn up field and get as much yardage as I can. We think of this as being a game of hide and seek."

Balance

A ball carrier should try to keep his feet under him at all times. "Anytime you lean too far forward," said Bass, "you place too much pressure on your legs. What I do sometimes, if I am falling, I try to run into someone. It seems kind of funny now to talk about it, but sometimes if I lose my balance, I try to run into someone. By hitting me, they stand me up to a point where I can get my feet under me again. They'll straighten me up so that I can continue on."

For good balance, a ball carrier runs with his feet apart and with a high-kick action. If he runs with his feet just slightly above the ground, he will stumble easily and be vulnerable to just a simple arm tackle.

Cross-over step

The Cross-over step is very effective on a waiting opponent. The fundamental to set up the Cross-over step is the head-and-shoulder fake. Instead of running straight ahead, the runner crosses his right leg over the left just before he makes contact with the tackler.

The ball carrier executes the step by driving a foot as close to the opponent as possible and crossing over with the trail leg. After cutting a 90 degree angle, he fades away from his opponent. As he crosses over, he shoves his right hand against the shoulder or helmet of his opponent.

Cutting

The Cutting maneuver is used to throw the tackler off balance, which often breaks his tackle. The best time to make a cut is when the defensive man crosses his leg. "I try to make my cut without losing any speed," explained Mason. "I can cut either in or out, thereby forcing the tacklers to change direction. I might want to lead in one direction with one leg, and then, with a short lateral step, go the other way."

147

C

B

A

Fig. 6-15. CUTTING. The runner must always be under control when cutting. The cutting maneuver is used to throw the defender off balance; this often breaks his tackle. Tommy Mason, above, leads in one direction with one leg, then pushes off the other way, with a short lateral step. The best time to make a cut is when the defensive man commits himself. If he doesn't commit himself, then a sharp fake will set up the cut.

D

An important rule for all running backs to remember is never cut more than once. After making his cut, the runner should not move too far laterally. As soon as the opportunity exists, he should head up the field.

On outside plays, some backs make the mistake of trying to get outside the entire defense. On sweeps, the ball carrier should turn up field as soon as he is outside the defensive end. As a result, he'll have more room to maneuver and can elude opposing tacklers.

Change of pace

This deceptive maneuver is most effective on tacklers coming laterally across the field. The ball carrier appears to be running at top speed; actually, he has some speed in reserve. At the right moment, he releases it to outrun the tackler. Or he may run at full speed, then slow down or stop

A   B

C   D

Fig. 6-16. CROSS-OVER STEP. The runner crosses his right leg over the left just before he makes contact with the tackler. After cutting a 90-degree angle, he fades away from his opponent. As he crosses over, he shoves his right hand against the shoulder or helmet of the opponent. This technique should be worked on every day. (Les Josephson)

149

A   **B**   **C**

Fig. 6-17. TURNING THE CORNER. In making a sharp cut to his right, Tommy Mason makes a quick pivot on his right foot, like "turning on a dime." He lowers his hips which lowers his center of gravity, allowing him to be on balance, under control.

D

to make the defender miss. Dan Reeves of Dallas uses this maneuver effectively.

The Change of Pace can be practiced by running at an object, an assumed tackler. The ball carrier approaches at three-quarter speed, then crosses away at full speed.

Straight-arm

This is almost a forgotten weapon. A good straight-arm can be useful for any ball carrier. It is a jabbing motion, in which the runner thrusts the arm nearest the tackler straight out from the shoulder with the elbow locked. Usually, the target is the helmet of the tackler.

The straight-arm is most effective when combined with a good pivot, cross-step, or sidestep dodge. At the moment of contact, all the weight should be taken off the feet to allow the legs and body to swing free.

E

Fig. 6-18. ELUSIVENESS pays off. Willie Ellison (33), Los Angeles running back, eludes the out-stretched arms of Cleveland's Bob Matheson (56) and goes in to score from the five-yard line in the 1968 "Play-off Bowl" in Miami.

Hanging on to the ball

Running with the ball involves proper carriage, with both points covered. "Any-time that I am in a crowd," explained Bass, "I always hold the ball with two hands. First of all, I carry the ball as close to me as I can to the inside area of my body. I like to lock my fingertips over onto the ball with the point inside of my elbow close to the body. As long as it is in there, it is hard for the defense to tear the ball away from me.

"Most athletes try to run like a track man, but when carrying a football, the ball carrier should run just the opposite," said Bass. "In track, an athlete will pull his arms down and work up; whereas in football, he will work the arms across, keeping the ball as close as he can to his body. This action prevents somebody from pulling his arms away from his body."

Getting hit and landing

No matter how tight a situation, the ball carrier can always manage to turn or twist one way or the other. "If I see a blow coming," said Mason, "I try not to take it so hard. I always more or less struggle as long as I can."

If he sees it coming and there is nothing

151

A   B

Fig. 6-19. RUNNING THE GAUNTLET. In this drill, each offensive back runs with the ball through two parallel lines of players, each of whom is trying to jar the ball out of the grasp of the carrier. Anytime you are in a crowd, cover the ball with two hands! (Dick Bass)

he can do, the runner might try to hit the tackler as the tackler tries to hit him. "I will often come off much better this way. If I just stand there and let him hit me, I'm just like a punching bag. Very likely, I will come out on the short end of the deal. Above all, when tackled, I want to be sure I have the ball safely tucked away."

"When falling, I always try to hold my elbows in," said Mason. "A ball carrier can get separated shoulders by falling on his elbows. If he hits the ground and he knows somebody is right by him, many times he will get hit after he goes down. So, he should just kind of roll up and curl up in a fetal position."

"Once I get hit," said Bass, "I try to explode again. Sometimes I can tear the tackle. In professional football, we often say a back is judged from the time he is

hit, how many yards can he gain after he is hit. Sometimes when a defensive tackle makes a tackle on me, he will clutch his arms, but momentarily, a second after he hits me, he relaxes. So if I can explode once again, I might break that tackle!"

Prevention of Injuries

Most knee injuries occur when a player fails to see people. Knee injuries come when his feet are planted. The cleats are planted into the ground, in an odd direction. Many injuries of the knee happen this way. "I have never had to worry about a knee injury from being hit," admitted Mason. "I could always pick my feet up and not get hurt."

152

A   B

Fig. 6-20. FOOTWORK DRILLS. Our offensive backs go through a series of drills twice daily. Fundamental drills are the ingredients which make a great back. (Les Josephson)

Bass felt the best way to prevent injuries is "never stop running!" "Most injuries occur when ball carriers stop running," explained Dick. "I feel if my legs keep going, a lot of good things can happen to me.

"If I want to strengthen my legs," continued Bass, "I try to run on hilly areas as often as I can. What I mean is to sprint hilly areas because it gives me drive in my thighs and hamstring muscles. Plus, it gives me that strength that I will need to have explosiveness when I get into trouble." Steps are also very good. They build momentum for that important second effort.

Drills

Football is a game of detail. Fundamental drills are the ingredients which make a great back.

Our offensive backs go through a series of drills which have proven rather effective for us. We set up about three bags about 15 yards apart, and we go through a series of four drills that we work on every day, twice a day. The boys use a crossover step with a straight arm. In another drill, he comes up to a bag and "gives the tackler a foot and then takes it away." As he gives him his foot, with the other foot, he drives away from the tackler.

In the Double Fake drill, the back comes up to the tackler and gives him the double fake. We feel a single fake is not that effective. A pass receiver going downfield or even a running back has to give the tackler two fakes. If his opponent doesn't go for the first one, he probably will go

153

Fig. 6-21. BLOCKING DRILL. The best way to teach the shoulder and body blocking technique is by the use of dummies. Above, Coach Ted Marchibroda checks the technique of one of our backs.

for the second one. Then, the runner should break away from him.

On the Spin drill, the back comes up to a tackler and spins away from him, turning his back, if necessary, and spinning away. Another thing we stress is lifting the knees high at all times.

Balance and maneuverability are the prime essentials we strive for in the fundamental drills. I believe that one of the best conditioning drills is running through ropes. We feel ropes are better than tires because they can be raised to various heights. Two methods of running the ropes are straight ahead or using the cross-over step. Our ball handling drills start with the quarterback handing off to a back who first hits straight ahead and then to the side. We like to use a center in these drills to perfect our timing.

The next drill should involve a faking back. After the backs perfect this phase of handling the ball, the quarterback should start handing off to either back.

Our backfield practice begins with starts. We use a center, quarterback, and two halfbacks in this drill. The cadence is called by the quarterback. The ball is snapped and the backs move straight ahead for 10 yards. The quarterback doesn't hand off the ball in this opening warm-up drill. The backs are just concerned with improving the quickness of their start.

There are few drills available to perfect blocking or tackling. A good tough scrimmage will give them the opportunity to show their wares in this department. The best way to teach the shoulder and body technique is the use of blocking dummies.

154

The Kicking Game

62 percent of all yardage made in the 1968 NFL season was the result of all phases of the kicking game.

7

No play in football wins or loses as much yardage as the kicking game. This is why the Rams work every day on kicking, including such fundamentals as protecting, covering, and returning, as well as the actual kick itself.

A strong kicking game is the easiest way to obtain good field position, a major factor in winning football games. The mastery of kicking can determine the position of the team on the field, offensively and defensively.

According to statistics, the kicking game accounts for over 60 percent of the lost yardage and 25 percent of the scoring in the football game, which shows how important kicking is. Frankly, I don't think a team can win a championship without it. A problem we have in Pro ball is that many players do not take a deep interest in kicking organization and practice.

I feel we can win two games each year on our kicking game, and those two might win us a championship. So we work on it every day, all through the training camp and through the season. Next to passing, if a team has a defense and a kicking game, they are going to win a lot of football games because the kicking game can be used as an offense. Nearly every year in the NFL, the field goal kicker leads the league in scoring. Our own Bruce Gossett set a record in 1967, and he led our team each year in the 1966–67–68 seasons.

Place Kicking

Field goal or extra point kicking demands a team effort. A successful place kick depends not only on the kicker and the holder, but also on the center and blockers working together. To be an outstanding place kicker an individual must have good leg power. He should also be well coordinated because kicking requires good timing and coordination.

A

B

Fig. 7-2. THE KICKING GAME. The Rams work on this every day. Coach Howard Schnellenberger is shown "timing" a kick by Bruce Gossett, while Pat Studstill, right, gets off a punt during pre-game practice.

We break down the place kick into a four-part machine.

1. *The center* has to get the ball to the holder low and over the spot, without wasting time.
2. *The holder* has to get the ball on the spot, and if he can put the laces in front, it makes for an easier kick. However, if he cannot, he should get the ball on the spot so the kicker can kick through it.
3. Of course, the kicking team has to have *blocking* first to make the four-part machine work.
4. Last but not least, the important *kicker* must kick the ball through the uprights.

Note that in place kicking a square-toed shoe is more effective than the normal round-toed shoe used in punting.

A kicker should try to kick extra points and 40 yard field goals the same way. He should try to kick straight and let the distance take care of itself. The worst thing a place kicker can do is to try and "overpower" the ball. Usually a kicker will try to kick too hard on extra long field goals that are attempted over 50 yards. It's still a natural swing and follow-through whether 30 yards or 50 yards. Every kick should be the same way, with the same rhythm. If he hits it right, the distance will take care of itself. The important thing is to hit it straight.

All the best kickers are talented. When a kicker goes sour, it is usually because he has lost his confidence and concentration. When this occurs, everything is lost—especially timing and rhythm, which are musts.

Fig. 7-3. A SUCCESSFUL PLACE KICK depends on the kicker and the holder and with the center and blockers working together. Here, Bruce Gossett, with his "educated toe," boots one through the uprights.

Fig. 7-4. A COMMON FAULT of all kickers is trying to overpower the ball. It has to be a natural swing with the leg and a good follow-through. Kick every ball the same way, with the same rhythm. This picture shows Bruce Gossett's follow-through on the kick-off.

159

Fig. 7-5. KICK EXTRA POINTS AND FIELD GOALS the same way. Kick the ball straight and let the distance take care of itself. In this picture, Bruce Gossett, with Eddie Meador holding, boots another three-pointer. Notice he still has his head down even though the ball is soaring toward the upright.

"Try not to worry about the ones you missed," advised Gossett. "Just think about the ones you made because it's a 50/50 chance. It either goes in or it doesn't, and you cannot bring it back and kick it over."

Stance

The place kicker lines up about three walking strides behind the spot where the holder is going to set the ball. These are just normal steps. Assuming a relaxed position, he stands with his right foot in front of his left foot, squaring his shoulders with the uprights. "I keep my weight on my rear foot," explained Gossett. "I like to line my right toe up with the spot on the ground and the middle of the goal posts."

"I keep my eye on the spot, and I can also see the holder's hands. When he throws out his fingers, I know the ball is coming back, and this is a clue for me to start up with my steps to move up to the football."

For extra point tries, the ball is set down about seven yards from the line of scrimmage. This is the ideal spot.

Approach

The approach to the ball takes the kicker a step and a half. Just before the holder receives the ball, the place kicker starts his move. He makes his initial step with the kicking foot. This is a short, momentum-gathering step on the imaginary line he has pictured downfield.

The second step is a lunging power

step, which comes to a point about six inches behind the ball. This is the step that will give a kicker the power to kick the ball far. Like on the kick-off, the last step is the most important step. His eyes are concentrated on the spot where the ball will be placed. He wants to see his toe hit this spot.

Contact

The kicking right leg should be swung in an arc, with the knee flexed; the kicker finishes with a snap of the lower leg. Immediately after contact, his knee joint is locked, and his toe is pulled up. The heel of the kicking foot contacts the ground first before his toe hits the ball. This helps to lock his ankle and lets him get more power and accuracy into the kick.

On his last step, the kicker's right leg, from the knee down, is almost parallel with the ground. After bringing it straight behind him, he forces the leg out, and it comes up about the same after he kicks the ball. It's more or less a half circle, from the start of the kick to the finish.

"On my extra points, I try to hit the bottom half of the football on the ground," said Bruce, "because I want the ball to get up in the air. On the longer field goal, I try to hit the middle of the ball so that I get a slow spin. With the wind resistance against it, it isn't as great as a fast spinning ball. So, I just pick out a spot on the ball where I want to hit it, and I hit it."

All field goal kickers concentrate on bringing their right foot straight through on a line with the goal posts and then setting the foot back. This way the kicker cannot get a truly bad kick.

In order to kick a field goal, the place kicker has to have terrific snap and rhythm in his leg. Field goal kickers have exceptional strength in the muscle right above the knee. This is the one that "snaps" every time a field goal is kicked.

On shorter field goals, from 30 yards in, the place kicker should try to get a lot of height on the ball so he tries to get under the ball. His heel will first contact the ground and drive the ball upwards. On a longer try, the heel will be pretty close to hitting the ground before the toe hits the ball.

On field goal tries inside the 40 yard line, Gossett tries to hit the ball just a little below the center. Beyond the 40 yard line, he tries to hit it in the middle or a little above the middle. This gives him a slower spin to make the ball go further.

Follow-through

After making the kick, the kicker must continue to keep his head down and follow-through. The type of follow-through depends on the type of kicker. Whereas Lou Groza of the Cleveland Browns had a tremendous follow-through, many kickers do not. They more or less punch at the football.

"My toughest angle for a field goal is anywhere on the left hand side of the field," said Gossett. "It just seems that I'm further away from the goal posts on the left hand side because I'm a right-footed kicker.

A

B

Fig. 7-6. PLACE-KICKING TECHNIQUE.

Holding The Ball. Prior to the snap, the holder always gives the kicker a good target. He focuses his eyes on the target spot. The index finger of the left hand is placed on the tip of the football. The ball is centered with the laces away from the kicker.

Contact. With the knee flexed, the kicker finishes with a snap of the lower leg. Immediately after contact, his knee joint is locked, and his toe is pulled up.

E

F

C

D

Fig. 7-6 (Cont'd.). PLACE-KICKING TECHNIQUE.

The Approach. Just before the holder receives the ball, the kicker makes his initial step with the kicking foot. The second step is a lunging power step, which comes to a point about six inches behind the ball and straight ahead.

Follow-Through. After making the kick, the kicker must continue to keep his head down and follow through. The right foot must be brought straight through on a line with the goal posts.

G

H

163

A

B

C

E   **D**

Fig. 7-7. HOLDING THE BALL. The holder's hands, which are reaching for the ball, should form a good target for the center. His eyes are fixed on the ball. If the laces need adjustments, the right hand does the job. The index finger of the left hand is placed on the tip of the ball.

The holder must not remove his finger until the kicker has swung his leg completely through. Although we use the left hand in holding the ball, we prefer the right hand. The kicker is able to see the ball better when the right hand is on top of the ball.

If I am on the right side, it looks pretty good. On the left side, it looks a little bit farther away from the goal post, particularly with a ball like mine which hooks a lot. The angle is cut down quite a bit on the left hand side of the field.''

Holding the ball

The holder and the center are very important in the execution of a successful field goal. In addition, there are ten other players, the guys that block for the kicker. Their importance is over 50% of a successful field goal. The snap has to be perfect, the holder has to get the ball down, and he also has to have the laces turned towards the goal posts. If they are on the side, the ball will go to the side the laces are on.

Many holders like to kneel and place their left knee approximately one foot from the kicking tee and to the right side. They may extend their right leg forward, bending it at the knee, to allow the right foot to be flat on the ground. Then they are able to move up, down, or to the side, if the snap is poor. Eddie Meador, however, prefers not to extend the right leg. His right knee is on the ground, while the foot of the bent left leg rests a half of a foot from the kicking tee.

His hands which are actually reaching for the ball, form a good target for the center. His eyes are fixed on the ball. After catching the ball, the holder focuses his eyes on the spot where he wants to place it. The tip of the ball toward the center should be placed on the tee. The ball is set in an erect position and held on the proper spot with one finger. The kicker then boots the ball from under the finger.

Kicking-Off

Essentially, the kick-off is the same kick that is used for the extra point and field goal. The prime difference is that the kick-off man has a longer approach to kick the ball. He usually takes a ten yard run at the ball to get a little more power behind him. I believe that most kickers would probably kick the ball just as well by lining up in their regular field goal position and kicking off.

On a kick-off, the kicker has the advantage of using a two-inch tee to kick the ball off of. "Your foot can hit the ball better," said Bruce, "and not have as much friction as a ball that's held right on the ground. Also, you can get your weight through better on the kick-off because you're coming at the ball a little faster, and it helps drive your body through the ball.''

"On the approach to the ball, I start off real easy over the first five yards," said Gossett, "and when I get past the five yard mark, I start speeding up. I make my last couple steps a little longer so I can really get my weight behind the ball.''

"If you're a right-footed kicker," said Gossett, "after the kick, you want to land on your kicking foot, and if you're a left-footed kicker, land on your left foot. This

A

B

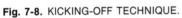

Fig. 7-8. KICKING-OFF TECHNIQUE.

The Run. With his left foot forward, the kicker starts at a spot approximately seven to nine inches from the ball. His first step is with the left foot. Using a two-inch tee to kick off from, he paces off the exact approach distance in strides. The last two or three steps prior to contact are a little longer so he can put more power into the kick.

Contact. The kicking foot should move in an easy, relaxed swing that reaches maximum velocity on contact with the lower leg snapping forward from the knee. The right ankle and knee should lock just prior to contact.

E

F

C

D

Fig. 7-8 (Cont'd.).

Approach. The kicker must start from the same spot each time and learn to approach in a straight line. He increases his run to three-quarters speed up to the actual kicking action when full speed should be started.

Follow-Through. Keeping the eyes continually on the ball, the kicking foot should follow through after the ball, never deviating from the line of the kick. Most kickers will always land on the kicking foot.

G

H

Fig. 7-9. KICK-OFF AT THE COLISEUM. Bruce Gossett kicks the ball deep into the opponents' territory. The important point is for the members of the kick-off team not to move until the kicker is even with them on his approach. Covering kick-offs is one of the areas we have to work on.

is the only way you can get all of your weight behind the ball on a kick-off. When you land on your kicking foot, you know you had to go into the ball hard."

If a ball is kicked 5 to 10 yards in the end zone, with a little bit of height, this is an excellent kick-off because they have to decide on whether to run it back or not. If they do, we're in good position to force a fumble or get them inside the 20 yard line. If they don't run it out, they would get the ball on their 20. The best kick-off would be out of the end zone where they can't run it back.

Normally, the kick-off should be high enough to give the kicking team the opportunity to get downfield. However, if the ball is high and on the 7 yard line, it's a poor kick. But if, as often happens, it is a high kick that is two or three yards in to the end zone, then this is an excellent kick.

"Last year, I believe I kicked the ball into the end zone more consistently than the other kickers that we played against," said Gossett. "That was the first year I've done this. I credit my improvement to 'reaching for the football and hitting the ball in the middle' because I get the slower spin and the ball will go farther."

When the kicking team is behind and must gain possession of the ball, the on-side kick is used. However, the ball must cross the opponent's restraining line before the ball is a "free ball."

After the kick-off

When asked what he does after he kicks the ball, Gossett replied: "First of all, I try to avoid the guy that's trying to

A   B   C

Fig. 7-10. RECEIVING THE KICK-OFF. Concentrating only on the ball, the receiver draws the ball into his body. He doesn't fight the ball. He brings it in nice and easy! It's much easier to catch kick-offs than punts, due to the height of the ball. However, the fundamentals are basically the same. Receivers should catch the ball on the move rather than wait for it.

knock me down, usually the center who is standing right in front of me. Eddie Meador is the safety, and I look to see which side Eddie is going to, and I go to the other side. There were times when I had to make the tackle or the guy would have gone all the way for a touchdown.''

''A runner coming out of the end zone doesn't know who I am. All he sees is the color of the jersey, and the runners will turn away from the color. If I'm on the outside, I will turn back to the inside where our pursuit can catch up with him and make the tackle.''

Kick-Off Returns

Returning the kick-off is perhaps one of the most overlooked phases of football.

Since a miscue can cost valuable field position if there is a bobble, the receiver must catch the ball at all costs. Kick-off returns are not only important tactically but psychologically: they can demoralize an opponent.

On kick returns, the ball carrier can use a long stride and glide around tacklers with no loss of speed. He has more room and time to maneuver from scrimmage than the ball carrier does.

There are only three basic kick-off return plays: run to the right sidelines, run to the left, or go up the middle. The play is called before the kick-off. Many teams use a wedge return to force everyone outside of the wedge by sheer numbers. The ball carrier tries to stay in behind the wedge as long as he can, and any time he sees daylight, he may break off to the

169

C   B   A

Fig. 7-11. RUNNING UP THE MIDDLE. On the kick-off, Ron Smith starts up the middle to draw the defense toward the middle. At the twenty yard line, Smith cuts to the left according to the play that was called.

outside. He shouldn't get out of the wedge too soon, though, and conversely, it will be a mistake to stay in it until he falls over his blockers. Whichever return is called, the runner must remember that the straight line still is the shortest distance to the goal line.

Normally, the kicking team's chief responsibility is to keep the ball carrier inside where there is heavier traffic. They want to keep him away from the thinly guarded sidelines.

On a sideline call, the receiving team aims for a lane between the number four and five men of the onrushing team. The kick-off men are numbered from the middle, or kicker, five on each side, to the sidelines. The number five man has the responsibility of hugging the sidelines and turning in all ball carriers. Normally, the receiving team tries to block him out and the number four man in. However, if the number four man hangs back, the sideline return could go through the number 4 and 3 men.

On the up-the-middle return, the receiving team employs cross-blocks. The blockers on both sides crisscross in their charge upfield, with the idea of knocking everyone to the outside and creating a funnel up the middle.

Punting

The value of a good punter cannot be overemphasized. His long, booming kicks can be most instrumental in keeping the other team deep in their own territory. When we won the championship with the Bears in 1963, we didn't have much of an offense. Bobby Joe Green, our punter, was our offense.

A powerful boot not only can get a team out of a hole, but can put the opponents on the spot, such as an accurate kick to the coffin corner.

A well-placed kick is sometimes better than a long gain on the ground, or a forward pass, because it puts a team in a

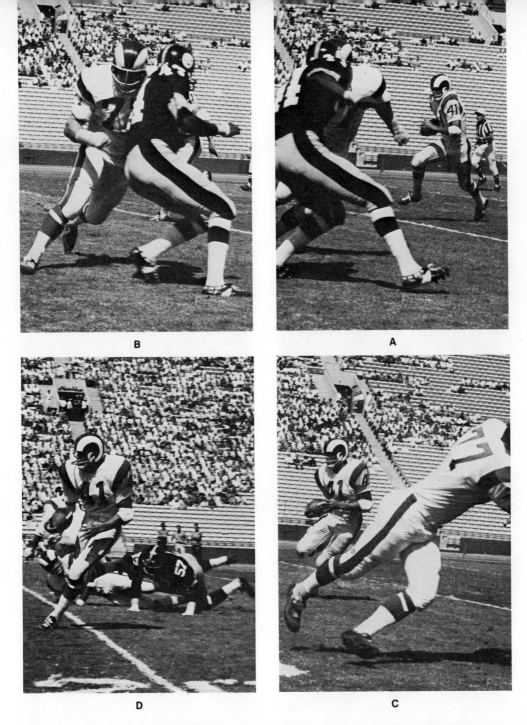

B

A

D

C

Fig. 7-12. BREAKING TO THE OUTSIDE. The blockers on both sides crisscross in their charge upfield, with the idea of knocking everyone to the outside and creating a funnel up the middle. Lineman Jim Wilson (77) of the Rams clears the way for kick-off return specialist Ron Smith.

D

C

F

E

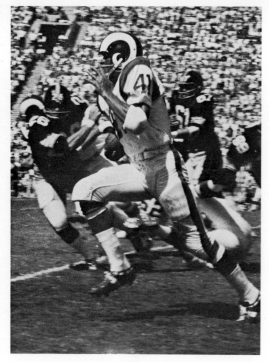

B

A

Fig. 7-13. TURNING ON THE SPEED. Ron Smith uses a long stride and glides around opposing tacklers with no loss of speed. Faking is done quickly and without effort in eluding the oncoming Pittsburgh lineman Ernie Ruple (73).

hole. And a team has a good chance to score if the defense can keep the opposition down there.

The big thing we want in our punter is to get elevation on the ball, so we can get down and cover the kick. We are more interested in getting the ball in the air than in having the man kick the ball 40 or 45 yards consistently. We don't care for the individual who is capable of kicking the ball 60 or 65 yards but is inconsistent.

Stance

In waiting for the pass-back, the punter should assume a comfortably erect stance from 14 to 15 yards behind the center. This distance is far enough back to eliminate the block kicks or keep them to a minimum. Most centers get the ball back to the kicker anywhere from 8- to 9/10 of a second. "I'm a three-step kicker," said Jon Kilgore, "so my left foot is forward. Many other kickers, however, have their kicking foot forward. I try to keep a balanced stance, in case the snap is to

173

Fig. 7-14. HOLDING THE BALL ON THE PUNT. The hands are placed flat along the sides of the ball. The left hand is near the front tip of the ball to steady it and is removed during the second step of the kick. The right arm is underneath the ball to allow for placing on the ball on the foot. The laces are turned up to assure consistency (Pat Studstill).

the right or left, high or low. In either case, I won't go off balance trying to catch it. I don't like to crouch because I find it constricts my kicking action. I like to stand with my feet slightly spread, the knees flexed."

The weight of the kicker is slightly forward over the forward foot. "Maybe it's a bad habit, or a good one," said Kilgore, "but I try to step into the snap, wherever it is. So, my weight is a little forward."

The hands are kept out in front, loose and relaxed, much like a receiver's would be. The thumbs are out and the palms up. "I try to give Kenny Iman, our center, a good target," said Kilgore, "I think this helps Kenny, and it helps me, too, because he knows I'm ready when I get my hands up and form the pocket for him."

The eyes are constantly on that ball, at all times, as the ball is passed back. Look the ball into the hands. "I like to receive the ball on my right side," said Jon. "My fingers are extended, kind of like I'm going to cradle the ball in. Very flexible, not stiff. You don't want to force anything, just bring the ball in very smoothly. The elbows should give slightly so as to cushion the ball. Don't fight it, but keep the hands relaxed and let them give with the ball."

Holding the ball

The hands are placed flat along the sides of the ball, with the fingers fairly close together. The ball should be held parallel to the ground, with the laces turned up. The left hand is nearer the front of the ball, and the right hand is near the back.

174

The left hand is placed near the front tip of the ball to steady it and is removed during the second step of the kick. Since the ball is cupped in the right hand, all the kicker has to do is turn the front tip slightly to the left, producing a spiral, with the nose of the ball slightly down.

As he drops the ball to the foot, the hand or hands fall away. "Don't pull your hand away," suggested Kilgore, "since this might deflect the ball and cause poor contact with the foot. Normally, I hold the ball about waist high, although this will vary with the type of kick. Holding the ball too high can prove dangerous because the wind may cause it to drift."

The steps

Most of the better punters today are three-step kickers. However, results are more important than the particular style a kicker employs. An excellent three-step kicker, for example, may hurt himself by changing to two steps. There are some who find the Rocker step effective.

The punter starts to move forward the moment he receives the ball. The initial step is nothing more than a comfort step straight ahead with the front foot. A long first step might pull the kicker off-balance and disrupt his timing and coordination.

Just prior to planting his last step, the kicker should drop the ball. Then his kicking foot comes up to meet the ball. "You want to place the ball flat on the foot," said Kilgore. "If I cannot drop it parallel to the ground, I want it a little nose down. If the tail end is down, you have a tendency to hit the back end of the ball before hitting the middle. As a result, you will get an end-over-end kick. So, the drop is very important."

The forward movement of the punter is similar to a fast walk. There should be no hesitation in it once it is initiated. It has to be smooth and precise.

The swing is a pendulum kind of swing. The punter should want his kicking leg straight on contact with the ball. As soon as he gets through, at the bottom of his pendulum swing, he should lock his knee.

Contact

The contact is, perhaps, the most crucial phase of the kicking action. The ball must be placed out in front of the kicker so that it falls directly onto the instep of the kicking foot. In order to assure proper arching of the foot, he should point the toe of the kicking foot down. He should place the ball right on the arch bone, maybe a little to the outside.

When contact with the ball is made, the knee of the kicking foot should be bent slightly. As the ball leaves the foot, however, the knee must be locked. The ball should be met by snapping the leg out straight with the ankle locked down. It's the snap in the kick that makes the ball travel. To get the proper snap, he carries the leg forward with the knee bent until just before the ball is struck. Then, he snaps it out straight and locks the joint as the foot meets the ball.

"If you place the ball right," said Kilgore, "the only pressure you will feel will be in the middle of your instep. The ball will feel real good on the foot."

| A | B | C |

Fig. 7-15. PUNTING TECHNIQUE. Pat Studstill is a 2½-step kicker, so his left foot is slightly forward in receiving the ball. The hands are held out in front, loose and relaxed. His first step is a short jab with the left foot; he then fullsteps with his right, followed by the left. Then comes the kick.

"Don't try to kick the ball too hard," said Studstill. "When you just depend on brute force, you ruin the smoothness of the kicking action and the long, easy follow-through which is so vitally necessary. Start your kicking swing slowly and continue with increasing speed until it reaches its maximum velocity just as the foot hits the ball."

Concentration plays such a vital role in successful punting. The kicker who takes his eye off the ball will be vulnerable to hooks, slices, and even blocked kicks. A good rule to follow is: "Never look up until your kicking foot comes back to the ground."

As the ball arrives in his hands, the punter fixes his target in his mind, then he trains his eyes strictly on the ball. He watches it as he drops it, as it contacts his foot, and after the ball leaves the foot.

Then he watches his foot as it returns to the ground.

"Above all, work on your drop," advises Studstill, "and be sure you are locking that knee and ankle. You will defeat yourself even before you start if you don't do these two things."

"You must kick the ball when it is only 12 to 18 inches from the ground. If the point of the ball dips down, you'll have a bad kick. If the point is up, it will also be a bad kick. You have to drop the ball absolutely flat."

Follow-through

After making contact, the punter should kick through the ball, allowing his kicking leg to carry through over his head. "You've got to drive your whole body into it," said Jon. "And I think getting the ol' rear end into it is all important . . . just drive

176

D	E	F
G	H	I

Fig. 7-15. PUNTING TECHNIQUE (cont'd.). While taking the two and one-half steps, Studstill adjusts the ball to his hands. Just prior to planting his last step, Studstill drops the ball, placing the ball flat on the foot. He wants to "look the ball all the way on the foot." Over 80 percent of the bad kicks in punting are caused by improper drop of the ball. Notice that the kicking leg is straight when it comes in contact with the ball. The toes are pointed downward and inward. Punting power comes from the right knee snap. At the bottom of his pendulum swing, he wants to get the knee locked. To kick the ball high, contact with the ball should be slightly higher than normal.

in up under it. It's just like making a tackle of a block. You have to get fully into it.''

During the kicking action, the punter's back should be bent and his shoulders rounded. When the leg begins to go up, he should straighten his back and throw his shoulders back. The eyes of the kicker should remain on the ball throughout the kicking process.

The punter should come up on the toes of his other foot with his arms outstretched at the sides. After completing his follow-through and bringing his foot back to the ground, the kicker should take a step or two forward to avoid any roll-back action.

It is most important to keep the balance foot on the ground and to stay up at the end of the kick, not fall back. Some kickers like to take a step or two forward after completing the follow-through.

Time to get ball away

The kicker must always be conscious of the amount of time required to get the ball away. But he must have the poise to remain calm in all punting situations. Most punts are blocked due to the kicker taking too much time. We like our kickers to kick the ball in less than 2.2 seconds from the time the ball is snapped from the center.

Height and distance

The punt should be kicked as high as possible. At the same time, the punter doesn't want to out-kick his coverage. He has to look at both of these in moderation.

A really high short punt isn't a good punt at all, but in the same sense, a long, low punt has a good chance of being returned by the opposition. They will run it right back down our throat. The ideal punt, probably, would be a punt that would stay in the air anywhere from 4 to 4½ seconds and go anywhere from 40 to 45 yards.

The good kicks are spirals. It's just like throwing passes. I'm sure if he threw the ball end over end, he wouldn't be very effective with it. A bullet spiral will travel a greater distance in the air, and when it hits the ground, the ball will likely roll fast and straight.

The test of a good punter is how well he can kick against a strong wind. Rather than a high boot, he must keep the kick fairly low. To do this, he should drop the ball a little lower and turn the front tip slightly down, and not follow through too far.

Quick kick

The quick kick can be a useful weapon in high school and college football. The Pro game, however, is a game of specialization. Every team in the NFL has a punter who does nothing else but kick. If he came into the game, for example, on a second or third down situation, it would be difficult to conceal his intentions. Furthermore, the Pros can score from long range on any given play, and they don't like to give up the ball until they have to.

There is no defense against the quick kick, and a team can pick up an easy 45 yards. This surprise move is usually on a third down situation with the wind at the back of the kicker. The kicker must not give any tip-off through his stance.

Moving quickly on the snap from his normal backfield stance, he takes an average comfort step back with his kicking foot. He doesn't want to roll back on the heel of his balance foot. The ball arrives in his hands the instant he comes back on his balance foot. This demands split-second timing.

The punter quickly throws his weight forward on his kicking foot, then he takes a full step forward on his balance foot and kicks. The kicking toe must be turned down, with plenty of snap in the leg. The kicker must stay up at the end of his kick. This helps get a bullet spiral with plenty of roll. Since he wants a low kick, about 20 feet in the air, the ball should be dropped a little lower with less follow-through, as if he were kicking against the wind.

The coffin corner

Angling a kick for the corner can be an important weapon, too. If, for example, a punter is on his own 45 yard line, he might draw a bead on the point where the 5-yard line intersects the right sideline. The right-footed kicker usually has a natural pull to the left, so an accurately placed kick might put the ball practically in the corner.

After receiving the snap, the kicker quickly sights his target and steps directly toward it. In order to get away a low one, he should drop the ball closer to the foot, keeping the toe perfectly straight and turned down. The instep should be flat.

Whenever the kicker stands near the middle of the field, he can aim for either corner. The natural pull varies with the individual, and, of course the wind is a factor, too. Only through practice can he determine the proper allowance to make.

Problems (flaws) in punting

When the punter is not getting the real good spiral effect, he can attribute this to a number of things. First, he might not be hitting the ball good on his foot and this could go back to the drop. He has to drop it absolutely flat on the instep. Maybe his drop is off just a little. Or, maybe he is not locking his ankle all the way.

Another flaw in punting is trying to overpower the ball. The kicker usually dubs it when he tries to kick it out of sight. The punter who takes his eye off the ball will likely kick hooks and slices. In trying to see how far he will kick the ball, he will look up too soon.

If a punter is violating the fundamentals, make him stop immediately and have him start kicking easily in slow motion. This usually will help him regain his form and find the solution to his problem. He'll soon realize that it's form, not force, that makes the ball travel.

Some punters have a habit of pointing their left foot to the left as they step through to kick. As a result, they usually move to the left, cross over with the kicking foot, and hook the ball.

Drill training

A punter should devote a considerable amount of time to work with a center. He must have a center snapping to him for his kicks. He might have someone make some bad snaps and practice reacting to them.

After he has mastered the basic fundamentals, he should be placed under as much pressure as possible, preferably during scrimmage. A coach can use a stop watch and have his kicker practice getting the punt away in less then 2.2 seconds. This is the only way to condition him for game conditions.

Kickers should not be overworked. They lose their effectiveness when fatigue sets in, so drills should be limited in time and scope. A kicker must be kept fresh and strong.

Off-season

Generally, a punting specialist will take a rest for several months before he resumes his kicking. "I probably won't touch a football until probably May," said Kilgore, "but I will do a good deal of running. By the end of May, I will kick the ball a little bit, but not much then. I feel like I need a center, and by just standing out there and kicking the ball, I'm defeating my purpose."

"To keep my legs strong, I like to run and do sit-ups," continued Jon. "Sit-ups are good because your kicking is done from the bottom of your rib cage down, and you do a lot of straining right through the mid-section in kicking the ball."

A typical work-out

Our punters start each practice doing the same thing that everybody else does, with our agility drills, warm-up form of exercises and the Exer-genie. "After I get through with the Exer-genie," said Kilgore, "I do considerable running. I run anywhere from 10 to 15 laps, and then we go out on our own field. Early in the summer training season in July, I don't kick a whole lot, probably 25 balls in the morning and 25 in the afternoon. That's not too many. I usually try to do as many of these with the center as possible. And later on during the season, I do most of my kicking early in the week, probably Tuesday, Wednesday, and Thursday. On Friday and Saturday, I'll cut way down, especially on Saturday, when I hit maybe 8 or 10 punts altogether. I try to be really fresh and crisp on Sunday."

"When I come out on Sunday, I'll probably kick 8 or 10 balls with the lineman going down field," said Jon. "I come out early before the other players come out and really loosen up, maybe another 6 or 8 balls. But these are usually one-half to three-quarter speed. This is usually about the extent of it."

Fielding the Punt

The punt can be a dangerous offensive weapon if the receivers do not handle the ball correctly. Actually, a punt can be a most difficult ball to handle, whether it be end-over-end, spiral, floating, or wobbling.

In catching a punt, two rules are of prime importance. First, the receiver must never be off-balance, and second, he should always watch the ball.

A   B   C

D

Fig. 7-16. FIELDING THE PUNT. The receiver must remember these points:

1. Get in front of the ball as quickly as possible.
2. Watch the ball leave the kicker's foot.
3. Make a basket of your hands and arms and tuck in your elbows.
4. One leg should be forward to assist if the ball slips through.
5. Put the ball away as quickly as possible.
6. Catch punts every day!

Most professional teams use twin-safety men. The man who is not receiving will advise the catcher about the tacklers pounding downfield. If they are too close, he'll yell, "Fair catch!" Otherwise, he'll tell him, "Plenty of room!" By providing this information, the receiver can concentrate strictly on the ball.

Generally, we tell our backs to "Fair Catch" a high punt and return a low, long one. A fair catch forfeits the receiver's right to advance the ball. He extends and waves one hand only above the head, and after catching the ball, drops one knee to the ground. He must catch the ball, otherwise the ball becomes free.

Most teams use two plays on a punt runback, right or left. The call is given for the punt by the defensive captain in the huddle. The simple left or right call becomes a necessity created by the peculiar blocking problems created by punting. The blockers on the receiving team must first break through the line to force the punt, then circle around and rush back down the sidelines to provide interference for the punt receiver.

When the receiver catches the football, he should hesitate for a split second. There are two reasons for this action. First, the receiver can get a quick look at his pursuers; it also gives his blockers time to get back to him. Then he can break down the middle, hoping to draw in the tacklers.

The duty of the other safety man is to block the first tackler downfield so the receiver can break down the middle. When the ball carrier sees the second tackler, he'll cut right or left toward the sidelines, according to the play. This maneuver will provide his blockers enough time to get back and pick him up.

We like our receivers to catch the ball with a combination of hands and chest. He will find it effective to lift up to the balls of his feet for the catch. We feel he can get a quicker take-off by doing this. But the most important point is keeping his eye on the ball until it's safely in his hands.

Every once in a while, a receiver will gamble and try to catch a punt on the run, but this is risky business. It is also dangerous to field a ball bouncing along the turf, but sometimes he has to take the chance.

Protecting the Kicker

Strong protection is of tremendous importance to the man kicking. Even when a kick is not blocked, his effectiveness is greatly hindered if he is hurried.

Punt Formation

The regular punt formation is of two general types:

1. *Tight balanced line.* The ends are split about 5 yards. The two backs protect the kicking side of the kicker, and one back protects the offside. The first responsibility of the interior linemen is to protect their inside seams toward the center. The outside foot and leg must remain stationary to prevent any leaking at the seams. Most punters, when using the regular

Fig. 7-17. A BLOCKED AND RECOVERED PUNT can be a great morale builder for any team. Here, Tony Guillory (88) of the Rams makes the "big play" as he blocks the punt attempt of Donny Anderson (44) of Green Bay, with only 37 seconds to play and with the Rams trailing 24 to 20. The Rams used the time to score seven points and win 27 to 24 on their way to the 1967 Coastal Division title. Rushing of the kick has been a strong point in the Rams' kicking game.

formation, will line up 10 to 12 yards from the center.

2. *Spread protection.* This type of protection tends to spread the defending team, diminishing the threat of a blocked kick. However, a team shouldn't employ this technique unless the center is able to snap the ball at least 13 yards with good accuracy.

Field goal and extra point protection

The team protection used in the field goal and extra point kick is identical. The kicking team will line up in a tight line from end to end. The responsibilities of the linemen are to protect inside. The offensive backs will line up tight behind and slightly outside of each end. Although they are primarily concerned with inside protection, they have a basic responsibility to bump any rushman going to their outside. The holder lines up 7–8 yards behind the center.

Rushing the Kicker

Rushing the kicker is of great importance to the defense. Indeed, a blocked and recovered punt can be a great morale builder for any football team.

The punt

Perhaps, the most effective method for penetrating the blocking pattern is overloading the defending halfbacks at one end

Fig. 7-18. RUNNING WITH THE LOOSE BALL, a moment after Guillory's sensational block, is Claude Crabbe of the Rams who returned to the five yard line. Observe that the Green Bay punter, Donny Anderson, is outnumbered by half of the Rams' ball team. The Rams had sent eight men through the line in an attempt to block the kick.

or the other. The tackle and end will often work together on the kicker's offside. The prime objective is for one of them to draw the back out of position, while the other rushes up the alley. Also, two linebackers might be sent in on one side with the hope that one will be overlooked.

Another technique is to drive directly up the alley either by overloading or by moving the center out of the way. In the roll-out procedure, one man will grab and pull the center out of position. This opens a hole for another defender to break through up the middle.

The place kick

The 8-man rushing line is generally used in attempting to block the field goal or extra point. As in blocking the punt, overloading and pulling stunts are used.

A

B

Fig. 7-19. THE FAIR CATCH. The receiver (Kel Winston, here) extends his arm fully up above his head, and after catching the ball, drops one knee to the ground.

Kick-Off Defense

The kick-off team must not only have speed but it has to have size in the middle to meet a wedge. The third men in from either sideline have to be speedsters since they are the ones who have to force the action.

The two outside men have to be strong enough and active enough to keep the play to the inside. These outside men have to stay on their feet and protect the sidelines.

Defensive Line

8

*The defensive line are paid to rush the passer,
and if they can't rush the passer, they're stealing!*

8

A team of hard charging, aggressive defensive linemen playing with determination and courage, and in top notch physical condition may get hurt a little bit against the run, but it is going to be a difficult team to beat at any place at any time.

The defensive lineman has to be in good physical condition to rush the passer. It's one of the most difficult phases of all of football. In every play, he is battling that offensive lineman; this takes a lot out of him, and we don't want linemen to take a couple of steps and stop and watch the pass being completed.

Defensive football is actually "hit and react" football. We like our linemen to concentrate on recognizing the moves of the offense, and then they must react to these moves. The important point is not where the rushman lines up but where he winds up.

An effective pass rush is the objective of all defensive lines. When the offense hits a long one, it usually means the pass rush has broken down, and the defensive lineman is just as much to blame as the pass defender.

The secret to winning in this game, therefore, is getting to the quarterback. That's the main job of the defensive lineman, though he has to defend against the run, too.

Tackling is to defensive line play just as blocking is to offensive line play. If a player cannot tackle, he will prove a weak defensive man regardless of whatever else he can do. Football is a game of "hit or be hit," and a lineman has to be willing to take some hard knocks and dish some out, too. But in order to make the tackle, the player must be able to get into position to tackle. This is where the maneuvers and stunts prove most effective. But unless a player is well schooled in the fundamentals of defensive line play, i.e. proper stance, the charge, and the hitting position, all his defensive maneuvers will be worthless.

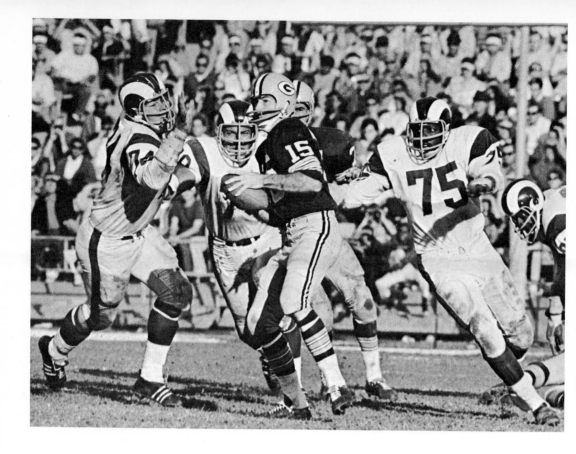

Fig. 8-2. CONSTANT PRESSURE from the defensive line makes the quarterback hurry his action. Even though Bart Starr of Green Bay doesn't see Rams (left to right) Merlin Olsen, Roger Brown and Deacon Jones, he can "feel" their immediate presence.

The inside (or "I") man's greatest asset is his quickness. A quick lineman, particularly one with good lateral movement, is more valuable than a man of great speed. He must have size, strength, agility, and alertness, but most important, he must be quick. *I value quickness more than any other skill a football player can have.* When a coach has a player who can combine size with quickness, that is Utopia!

A huge factor in successful defense is good preparation. On a given Sunday, we want our players to know their opponent's offense like a book.

Qualifications

Quickness is more important to me than height in our outside (or "O") men. We also like a rangy athlete with quickness, although not necessarily blessed with long range speed. If a lineman has good height, he can get his hands up high and bat some balls down.

Strength is another important quality. We find that all NFL linemen possess good strength, but the great ones have quickness and quick reaction. This is why we work on reactions to situations, reading

Fig. 8-3. DETERMINATION and courage are among the essential qualities of top NFL linemen. Above, Rams stage one of their patented goal line stands.

rules almost every day. The defensive lineman has to continually work on this phase of the game in order to increase a player's reaction to a play.

To be a successful football player, a lineman must have a strong desire for bodily contact, to want to knock somebody down. We like the overly aggressive type who can also take it. In the course of a 14 game schedule, a defensive tackle (we call them "I" men for inside) will take approximately 1000 or more licks, not counting special teams. In other words, they are getting hit on every play. The defensive ends are the same way, with the

exceptions of sweeps away from them when they have to pursue. If these licks are added up over the season, it means that these linemen will have to take quite a bit of hard contact. So, they must be real tough to be able to take it physically.

Actually, it takes as many years to develop a top-flight defensive lineman as it does a quarterback. Intelligence, determination, concentration, deception, agility, and quickness are as important as size and toughness.

Defensive linemen must be aggressive, alert, and mean. There is always the possibility of blocking a punt, intercepting a pass, or recovering a fumble. A quick thinking, alert lineman can be an asset to any team.

"We have our own code of ethics," explained Olsen, "violence, viciousness, and brutality are built into the game, but there is a line drawn between what you can and cannot do if you wish to keep your head screwed in place."

A player must have this desire for body contact because it's hard to instill this strong desire to hit people and get hit. Of course, if the player who is not too aggressive plays with a group of people that are aggressive, this can rub off.

Basic Responsibilities

The responsibilities of those on the defensive line will vary according to the defensive line charges that we employ. Basically, our defensive ends, who are our pass rushers, have run-hole responsibility. The defensive end is responsible for the 6 or 7 hole, which is immediately outside the offensive tackle. On the snap, he has to read certain reading rules, and this can change on the run. That's where quickness and reaction plays such an important part. He has to charge across the line of scrimmage and, in an instant, has to change his responsibility or his reactions to the play.

We have our inside people do more things than we do with our outside men because the defense cannot sacrifice their outside pass rush. However, I'm not saying the "O" men don't have reading rules. They have just as many, but they aren't as complicated as those of the "I" men. The inside people, on occasion, will pinch the offense. We send one lineman one way and one another way. We will do stunts inside with them. If it is a basic line charge, about 65 percent of the time their responsibility is to shoulder outside the offensive guard.

Once the linemen charge across the line of scrimmage, they must pick up their reading rules instantly and take off. In short, they do not just come off the ball. A defenseman should have good pursuit. He must be able to chase the ball carrier with quickness.

All defensive linemen must master the following individual fundamentals:

1. *The ability to move.* Every defensive player must move on movement. Instead of watching the ball, he watches the blocker opposite him, and he *moves as he does!* Speed and accuracy of movement are highly important.

2. *The ability to protect himself.* The best way for a defensive lineman to protect himself is to deliver a blow. His prime objective is to strike a blow, neutralize the blocker, get rid of him, pursue the ball carrier and make the tackle.

3. *The ability to tackle.* The ability to tackle is perhaps the most vital defensive requirement.

4. *The ability to fight pressure.* The defensive lineman should always fight around the blocker's head to get to the ball.

The reading and charging theories of

Fig. 8-4. THE FRONT FOUR. Three of the Rams' famous "Fearsome Foursome" are shown in "pursuit" action (left to right): Merlin Olsen (74), Deacon Jones (75), and Roger Brown (78); Lamar Lundy cannot be seen in this photograph.

The defensive Front Four have to close the middle against running and put heavy pressure on the quarterback in a pass play. These men are the defender's best friend.

defense are most prominent in football today. A reading defense will hit, then wait to try to read the play. The Dallas Cowboys do a fine job with this style of defense. The defenders flow with the movement of the ball. A charging defense, on the other hand, "bangs" straight ahead across the line of scrimmage as quickly as possible.

Each theory has its advantages and shortcomings. An aggressive, hard-rushing line can be trapped, but it can also place tremendous pressure on a passer. I much prefer the "Jet style" of defensive line play.

For each formation and club, we have different reading rules that might change from week to week. This is in order to give us more effective stopping of a certain play or formation.

The Front Four

The defensive Front Four of the 1968 Los Angeles Rams, comprised of Lamar Lundy, Deacon Jones, Merlin Olsen, and Roger Brown, represented a combined weight of 1085 pounds. This is slightly more than half a ton. Their tremendous rush has made life miserable for opposing quarterbacks. In 1967 when the Rams defeated the Colts 34–10 to win the Coastal Division title, Johnny Unitas was caught seven times and lost 48 yards attempting to pass. On two other plays, the Rams' fierce rush led to interceptions. In 1968, our Front Four sacked opposing quarterbacks 51 times; this was tops in the NFL.

The Front Four have the responsibility of closing the middle against running and putting excessive pressure on a quarterback on a pass play. Behind the Front Four are the three linebackers. The middle linebacker plays two yards back from the center. The corner linebackers play head on with the offensive ends and often harass them when they try to go downfield for a pass.

Should a high school or college team employ this defensive alignment? First, they would have to have the personnel. Generally, a coach shouldn't copy another team because quite often, he doesn't have the players to do certain things. Most important, however, his players do not understand the entire defense.

We have great personnel on our front line who can react to a variety of plays. We don't have to use too much trickery, although when we do use trickery, it's quite effective because the opposition doesn't expect it. But our Front Four are so agile and quick that it isn't necessary for us to sacrifice going against the grain.

Defensive ends ("O" men)

The primary job of the "O" men is to get at the quarterback, to rush and harass him. They have to be strong enough to hold their ground against running plays and be able to stack up the interference. They must be able to counteract double team blocking.

On the pass rush, the outside men have options to go inside, outside, or to go over him. Basically, his initial movement is outside. If an "O" man has a man set up who is dropping outside to him, he just has to come back to the inside. That's the

only way he is going to have the offensive tackle come back and play it honest. It is to his advantage if he can beat him to the inside. If the offensive tackle is dropping off to the outside and he is giving the "O" man the inside, he should take it.

Defensive ends have to be big, particularly on the four-man line. Along with quickness, the "O" men must be counter punchers, reacting to the maneuvers of the offensive tackles. Therefore, they must be able to read the tackle. Some tackles telegraph the way they are going to block, so a defender should observe how he sets up for pass protection and the stance he employs.

Some offensive linemen put a little more weight forward, while others may put a little weight backward. If a lineman really wants to blow out, he may put his right foot back a little farther back, or he may get his buttocks a little higher.

Defensive tackles ("I" men)

A defensive tackle should have quickness, the ability to slide around opposing linemen.

These men do not have to be as rangy as the outside men, though. Although they don't need as much mobility, they should be stronger because of the plays hitting directly at them. Quickness, rather than speed, is the quality I prefer. They don't have to worry about containing.

On runs aimed at him, the defensive tackle should be strong enough to hand-fight his guard, then slip through to make the tackle. He often gives the blockers what we call a hand swipe. He hits them

A

B

Fig. 8-5. STANCE. We prefer a three-point staggered stance, with the weight definitely forward, to allow the rushman to explode off the line. A strong, balanced stance (demonstrated here by Merlin Olsen) enables the defensive lineman to deliver a quick, powerful blow.

in the head with a forearm, then takes the inside. The exceptionally quick tackle can go to his outside as well as the inside, and still be able to get to his objective.

Everyone on the defensive line should know what every man is doing. For instance, if the "I" man has an inside spot between the two inside men and if he is going to stunt, his own men should know this.

If he is very quick, a defensive lineman can make a move to the outside and take off back to the inside. The chances are there is going to be a tremendous pile-up in the middle area with the stunting action. This will leave an awful big hole for the defensive end to react to. He will then have plenty of room to the inside.

If the tackle is rushing to the outside, the defensive end knows the tackle is going to beat him to the outside, and he won't be able to react back. But if he knows the man inside of him is going to the inside, he might tell his own man that he is going to the inside. This is a good

opportunity to use the option of going to the inside. However, he has to know when to do it, and what charge to employ that will allow him to do it.

Stance

Since a defensive lineman must meet, stop, control, and release an offensive blocker, he should employ a wide stance, staying low and on balance. A strong balanced stance is important, because it enables the lineman to move forward or in slanting directions and deliver a quick powerful blow.

The most common defensive stance used by linemen is the three-point stance. Some coaches prefer to have their guards in a four-point stance. Linemen using the four-point position, however, should not let their knees touch the ground.

A common mistake many coaches make is placing too much emphasis on a rigid type of stance. When it comes to stance,

195

everyone cannot be the same because their physical characteristics are different. The only thing that I want is that the weight should be forward, his feet out in a sprinter's stance. He should line up in a position that does not tip off his intentions. "When he gives cues to the opposition, he is allowing the offensive man to place his hand on his wallet."

I'm only interested in 10 yards—who can get there the quickest, regardless of stance. However, his feet should be slightly close together, weight forward, and he has his buttocks up. When he does this, he will come out low. By keeping his feet up under him, on the snap, the chances are that he will come straight up, and this is what we don't want to see. We are always working on getting them low and stretched out, so that on the snap, they can get across that line of scrimmage. That's where the games are won.

In getting the job done, my recommendation is to allow the best stance for the player and let him come on across. He should not want to copy stances because the arm length, body and leg length are different. The coach just has to experiment and time the guy. We like to time our rushmen a lot in training camp. Have the linemen experiment with different stances, then select one they perform the best with the fastest time.

When Deacon Jones came into the league, he had a problem with his three-point stance. When the blockers would "M-block," fire away right at him, he seemed at a disadvantage. He found that he couldn't get anywhere with someone's head in his gut. So his stance was changed around until he was comfortable and could get out quick. Now, he can hit them first and go past them, before they can hit him.

Actually, the stance on defense is similar to the one used on offense. The chief difference is that the weight is more forward since the lineman does not have to pull laterally to the line of scrimmage. The feet are placed about shoulder width apart with one foot slightly back in a staggered position, one or two hands on the ground with the weight forward on the hands. When on defense, the body of the lineman should be closer to the ground than on offense.

Some defensive ends assume a two-point stance, facing the line of scrimmage with the inside foot forward. However, whenever they are playing tight with a linebacker covering to their outside, they use a three-point stance.

Use of the Hands

All good defensive linemen use their hands to keep the offensive blockers away from their body. *This constitutes the only advantage the rules provide for defensive players.* The hands are used to ward off blockers and to allow the defensive players to get to the point of attack.

The term, "use of hands," means the use of hands, forearms, and shoulders to keep an offensive man away from the defender's legs and body long enough to permit him to read, diagnose, react,

A   B   C

Fig. 8-6. THE CHARGE. A team of hard charging linemen is always hard to beat. We have seven different defensive charges on the Rams. The one Coach Allen prefers is the "Jet" charge, demonstrated below by Merlin Olsen. Ole takes off quickly, low, and aggressively, with strong arm and leg drive. Note that his head and eyes are focused directly ahead.

and get to the point of attack. Many times a defender may not be able to play off a blocker with his hands, but he can play himself off a blocker.

Don't ever forget this! If a rushman fails to make use of his hands, he is never going to reach his potential as a defensive player. Use of the hands is necessary whether a lineman is playing a run or rushing the passer.

Rushmen Maneuvers

In this modern day of pro football with the multiple attacks employed by the offense, the charging maneuvers of defensive linemen demand not only quick thinking but strength and maneuverability as well. From the skill standpoint, I'm more concerned about the rushman's quickness than any other single characteristic that he possesses.

Every defensive lineman has his own favorite maneuvers. We like our young players to experiment and practice all the methods used for defense to see which are the most natural and which they can execute best. In deciding which maneuver to employ, the lineman should first consider the down and tactical situation. He should keep his opponent guessing by mixing his maneuvers. Above all, he should be in position to tackle after he executes the stunts or maneuvers. Quite often, a player might develop his own maneuver. However, new maneuvers should be tested and proven in practice before they are tried in game action.

Certainly, teamwork is necessary to make any defensive line a success. Our linemen have special signals, in which they let each other know what they are going to do. Maybe two will fire in so the other two lay back. Of course, since things change a lot, they have to change

A   B   C

Fig. 8-7. ARM RAISE TECHNIQUE. The rush-man (here, Lamar Lundy) charges forward, and before making contact with the defender (Merlin Olsen), he lifts his right arm high into the air and over the head of his man. As he raises his arm, he pushes off his right foot to the outside of the defenseman. A good job of faking and quick footwork is necessary if this charge is to prove successful.

D

what they start out to do. But they have played together long enough now so they know instinctively how each other is going to react to something. And they always cover up for each other.

Getting off on the ball

This must be drilled upon every day both in training camp and during the season. Defensive men should not listen to the signal-calling cadence of the quarterback. They must take their initial starting signal from what they see, not what they hear.

There are two ways to perform this vital phase of defensive line play. One method is to key the ball and move when the ball is snapped. The other is to key the offensive player and react on his movement. Actually, some players use a

A   B   C

D   E   F

Fig. 8-8. THE STEP TECHNIQUE is an effective charge used by defensive linemen. When the outside foot is back, the step charge is a jab step with the inside foot, as contact is made. The lineman should come out using his hands, taking a good hard swipe at the offensive lineman with as little lost motion and time as possible. Defensive linemen have a common fault: they make too many moves.

third method in that they combine both keying the ball and reading the offensive man's movement.

Let's say the charge calls for the outside shoulder responsibility of the offensive lineman. We want our defensive man to get there as quickly as possible. We want him to more or less ignore the run and "come off the ball" as fast as he can. If a team drills enough on their reaction to running plays, if it happens to be a run, then they will not likely get hurt.

Shoulder charge

The shoulder charge is used in extremely short yardage situations. Some linemen like to charge straight into the blocker and jolt him with both hands on the shoulders. The lineman wants all his weight behind his shoulders to drive his man straight back. When using the shoulder charge, we want the rushmen to combine it with the forearm flipper. If he goes just with his shoulder, chances are his arm will be

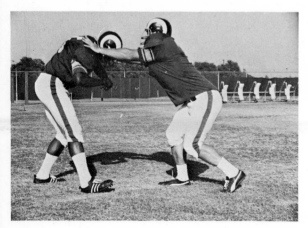

D

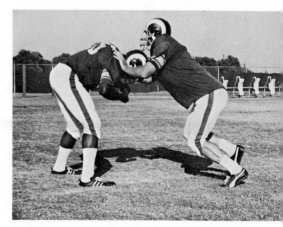

C

behind him, and the offensive man can get under him. Whereas if he comes out real low, using his shoulder and his flipper, he might be able to bring him up as he hits him across the chest. He can bring him up and still stop his movement.

A defensive lineman has to gain control of the line of scrimmage before he is ever going to stop the play. If he comes out with the shoulder alone, we think he will not be as effective. We want him to meet the blocker low with the shoulder and neutralize him. Then he should raise him up and control him with his forearm and other hand. After he whips him, he should release him and make his tackle.

The defensive lineman must always watch his target so he can get a solid blow. After making contact with the blocker, he then should locate the ball carrier. He

cannot perform this procedure in reverse or the blocker will have the advantage.

Hand shiver

The forearm shiver is a straight-out shot executed by the defensive lineman using the heel of his hand, and then locking his elbows. The forearm shiver is usually used when he is in pursuit, and a back or guard is coming out to get him. He should extend the palm of his hand out and lock his elbow and give him a real jolt and try to knock him off balance and down. Quite often when they are running, it doesn't take an awful lot to cause them to lose balance.

The forearm shiver is similar to the hand shiver. The difference is that the lineman allows his forearms to make the initial contact with the opponent. He should

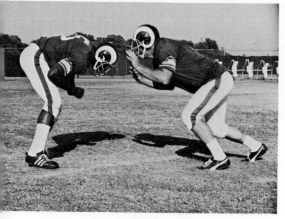

B

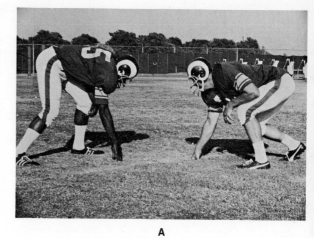

A

Fig. 8-9. HAND SHIVER. This is a straight-out shot using the heel of the hand, and then locking the elbows. This allows the defender to "read" the play and keep the blocker away from his body. It is an effective technique for linemen who possess exceptional quickness. Above, the rushman (Merlin Olsen) gives an real jolt and tries to knock the blocker (Lamar Lundy) off-balance and down.

bend the elbows to a 90 degree angle. The forearm shiver is more popular than the hand shiver because the individual who uses the hand shiver must have exceptional strength for satisfactory execution.

A shiver involves a straight lock with the elbow and getting the shot there. The lineman should come out with the elbow locked, and he should try to stun his opponent right there so he can react to the play. The forearm shiver is done with both arms and is a protective maneuver to maintain a relative position on the line of scrimmage until the ball is located.

One hand is placed on the opponent's shoulder, and the other is on the head. The defensive man should step into his opponent with his back foot, always keeping his feet and legs well back of him.

Thrusting his hands forward in an upward movement, he delivers a blow with the base of his palms.

The forearm shiver is often applied in cases where the opponent is trying to use a side body or reach block. It is an effective counter when the center attempts to block the I-man. The arms are extended and are locked. The locked-arm position helps to keep the blocker away from the defensive lineman's body.

Forearm lift

This maneuver is used mostly on close-in blocks, where the blocker reaches the defensive man much quicker and with much more power. It is also effective when a rushman attempts to run through a pass protector who is using an upright blocking stance. The rushman uses the forearm

A   **B**   **C**

Fig. 8-10. FOREARM LIFT. The defensive line-man (here, Merlin Olsen) meets the power of the block in a lifting action. This maneuver is effective in destroying the force of the offensive block. His target is the chest of the blocker (Lamar Lundy) and he drives his forearm hard under the chest.

D

nearest the blocker, aiming his arm be-tween the neck and shoulder, under the chest to lift up the blocker.

The defensive lineman comes out of his stance, and he doesn't immediately draw back. He comes right out of there and gets real tension on his arm. He tries to make contact along the shoulders of the blocker or up to the chin or possibly the head. He uses a very quick shot with his forearm and tries to knock his man off balance, and then he reacts to the play. He is thinking about a run, *and he is not thinking about avoiding the man so*

much as he is beating him right there on the spot to protect his area.

In using the forearm lift, the lineman meets the power of the block in a lifting maneuver. It is applied in most situations where the opponent is using a shoulder block. This maneuver destroys the force of the offensive block. The arm is driven hard under the chest of the blocker, which forces the offensive man to rise up. He wants to rid himself of the block so that he can get to the tackle. He must avoid a stalemate because if that occurs the offensive man usually wins.

A   B

Fig. 8-11. HAND SWIPE. The rules allow defensive players to use their hands. It's the only advantage they have over offensive players. A defensive lineman must use his hands to keep the blockers away from his body. Using the heel of his hand and locking his elbow, he gives the blocker a powerful hand swipe on the side of his helmet. After completing the technique, he must rush the passer without wasting any time and without any lost movement. (Roger Brown)

Hand swipe

This maneuver is used by linemen who are quick and agile, both against runs or passes. The rushman executes a fast jab step in one direction as the blocker reacts to meet this fake and comes in the direction of the fake. He uses his hands to swat or swipe him on the head and body compelling him to continue in the direction of his fake. At the same instance, he changes the direction of his feet and goes behind him to the point of attack. If he doesn't go to the fake, the rushman uses his hands on him from the inside and continues in the direction of the original fake.

Submarine

The submarine maneuver is used primarily for extreme short yardage and generally down in tough territory, when the offensive team is close to a touchdown. The lineman takes a real low stance, usually a four-point stance with both arms on the ground. The submarine technique is particularly effective against wedge blocking.

A

B

Fig. 8-12. SPIN OUT. The defensive lineman (left) comes out of his stance and charges into the offensive blocker. He uses a forearm lift, aiming his thrust under the chest to lift up the blocker. After making his initial charge to the outside of the blocker, the rushman makes a quick pivot of his forward (right) foot and spins around in a reverse action to the inside lane of the offensive lineman. This maneuver must be done quickly and be preceded by a hard straight shoulder charge. (Here the rushman is Merlin Olsen and the offensive lineman is Lamar Lundy.)

E

F

204

C

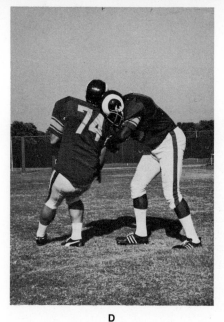

D

Fig. 8-12 (cont'd.). The defenseman must come out of the reverse spin maneuver down low, on balance, and must be ready to move in any direction. Although alert and primed for a running play, he will continue his charge and put pressure on the quarterback if a passing situation shapes up.

I value quickness more than any other skill a football player can have.

G

H

On the snap, the rushman must come out real low and fire right at the offensive man's knees. He should not go any higher than the knees because if he does, they will drive him back. The prime objective is to create a big pile-up right there, hoping the runner will run into the heavy congestion. Someone then will likely be able to react to him and prevent him from progressing.

Against certain opponents in specific instances, the lineman will find it effective to fake a high charge, then dive under his opponents. As the opposing player of players charge, they will invariably slide over the back of the rushman. He then raises himself up and is in position to make the tackle. Caution should be taken not to drop to the ground and stay there. It is essential to bring the feet up under quickly so to be in position to rise after the initial charge.

Slanting

Slanting is a maneuver used when the defensive line has picked up a frequency, a certain formation, and they know—a high percentage of the time—they are sure of the situation. The defensive line can be slanted one way or the other, and each man is given a definite hole responsibility. Slanting is employed when the defense expects a run, not a pass, and on the snap, they hit their holes just as hard as they can.

We want the defensive line to get there quickly and disrupt the blocking pattern by the offensive team. Every man must execute his responsibility without hesitation. If he is right, it places him in tremendous pursuit of the play and, usually, he will come up with a loss.

Going over the top

This maneuver involves jumping over the two blockers. He either goes over leapfrog fashion with one foot out in front and the other trailing, or he merely dives over headfirst. This, of course, is a maneuver not restricted to linemen alone. Our linebackers sometimes use this when dogging to defeat a backfield man who blocks low.

Defeat the two on one block

A common defensive mistake is trying to play both blockers. The defender should play either the lead man or the post, but not both. No one is strong enough to defeat two good blockers. Four types of maneuvers used against two offensive blockers are the split, the submarine (in short yardage situations), the limp leg, and the spin-out.

Stunting

Stunting by rushmen can be very effective if used intelligently and with moderation. Basically, stunting is exchanging responsibility with someone else. The rushman must make sure he does not get cut off. If he doesn't replace the man he is supposed to, the defense is vulnerable to a large gain and perhaps a score.

The stunt, or loop, is a quick-change maneuver which Jones and Olsen per-

Fig. 8-13. THE LINEMAN must have a strong desire for bodily contact, to want to knock somebody down. Above, Roger Brown (78) and Irv Cross team up to stop Ken Willard of the 49ers after a short gain.

form to perfection. Just before the snap, Deacon steps to his right—to the inside, and Olsen loops behind Jones, to the outside. The two rushmen quickly change places, Jones going inside and Olsen, in protecting the now exposed flank, going outside.

By stunting, it is possible to upset the blocking patterns against the run or spring someone loose to harass or sack the quarterback. By upsetting the running game, offensive blockers begin to hesitate before coming off the line, thereby upsetting their timing and charge. However, stunting is not easy to perfect.

As the offense adjusts to the strengths of our defense, occasional stunts become very effective. This is particularly true if a team is trying to adjust with splits in the line. By doing this, they are weakening some area that we should take advantage of. The best example of defeating splits is when the offensive tackle has widened up because the defensive end is beating him outside. The end jumps inside and blows, with the defensive tackle then covering.

The defense should not stunt just to be stunting. They must have a definite reason or objective. Variations are many and change with various teams, so it is important that they determine the most effective type stunts or proper adjustments. Above all, the complete defensive structure must be considered.

Tackling

Good technique in tackling is most essential in playing defensive football. Actually, the tackling procedure is similar to blocking, with the added advantage of using the hands and arms. Tackling is basically one of balance, and this is acquired through flexing of the knees, keeping the head up and distributing the weight evenly on the balls of the feet. In order to maintain a comfortable position, the feet must be spread. To be a deadly tackler, an individual must have an eagerness for contact and he must be proficient with either shoulder.

The type of tackle used by the defender depends on who is carrying the football. If there is a big strong runner coming at him, the tackler probably will hit him low. If a player has tremendous footwork, he

207

A	B	C

E	D

Fig. 8-14. TACKLING TECHNIQUE. As he approaches the target, the tackler (Diron Talbert in this photograph) must keep his eyes focused on the belt buckle. A tackler should always have a target. Dipping his shoulders just before contact, he slips his head to the side, clubbing the arms. As he makes contact, the tackler should wrap his arms around the target and lock his hands, if possible. He should hit with a lifting, driving motion to put the runner on his back. He must continue to drive with short, choppy steps.

might want to go high on him. If he is a real scatback, he has to go high on him, otherwise he might be faked out.

When a team is behind and has to catch up, gang tackling is a must. Even if they are not behind, they should go for the football. The tackler might find it effective to come on in with one arm; while he is making sure he gets the runner down, he goes for the football. Besides the possibility of a fumble, he will give the runner some good punishment.

Head-on tackle

Every tackler must always have a target —this is a must! If a defensive lineman has a ball carrier coming straight on, he should "stick his head right in the midsection at that belt buckle." He will not get faked out if he sticks it right in the belt buckle. He must keep his head up, his seat down, and keep his feet working. The feet should be spread, back bent, and the arms out from the body. He should move toward the runner and keep his eyes focused on his mid-section. The defender must be the aggressor and not wait on the runner. He must go right on into him as soon as he can get the shot. Contact should be made with the shoulder at the break of the hips and stomach. He should dip his shoulder just before contact. The head slips to the side of the ball carrier and remains snug against his ribs. As he makes contact, he should wrap his arms around the ball carrier and lock his hands behind him with a wrist lock, and drive right on through him.

The tackler shouldn't stop there! He must dig his hardest at the moment of contact and continue to drive with short, choppy steps. He must try to carry the ball carrier at least three yards and drop him on his back with a driving thrust to the turf.

If the defender is going in belt high, sometimes, he can cause a fumble. The ball carrier has the ball under his arms at the waist, and if he is lucky, the tackler's helmet might go right at the ball.

When he faces a man head-on, the defender doesn't want the runner to fall forward on him or to break through. So, he must stick that shoulder in his stomach and drive right on through him.

Side tackle

The key point in making a side tackle is to take the correct angle of pursuit and be under good body control. The right angle should always be in front of the ball carrier, and the defender should try to anticipate the route he might travel.

We want the head in front of the runner and then the defender should make a hard-driving shoulder tackle. As far as hitting him low or high, again, it depends on the ball carrier. But the important thing is to get the head in front of him because all the runners in our league are very powerful people, and if he has his head behind him, the chances are he won't make the tackle. Besides, as he goes into him, the side tackle is the only way that he can wrap his hands around him. It's just too hard to get his arms around him if his head is behind him. Also, by getting his head in front of him and the goal line, he will be able to get his shoulder into better play and wrap his hands around him. The other way, the runner will likely break his tackle because he will never get one hand to the other for a lock.

The tackler should hit the ball carrier at the break of the hips. After contact is made, *the feet should continue to move in a driving motion through the target.* He then drives the runner into the ground.

High sideline tackle

A high shoulder tackle may be used occasionally when the ball carrier has turned the end and is racing down the sidelines. The tackler must have proper balance and good angle on the runner and attempt to drive straight through him. But he must get his head in front of the runner. The tackler must give him a good enough shot, so that the runner will be knocked out-of-bounds.

In executing this tackle, the proper angle of pursuit is very important. The tackler

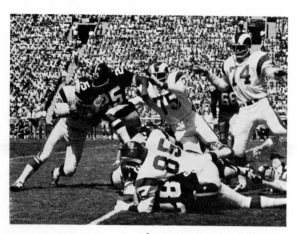

A

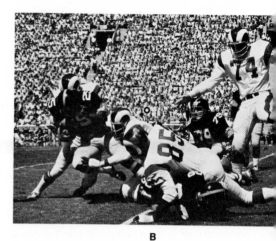

B

usually moves in on a 45 degree angle from the line of scrimmage. His eyes should be focused on the runner's neck and shoulder area. He should strive to hit the runner with a strong forearm shoulder lift about shoulder high. The tackler's prime objective is to hit the ball carrier with a powerful lift action in order to send the runner off the ground and sprawling into the sideline.

Recovering Fumbles

Recovering fumbles is not accidental. The team getting the ball, invariably, is the team which is always after the ball. Recovery is dependent upon *alertness* and *speed*.

The ball is not picked up, but is scooped in. The player actually slides into the loose ball. The dive is low, dragging the hip close to the ground. A pocket is formed by the player's legs and body, and one hand and arm are extended to gather in the ball.

The player must remember to scoop it with this extended hand and draw it into the pocket. To protect the player from the impact of other players, he should draw up his knees.

After scooping in the ball, most players find it advantageous to curl up, thus lessening the possibility of injury to the shoulder.

The Proper Mental Stance

The defensive lineman must believe that he can get out there and do the job. He has to want to get out there. I want to see a man raring to go before a game. During the week, I want to see him just itching to get to the game and to enjoy the warm-up, the game, as well as the accomplishments which go with it.

A coach must try to get a unit together that enjoys these different challenges—getting the quarterback, forcing fumbles, "sacking" the passer, and maintaining good pursuit. They must work very hard

C

D

Fig. 8-15. GANG TACKLING and pursuit, a trademark of the Rams' defense, can be demoralizing to any football team.

Myron Pottios (66), Deacon Jones (75), and Irv Cross (27) combine to stop the Steelers' Don Shy (25). Jones hangs on to Shy's legs as Cross and Pottios move up from the defensive secondary. Although being blocked, even Lamar Lundy (85) is still not out of play.

E

and be able to sustain the same level of work throughout the game. A football player has to have the stamina to go 60 minutes! *Every play is a big play!*

Most linemen are more effective if they can develop a sense of meanness, to be tough and ornery on the field. However, this mental stance cannot be achieved just by a pre-game pep talk. The conditioning of the mind has to take place throughout the week and on up to game time.

Playing a Run

The first objective in defensive line play is to get across the line of scrimmage, getting across with the feet as well as with the hands. Each man on the line is charged with an individual responsibility to protect the ground on which he stands or immediately in front of him. However, before he offers help to anyone else on the

Fig. 8-16. TACKLING FROM BEHIND. Speed, of course, is the key factor in tackling a ball carrier from the rear. In tackling the runner from behind, the defense should start high, lock his arms, and slide down, tying up both legs as demonstrated here by Jack Pardee.

field, the lineman must first protect his own territory.

After protecting his own territory, the lineman then should go for the ball. A good rule is always to fight resistance. If a blocker is working on his inside, a lineman can be pretty certain the play is inside. Therefore, if he always fights in the direction of resistance, the defensive lineman will be going for the ball.

On the guard pulling to his own side, the "I" men might drive into a tackle on that side with a hand or forearm shiver.

An outside rushman should always assume a play is coming back his way even though the flow is away from him, unless he sees that the quarterback has the ball and is retreating to pass. The "O" men

must remember they are the safety valves on all comeback plays.

Pursuit

Pursuit is the backbone of all great defensive teams. I have never seen a great defensive team at any level of competition that didn't have great pursuit. Alert pursuing action of the defensive lineman can keep running and passing gains to a minimum of yardage. Relentless pursuit by eleven men can make up for weaknesses in other areas.

The correct "angle of pursuit" is the key problem. The player who moves along an incorrect pursuit angle will find him-

Fig. 8-17. THE SECRET TO WINNING in this game is getting to the quarterback. Although Deacon Jones (75) and Merlin Olsen (74) were not able to tackle John Unitas of the Colts (19) before he threw the pass, their efforts paid off in an interception by the Rams' Eddie Meador (21). This was the "big play" of the game against the Colts as Baltimore was driving for the lead touchdown. However, the Rams scored and led to the big win, 34–10, for the 1967 Coastal Division Championship.

Fig. 8-18. A STRONG PASS RUSH is the "best pass defense" in football. Merlin Olsen, Los Angeles Rams' defensive tackle, stretches high into the air to block a pass by Baltimore's John Unitas. Lamar Lundy (85), Rams' defensive end, puts added pressure on Unitas from behind.

self removed from a possible tackle. A correct angle of pursuit will bring the player to or in front of the ball carrier, not behind him. The best time to develop the correct angle is during practice while the offense is running plays.

The angle of pursuit depends upon the speed of the offensive players. The defensive lineman must consider his running speed in relation to the runner and the particular path he wants to follow to intercept the ball carrier. He should always stay one step behind the ball carrier while on the pursuit angle.

Playing Screens

A defensive lineman cannot be an effective pass rusher and be thinking about dropping off to play screens, unless that is his specific assignment. However, if he senses a screen, he should be tough on the receiver and try to knock him down or off balance on his way to the passer. So, he must jam any potential receiver he can reach without going out of his path.

After rushing the passer successfully, outside linemen should look for screens their way. They must play the screen the instant the ball is thrown.

Rushing the Passer

Rushing the passer is the most important part of defensive line play. *A team will do more rushing of the passer than any other single maneuver on defense.* Many coaches and players don't realize this.

The big "Front Four" have to get after that passer. Having a strong rush line cuts down the necessity of the blitz. Thus, the red dog can be a surprise move rather than an over-used move that many teams have to make to get to the quarterback. But we rely on our "Front Four." They have one job: get the quarterback! Everything else is reaction. If there is a run, they react to a run, but they first start off rushing the quarterback. That's my theory on rushing the passer and playing defense.

A pass rusher should be thinking of four things:

1. Line up as close as possible on the ball.
2. Have several possible moves in mind before taking a step.
3. When the center moves his hands, fire through.
4. Come in high, arms waving, to cut off the passer's view.

The down and distance will predetermine every move. On a second and twelve situation, a pass play is most probable. When he decides it is going to be a pass, he determines the type of rush he will employ. Defensive linemen should learn all the "pass giveaways" they can.

There are two basic types of pass blockers:

1. *Riders* The rusher sits back and waits for the defensive man to come to him. While he never hurts him, he still manages to screen him away from the passer.
2. *Fire and Recoil* This type will fire out on a defender, then move back and set up for his first charge. Here, the pass rusher should wait for him to fire, then shoot the gap and let him have a limp leg. If he doesn't knock him down with his initial punch, the pass rusher tries to get by him before he recovers and can set up again.

When the offensive man recognizes the move of the defensive player, in most cases, he will react a certain way to it. Usually, he will come right at the hand of the defender, duck his head, or something. "Once he ducks his head, he has lost sight of you," said Marion Campbell, formerly our defensive line coach, "and that's to your advantage."

"You may have your right hand up," continued Coach Campbell, "and you would like to come back to the other side." Here is where your planning will come in. You

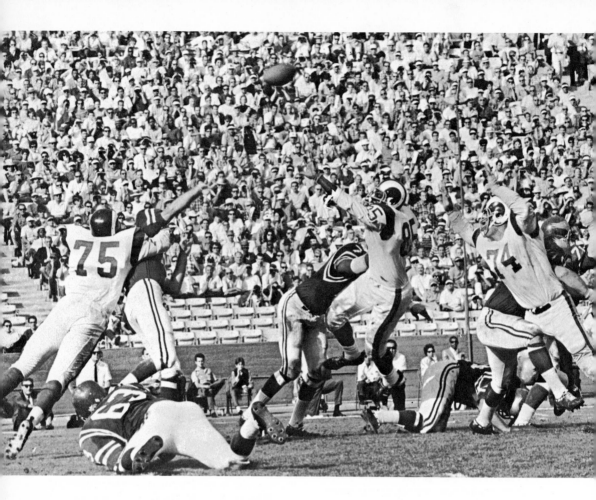

Fig. 8-19. PASS RUSHING. The all-out pass rush is the Pro's best defense against the pass. Constant pressure and pursuit by Rams' Deacon Jones (75), Lamar Lundy (85) and Merlin Olsen (74) make Norman Snead of the Philadelphia Eagles throw the ball off-balance. This type of defensive play can result in interceptions and become the difference between winning and losing.

know you are going to make this move, and you want to get more power and speed. Now, you want to use your left, and you want to slap him real hard because you have him off balance to the other side. You should duck your inside shoulder as quickly as possible and drive real hard at the quarterback. Many times you will break clean from the man. As soon as you make that second move, you will be gone, and he will be off to your side. So, now, you just sprint for the quarterback.''

Pass Rush Techniques

The most important skill that I want my defensive line coach to teach our rush-men is pass rushing techniques. They cannot get too much work on it. We want to start in training camp and go all through the season. We may even want to do it after practice. If the defensive line coach doesn't emphasize pass rushing techniques in our league, then he is missing the boat, and we are all missing the boat.

In our league, we live or die on our ability to rush the passer. And everybody can improve their pass rushing techniques, no matter how big or slow or strong, fast, or quick they are. This is something that isn't taught too much in high school or college because of the emphasis on the running game.

Pass rushing techniques are essential for any defensive lineman that hopes to stay in the league and make a career out of pro football. *The day of just stopping the run is over.*

1. *STEP TECHNIQUE* This charge is used most effectively by defensive linemen. When the outside foot is back, the step charge is a jab step with the inside foot, as contact is made. The lineman should come out using his hands, taking a good hard swipe at the offensive lineman with as little lost motion and time as possible.

2. *JET TECHNIQUE* The defensive lineman takes off as quickly as he can, low and aggressive, with strong arm and powerful leg drive. On the "jet technique", he drives through the pass protector any way he can. His weight should be forward to meet the block of the offensive guard or tackle. In addition, if he has enough weight forward, he will not be driven back or raised up too high by the pass protector. He must keep his eyes on the passer and not be so reckless that he takes himself out of the play if the passer decides to run or scramble.

3. *ARM RAISE* (see page 198).

4. *SIDESTEP TECHNIQUE* Linemen who are quick are continually using this technique. The lineman will feint a sidestep to one side and then quickly sidestep to the other. As the ball is snapped, he moves either foot about six inches to the side.

The initial charge must have the force to move the lineman attacked, backward and to one side. To accomplish this, he takes his stance in front of the man he expects to side step.

In making the fake, the body need not be moved more than is necessary to draw the charge of the offensive lineman. It is similar to a basketball player faking with his head and stepping in one direction and then dribbling off in another direction.

Playing two Blockers. A lineman should never try to overpower both opponents in front of him. One man at a time is difficult enough to lick. If he wants to play straight through, he must concentrate the force of his charge on one opponent rather than spread it over both. While he attacks one opponent, he must try to elude the other. It is important that the feet move across, causing the other lineman to miss. If he has executed the maneuver properly, he will find himself free and ready for the tackle.

5. *SPIN OUT AND SPIN IN* (see page 204).

6. *HEAD FAKE* A head fake is also effective in rushing the passer. The defensive lineman shouldn't drive straight in all the time. When he comes up on the line of scrimmage,

he can make a quick head fake to one side and take off on the other side. When he does this, he should reach with his hands and grab his opponent's shoulder and pull him in the direction that he is facing. To do this, he has to have good speed. He can set up these different moves and then come back with something else, something the pass blocker isn't expecting.

7. *SHOULDER DIP TECHNIQUE* This is the technique used by the defensive ends. Some outside linemen find the shoulder dip highly effective in rushing the passer. However, it has to be used when the offensive tackle has been set up for it.

The defensive end explodes off the ball, dipping his inside shoulder low and hard, allowing the offensive tackle less blocking area for contact. He aims directly at the point where he expects the quarterback to set up for the pass.

8. *LOOSE LEG TECHNIQUE* This technique is more effective for the I-men. The rushmen dangles the leg at the offensive man and as the blocker makes contact with that leg, he loosens it and allows the leg to accept a portion of a block and then he proceeds aggressively after the passer.

Most good defensive linemen perform this technique without actually realizing it. People that use the loose leg technique are extremely quick. They are so quick with their feet and legs that they drive one leg into a man and then take that leg away.

All these pass rush techniques have to be practiced, day after day, all season long. We expect every lineman to know the down, distance, score, and time remaining, as well as the formations.

Penetration

Every move that a defensive lineman makes has to be penetration. He cannot make a lateral step one way and go in the other direction because the guard is already set up there, one to one and a half yards, and he is waiting while the defensive man is doing all this. The rushman has just so much time to get to that quarterback, therefore, he must make sure that he makes every move with his foot across or in the direction of the quarterback. "If you come across the line of scrimmage," said Campbell, "you will make the offensive man drop back another step. When you come back the other way, he will drop back another step, putting you closer to the quarterback."

The rushman should try to get his man on the run. Also, he has to recognize the depth he sets up. If he is setting up short, he should use one technique. If he is dropping back, he should use another.

Sometimes the defensive tackle will fake to the inside, grab the blocker real quick and then cut to the outside. However, the inside move is the best for most linemen, and it is the quickest path to the passer.

If two protectors set up to take him, the rusher should go through the outside one. If two protectors set up wide, he should go for the inside one, then change his course and drive over the outside one. This will diminish the chances of the good roll-out quarterback's taking off to the outside.

If the protector likes to throw a body block, the rushman should veer more toward the middle so that he has to throw his block quickly. Then, he will have an easy path to the passer. If an offensive back attempts to block him, he must not fade. He should drive over him, then veer off his outside.

The quarterback run threat should be disregarded against a quarterback who rarely runs with the ball. Instead, the rushman should do everything possible to hurry the passer or prevent the pass from being thrown. Quarterbacks should not be tackled low or around the waist or chest. If he is close enough, the pass rusher should come down with his out-stretched arms on top of his shoulders and passing arm. If he isn't close enough for that, he should get in the line of the throw and jump as high as possible with his arms outstretched and waving. The quarterback should be forced to throw high over the rushman or around him.

The Goal Line Stand

In professional football, the most widely used goal line defense is the 6-1, with everyone pinching to the inside. We also remove our linebackers and use a 6-1 jumble by substituting two rushmen for the linebackers. There are many other good goal line defenses, but this is what we prefer at the present time.

All goal line defenses have one thing in common—*penetration*. The defense must penetrate into their opponents' side of the line of scrimmage. Pursuit is not of much value. Penetration is not easy to achieve because most goal line offenses tend to close down, so then the defense must apply leverage. The front line must not only drive for penetration but must drive lower than the blockers on the offensive line. This action creates piles, and more running backs are stopped by their own linemen than by any other method.

Eight Dumb Ways to Get Clobbered on Defense

Every year in training camp, I go over these eight ways to lose on defense. I want my players aware of these critical errors. While there are a lot of ways to get beaten, these are the critical ones and seem to be the most popular:

1. Don't play the Defense in the huddle.
2. GUESS where your coverage is. GUESS what type of pattern your man is going to run.
3. When rushing the passer, STOP when you are blocked. Hope the pass will be incomplete.
4. STOP PURSUING because you expect someone else to make the tackle.
5. JUMP OFFSIDE, or LINE-UP OFF-SIDE. Give your opponents an easy five yards to keep their drive going.

Fig. 8-20. DRILLS are most essential in developing the various skills of the defensive lineman. Here, defensive standout Merlin Olsen receives a workout with the shiver machine, under close supervision of former line coach Marion Cambell.

6. FOUL YOUR OPPONENTS when they are giving you the football. The best ways are holding, pass interference, etc. These are unnecessary penalties.

7. BE GUILTY OF A MENTAL MISTAKE. The best way is by not knowing, or not understanding your assignment in the defense. The defense breaks down because of mental errors.

8. LOSE YOUR POISE AND START A FIGHT, and get kicked out of the ball game. Not only do we get a 15 yard penalty, but we also lose a regular player. You don't have to take anything from your opponent, but remember that the player who retaliates is always the "one who gets caught."

Every season more and more defensive players are getting themselves and their team in trouble because of the above violations. If a player ever catches himself doing any of these dumb things, he should "STOP" in a hurry, because his team could lose a ball game through his stupidity. A player should check himself after each game and see if he is guilty of any of these errors.

Drills

Generally, defensive techniques are first taught in a single dummy situation. We then go to the blocking sled and individual scrimmage drills. Next, we come to the 7 on 7 drills for pass offense and pass defense, running offense and defense. Finally, we work together as a team in 11 on 11 dummy and 11 on 11 scrimmage situations.

Linebacking ⁹

90 percent of being a good tackler is having the determination and desire to really smash into an opposing ball carrier.

9

Good linebackers have been a major factor in the success of the great defensive teams of the National Football League. In fact, the linebackers are vital in the defensive unit of every football team.

In my opinion, linebacking is one of the most difficult positions to play in football. A lineman must worry about stopping runs, while a defensive back has to think primarily of pass coverage. The linebacker has the responsibility of stopping both runs and passes. This means he has to be quick, rugged, and a sure tackler. The decisions he makes and his reaction to play situations must be made without hesitation, whereas a deep back has time to "read" the receivers.

Generally, I prefer that one of the linebackers act as the defensive general.

Therefore, they must possess strong leadership qualities.

While coaches in the past have selected linebackers primarily because of their ability to defend against the running game, I prefer to select our linebackers because of their pass coverage. I'll sacrifice something on the running game to stop the passing game.

Qualifications

The linebacker has to be the best all-round athlete on the defensive team. He has to be fast enough to cover passes and strong enough and big enough to stop runs. I look for a player who is about 6'2'' and 225 pounds. I feel this size is just about right for an outside linebacker.

Fig. 9-2. For most football teams, the linebackers are key men in the defensive unit. They have to be fast enough to cover passes and big enough and strong enough to stop runs.

Now, if he is not that big, he can still play for us and do a good job. If he is a little larger, like Dave Robinson of Green Bay, that's all right, too. The middle linebacker should weigh about 245, and a height of 6'3" is ideal.

Any one who plays in the secondary, whether a linebacker or a deep back, must have quick feet. They have got to be quick starting, whether they are red-dogging or coming out of their coverage or getting into their hook spots. He should have "first-step quickness." He must be quick-moving laterally forward or backward with his first few steps. This is why I feel the

linebacker should have the footwork of a boxer.

Another factor in the qualification of a good linebacker is instinct, the knack of sensing plays. We prefer to call it "instantaneous reaction and recognition." They always seem to know what play is coming and where it is going. Many linebackers seem to have this instinct the minute they walk on the field, but this sensory perception can be trained and does come with experience by watching the same thing over and over. On the other hand, the linebacker should not commit himself too soon.

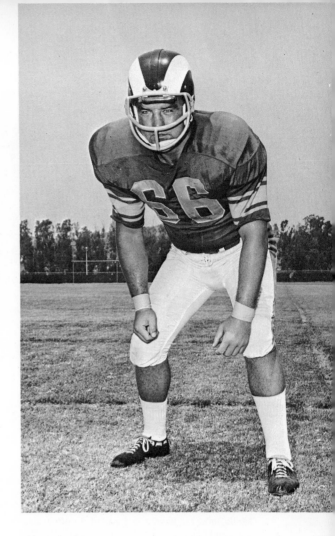

Fig. 9-3. THE LINEBACKER must be able to diagnose plays quickly. He must be decisive, aggressive, and hard-nosed. Quickness is more important than speed for a linebacker. He gets more tackles and is in more defensive plays than any other man on the team. He (like Myron Pottios, shown here) should have the footwork of a boxer.

The middle linebacker has to be agile enough to drop back for passes. He also must have good pursuit from inside out. He has to be a sturdy guy because generally he is facing bigger blockers than the outside linebackers. He is usually fighting off a center, guard, or tackle, sometimes two people. This is why we prefer a bigger man. He must also have the strong hands and arms to shed blockers rapidly and reach the ball as quickly as possible. In addition, he has to have the quickness to rush the passer. This is usually a short-coming in most middle linebackers.

In short, the linebacker must have a strong desire for physical contact. He must be physically tough enough to be knocked down and get up and knock someone else down.

Stance

Before he learns any of the many technical skills of his position, the linebacker must perfect the correct stance. As he waits for the play to develop, the linebacker is low and in a poised position. His feet are staggered, as wide apart as his shoulders, and the inside foot should be forward. The outside foot is kept back to enable him to move without being cut off by some blocker on his side. He has his balance under him, his weight on the balls of his

225

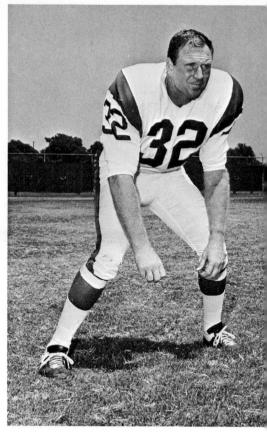

A

B

Fig. 9-4. STANCE. The linebacker is low and in a poised position. His feet are staggered, as wide apart as his shoulders. He has his knees flexed, and his weight is forward. Looking into the backfield, he is "cocked" ready to go. Good linebackers excel in the use of their hands. (Maxie Baughan (A) and Jack Pardee)

feet. His hands and arms are low enough where he can shoot them real tough into the first blocker. They are hanging loosely along the side of his body with the fists clenched, ready to strike a blow at the proper time.

The outside backer generally is playing on a tight end, about half the game. Since his man is only a foot to 18 inches away from him, he can get to him very quickly. Therefore, the linebacker has to be ready for the block immediately.

As the ball is snapped, the linebacker takes a short jab step forward, from six to eight inches, with his inside foot. This action places the feet in a heel-instep or heel-toe position. With the toes pointing straight ahead, the knees should be pointed straight ahead and are bent slightly. The hips are flexed, his body crouched slightly in a comfortable position.

Use of the Hands

No player uses his hands more effectively in Pro ball than the outside linebackers. The linebacker must keep opposing

A   B   C

Fig. 9-5. USE OF THE HANDS. Linebackers must use their hands well, keeping their elbows locked, or almost locked, and pushing the blockers off of them.

Strong forearms and wrists will do much to keep the blockers away from the legs. Above, linebacker Maxie Baughan (left) keeps lineman Dave Pivec away from his body. Maxie's outside foot is back, and he never crosses his legs.

D

blockers away from his body. If he allows a blocker to get into his body, whether he is blocked completely out of the play or not, he is going to get tied up for a second, a second and a half, or longer, on a well-timed play. By that time, the offensive team has the runner through the hole, and it is a matter of chasing him until they catch up with him.

So, we try to work with the shoulder, forearm, or a hand shiver to get the blocker away from him. He might give a little ground but must not be completely taken out of the play. We use the defensive reactor in training camp and try to work on it once a day.

The type of block will determine how the linebacker will try to offset the maneuver. If it is a real low hard-driving block, sometimes it is easier just to shove the man right on down to the ground, but if he is coming in waist high, possibly he can get up under him and raise him up and take his balance away from him where he has no more driving power. If the block is high, then the hands alone might take

227

care of it. So, the situation which confronts a linebacker will often dictate how he has to play the block.

Hand shiver

The hand shiver is done with the butt of the hand. The linebacker should wack the helmet or the shoulder pad pretty hard with the heel of his hand where he gets more power. Naturally, it doesn't always effect a big man, but if he can hit him with a lifting blow and if he is high enough, he can straighten him up and stop his momentum.

Forearm shiver

If the blocker is at a spot where he cannot get under him or knock him down, then the linebacker has to use a little bit more strength in taking on the block. This is where we use the forearm. The forearm shiver is the most common tactic he can use in playing off the block. Many linebackers are not strong enough in the arms to stop a blocker with the hands alone.

Our linebackers on the Rams really are not big people. They are very active with their hands, and they can often be seen using their forearm and the shoulder pad to take on the block. Actually, we work on the hands and wrists every day in camp and try to use the reaction machine at least once a week during the season.

Responsibilities of Linebackers

A linebacker must remember that he has a job to do on every defensive play re-gardless of whether the opponents choose to run or pass. If he follows instructions on each play, he should be a factor in almost every play.

Strong side

The first responsibility of a strong side linebacker is a running play outside the O man. His second responsibility is buzzing to the out-zone, and he must watch the passer as he does it.

On sure passing downs, he should line up deeper and wider for pass defense, unless the defense calls for him to jam a receiver or to red dog.

Weak side

The first responsibility of a weak side linebacker is a running play inside or outside of his O man. His second responsibility is buzzing to the out-zone on his side on passes. Keeping his eyes on the passer, he should run backwards at an angle.

Receivers must be kept from getting deep down field, so the linebacker must prevent them from doing so by bouncing, grabbing, or shoving them. The linebacker must never let a screen get outside of him.

Getting to the point of attack

The linebacker usually lines up as close to his O man as he can without being "hooked" or "turned in." The distance will vary according to the defense called and the formation used by the opponents.

Taking a medium, controlled stride with his inside foot, he moves to his point of

Fig. 9-6. THE MIDDLE LINEBACKERS in pro football are always moving laterally with force at an angle into the hole. Above, Myron Pottios (66) assists the Front Four in stopping an opposing ball carrier.

attack which is right behind the offensive line of scrimmage. He must be low when he reaches this point and shouldn't raise on his first step.

The quicker he can get to his point of attack, the quicker he can start his next movement.

Meeting inside plays

The success of stopping the play will depend on how quick the linebacker can get to the point of attack and his quickness in play diagnosis. This will come with study and experience.

Keeping low and closing his inside foot quickly, he goes to meet the blocker. He plays through the blocker and keeps his feet moving as he makes contact. On trap plays, he should strike a low, lifting body blow on the trapper. It is important that he see the ball carrier as he plays the blocker.

On inside plays away from his area, when either the fullback or halfback go up the middle, the linebacker must hold his ground until he sees the ball. We want him to take a pursuit angle where he will be a factor in the play. By going too deep behind the offensive line and chasing the play, the linebacker eliminates his chances of making the tackle.

Meeting outside plays

Again, the linebacker must be completely under control at the point of attack. He must not allow himself to be hooked in *at* or *near* the point by one blocker. We tell our linebackers we cannot afford to trade one for one.

The linebacker must not anticipate the outside path of a ball carrier. He should close the inside first. He doesn't want to change his direction until he actually sees the ball and the ball carrier outside him.

229

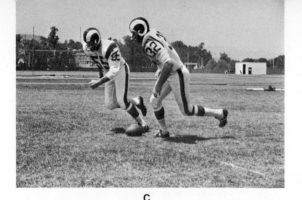

C

B

A

Fig. 9-7. RED DOG. The linebackers must react on the snap of the ball. They must take off as if "shot out of a cannon" and must make no false steps. They must stay down low on balance. Maxie Baughan, left, and Jack Pardee are two of the best in the business.

Then, he should go out laterally and get in position to make the tackle if the runner delays or cuts back.

Once he is certain he sees the ball, he must be sure not to be outside the ball carrier. He should play off blockers and prevent all runners from cutting back inside him. He should try to force the runner and blockers as deep as possible so that his teammates have a chance in the pursuit, but he doesn't want to open the gate between his position and that of his O man.

In defending against an outside play, the linebacker must make the tackle if he can, but he shouldn't go around any blockers to do it. He should always keep his hands in front of him to ward off blockers, and good footwork will help him avoid them.

On wide plays, he must not crash his way over blockers or else the play will likely be too far past him by the time he gets himself under control.

On quick tosses, in which the ball is immediately exposed, he must change his normal tactics by taking a direct line out to where he can meet the runner from the outside.

When he is sure the flow of the backs is away from him, and there is no back in position to execute a counter play, the linebacker must not chase the play to the opposite flank behind the offensive line. He might "slink" behind his own line, but he must always expect a counter play. He has to make sure the play is not coming back to his side before he "slinks" behind his own line to cut off the runner. As long as there is a near back on his side, whether strongside or weakside, he must be cautious when leaving his spot.

Defensive Techniques

In carrying out his responsibilities, the linebacker employs the following defensive techniques:

C　　　　　　　　　　　B　　　　　　　　　　　A

E　　　　　　　　　　　　　D

Fig. 9-8. DROP TECHNIQUE. The linebacker must be under control at all times. On the stance, his outside foot is back, and he glides quickly to his responsibilities. Generally, he will use a cross-over step. It is a matter of running with his body turned, and he has his head turned back in the direction of the passer to see what is developing. He is ready to adjust quickly if his key changes. (Maxie Baughan)

Red Dog

The Red Dog, or blitz, can be a valuable part of any defense. When he goes in too often, the linebacker leaves himself open for a long gainer, but we just "dog" enough to keep them honest. We particularly like to "dog" when they don't expect it. With our strong "Front Four," however, we don't have to blitz very often.

As the quarterback yells out the signals, the linebacker has to be very careful not to tip off the fact that he is going to red dog. The quarterbacks are sharp people, and they look for it from the way a man lines up. If one hand might be quivering, he might pick this up. If he anticipates a red dog, very likely, he will change his play and get himself some protection. Or, he will change to a running play which will take advantage of the red dog situation.

If a team has the balance and can get the good pass rush with their Front Four,

231

A   B   C

Fig. 9-9. BUZZ VS. PASS. In his coverage against the forward pass, the linebacker must never turn his back on the quarterback. He will get many more interceptions if he develops this practice. Above, Maxie Baughan uses a cross-over with his inside foot as he moves quickly to a hook zone. After he reaches his responsibility, he settles in a balanced stance so he can react quickly in any direction.

a linebacker does not have to red dog, thereby placing much less pressure on the deep secondary. No pass defender in football can continually cover speedsters if the quarterback has a long time to throw the ball.

We try to teach our linebackers to try to fool the quarterback. We do not let him know when we are coming, and conversely, we try to have him think we are coming when we are not. So, a linebacker must not tip off the red dog unless he is in a situation when the quarterback has completed his audible system. He has the signal caller in a spot when he cannot audible, and he is stuck with the play that he has called. Maybe, then, he can step into a hole in the line where he can get to him a little quicker.

Drop technique

We use the term "buzz" when our linebackers go to a certain area, whether it be an outside area or hook area. It is extremely important for them to get back there as fast as possible and still see everything that is going on. This technique is particularly effective in playing against the screens and draws.

From pretty much a parallel stance, our linebackers generally use a cross-over step. All our linebackers are fairly parallel as far as their feet are concerned, and as soon as they have diagnosed a pass, they

D   E   F

use a cross-over with the inside foot if they want to go out.

Keeping his eye on the passer, he must get to the area he has to protect as quickly as possible and get himself set. Once he approaches this area, he must get himself set under control where he can get his bounce back where he can move laterally, sideways, front, back, instead of just continuing his running.

Buzz vs. pass

A buzz is actually the coverage of linebackers against the forward pass, getting them out into the hook zones and into the flat zones, getting into those covered spots that the quarterback does not expect them to be in when he is running certain plays.

The buzz, for example, is quite effective against a button-hook type pass. Maxie will call defenses that will be most advantageous to us in getting a linebacker to be right in the line of flight of the ball for that hook pass. He can either pick it off or, if it is complete, he can help punish the receiver so he does not want to catch the ball anymore.

When covering, a linebacker must never turn his back on the quarterback. He will get many more interceptions if he develops this practice. The faster he can get back, the more time he will have to recover and play the ball. So, he should

Fig. 9-10. PASS COVERAGE. Maxie Baughan (55), Ram corner linebacker, covers halfback John David Crow (44) of the 49ers on a deep pattern. Executing one of the linebacker's toughest jobs, Maxie is in good position to knock the ball away.

In covering a receiver, the defender must never turn his back on the quarterback. As he retreats in his coverage, he is always looking through the quarterback.

always lock through the quarterback as he retreats in his coverage. The deep backs will communicate with him on two calls: "In, In, In," and "Out, Out, Out." The linebacker must also do his share of talking to help them. When he loses sight of the ball, he should stay at home.

The opposing team can be punished much worse on defense, so a defender should punish a receiver every pass he catches. He must want to make him cautious the next time he tries to receive a pass.

We like our linebackers to do a lot of "window-dressing," in which they jump in and out of the line of scrimmage. We want the offense to look at a defense they are not going to see when the play develops.

Play Recognition

Linebackers must read their keys quickly and effectively. Keys tell them the direction and nature of the play. The more they repeat on their ability to recognize what is developing, the faster they can read their keys. Never should a linebacker hesitate on defense! Sometimes, he will have

Fig. 9-11. AN ALERT LINEBACKER can accomplish feats such as this by being in the right place by "playing the defense called." Jack Pardee of the Rams, after intercepting a pass, is brought down by a San Francisco tackler.

to act without thinking and without hesitation. If a player hesitates on defense, even for a second, he will be in trouble.

The linebacker must never commit himself until he knows where the ball is. If he does not know where the ball is, he must not move. By playing keys, he usually knows where the ball is. The keys usually go through a triangle from the center on out—the center, quarterback, two guards, and the fullback. He watches which way the guards are going and the way the fullback is leading in.

Other mannerisms which linebackers watch for:

1. Leaning by linemen or backs.

2. Staggered position of the QB.
3. Backs cheating up or back.
4. Double-team blocking.
5. Splits taken by linemen.
6. Adjusting of hands or feet by linemen.
7. QB wetting his fingers.
8. Looking in the direction of the coming play.

Jamming the Receiver

By jamming, the linebacker is trying to hold up a potential pass receiver. By staying

Fig. 9-12. TO OBSTRUCT AND HOLD UP a fast receiver is part of the linebacker's job. With the big emphasis on the passing game he must be able to defend against big and fast receivers. Here, Maxie Baughan of the Rams shoves Chuck Logan (83) of the St. Louis Cardinals and makes him lose his timing and pass route. This is perfectly legal as long as the ball is not in the air.

with him as he goes along, he can delay his progress down the field. He can either push them out or let him get by him and kind of give them a pull. He can sometimes send them on their face. Or, he can "chop them down" the minute the receiver releases.

Our linebackers have got to be tough because we don't like to see these receivers get out where they can hurt us. Their timing into their pass pattern must somehow be thrown off, whether it means knocking them down, holding them up or jamming them.

Many times, the receiver, in an effort to give himself some space to get a better release, splits out about two or three yards.

Now, he has a two-way go on the linebacker, and it does make it difficult for the linebacker to jam him. It is very hard to hold up a man if he takes a wide release or with a three to four yard split. In this situation, we like for the linebacker to jam the man real tough with his hands, and if possible, try to straighten him up.

The running procedure for any runner is a leaning forward motion. He is faster this way. So, if we can straighten the man up, he cannot run quite as fast. The rule says that we can jam him as long as we keep him between us and the ball. Once he gets beside us or behind us, then the hands must be off. The defender cannot do anything more. He cannot trip him or

A   B

C   D

Fig. 9-13. JAMMING THE RECEIVER. When the end is tight, the outside linebacker generally plays him head on and tries to chuck the receiver, jamming or slowing him down. Linebacker Jack Pardee, right, shoots for the pads or up under the pads. He tries to get tight end Dave Pivec straightened up so he will lose some of his momentum and speed. All the time, he is still looking directly into the backfield to read the play.

grab his shirt, or anything like that. So, it all has to be done as he starts his release. The man must be controlled quickly.

On certain defenses, the No. 1 Sin for a corner linebacker is to let the tight end get an inside release. On many occasions, the safety man who is playing behind the outside linebacker, is positioned a little on the outside of the tight end. If the tight end gets a free inside release, the quarterback merely has to toss the ball three or four yards to get it to him, and the safety cannot recover quickly enough to knock the ball away before it is caught. John Mackey is the best in our business at this. So, the corner linebacker has to slow down that tight end on his inside release until our safety adjusts, if it is necessary.

Fig. 9-14. HIT HIM LOW! The best way to tackle a big receiver like Billy Truax (87) of the Rams is to get down low and lock yourself on his legs. Above, Alvin Randolph (27) and Dave Wilcox of the 49ers put that knowledge to good use.

In tackling, the secret is to always have a target and keep your eyes open.

Tackling

A linebacker has more opportunities to tackle than any man on the football team. Therefore, he must work on his tackling technique at every opportunity. Actually, 90 percent of being a good tackler is having the determination and desire to really smash into an opposing ball carrier. A good, hard tackle can give a team a real lift. Jolting tackles can also slow down the opposition.

The secret in tackling is: always have a target and keep your eyes open. "I try to hit him in the thighs or the knees," said Baughan. "Drive upward hard. Do not go to your knees. On hitches, hooks, curls and all short passes, hit the receivers hard. You want to jar him loose from the ball."

Smaller linebackers, when tackling big backs, should hit them low. A big, strong linebacker like Dave Robinson can always hit high and overpower the runner.

If a receiver catches a pass in front of him, the linebacker must tackle him hard enough so that the next time he comes out he will be cautious.

On an inside tackle where a ball carrier is coming through a hole, although the linebacker has some lateral restrictions which confine his movement, he must make a good solid hit either with the

Fig. 9-15. A SKILLFUL TACKLER is what a linebacker must become, because of the many key tackles he is called upon to make. He often must defend against a good ball carrier in the open field in a one-on-one situation. On the left, Rams corner linebacker Jack Pardee brings down Tony Jeter of the Steelers.

shoulder or with his helmet. Above all, he must never take for granted a man is tackled.

Open field tackling

When tackling in the open field, the linebacker *must be sure!* He has to get a hold of the runner and bring him down because if he misses, more than likely, it will be a touchdown. Here, the tackle is higher and not quite so aggressive, but just a sure tackle.

In teaching tackling technique, there are several points which the coaching staff stresses on the Rams' practice field.

A tackler must secure a good base since he cannot tackle with his feet together. In fact, I imagine the players sometimes hear them in their sleep. We emphasize the "good explosion," getting enough "pop" into the tackle to stop the ball carrier's momentum. As far as the arms, we continually scream: "Lock up, lock up!" When they get the arms around, we urge them to get a good lock on the other arm behind the man and keep their feet apart. If they cannot get the good lock, however, there is the "squeeze tightly!," grabbing hold of some part of the man's shirt or pants.

"Lock up" means for the tackler to squeeze as tightly as possible and pull the man's legs into his chest. If he has hit his man with a good lifting motion, he can take his man right up off the ground. He cannot run very well with his legs locked up against his chest. Now, the tackler must pin him down and drive him into the ground. He must keep after it!

Playing a Screen

We want our linebackers to turn that screen in. In other words, just as quickly as they see the screen coming, they must commit themselves to the screen, in terms of getting it turned in. If the linebacker blows through the gap and gets picked off and the screen man gets outside, then, all of our interior people, about 8 or 9 players who probably are chasing this screen, will have to run anywhere from 10 to 20 yards farther before they ever get to the ball carrier.

The screen situation is very similar to the sweep, except it is a delayed thing. It must be turned in to those people who are coming on pursuit angles.

Defensive Signals

Verbal signals are the principal means of calling and controlling defensive formations and movements. Defensive signals are, as far as possible, made up of easily heard and distinguishable sounding numbers, letters, words and expressions.

Signals are comprised to two digit numbers, letters, names, and expressions.

They are frequently made up of three parts: one part primarily for the rushmen, one part for the linebackers, and one part for the deepbacks. Although each of these defensive groups is controlled separately by its own part or parts of such signals, quite frequently one signal instructs all three groups.

The defense must be able to RECOGNIZE and IDENTIFY INSTANTLY what formations and maneuvers the offense is using. Then, the defensive players must be able to COMMUNICATE with each other easily, accurately, and rapidly what they observe. This ability is of the utmost importance in helping the defense to determine, ahead of the snap, what plays the offense will, or will not, use and in coordinating the efforts of the various defensive players in meeting such plays.

It is also important for the defense to IDENTIFY THE KEY OFFENSIVE PLAYERS AND THEIR POSITIONS, to communicate such information to each other and to adjust their defensive maneuvers to counter the abilities in order to attain adequate pass coverage and pass rush.

Common Faults of Linebackers

1. Letting an end get inside too freely when he is tight.
2. Looking at the passer and not reacting to a man looking or crossing right behind him. The linebacker must react to the deep back's call.
3. Not protecting outside on red dogs. The passer has made it to the outside in many instances.

Fig. 9-16. WORKING AGAINST THE SHIVER MACHINE. In order to be a good linebacker, a player must use his hands and forearms. This is a drill which must be practiced every day in training camp (Gene Breen).

4. Poor position on a pass when covering a halfback. He must keep him in front of him at all times. Be squared up initially with him.

5. On a quick pitch to a strong back, not being conscious enough of a crack back block from the flanker.

6. Not being tough enough with the end on goal line and short yardage. Control him.

7. Not harrassing receiver in his territory.

8. Not converging on the ball.

9. Buzzing before a draw threat is eliminated.

10. Not communicating on the screen or draw.

11. Not jamming "near" ends and controlling their release when possible.

12. Not being in position for tipped or batted balls.

13. Not blocking for interceptions.

14. Failure to alert others of a fumbled ball.

15. Lack of dedicated pursuit (earnest pursuits)

16. Not calling the position of the split ends.

17. Not moving around when possible, giving the quarterback something to think about (window-dressing).

18. Not calling out "pass, pass, pass" on play action passes. Call as soon as it is recognized.

19. Not getting depth quickly after a draw is eliminated.

20. Not punishing certain backs when dogging.

21. Overrunning plays away when cutback threat is possibility.

22. Tackling too low in open field.

23. Looking into backfield too much and getting chopped down too easily by the slot end.

Drills

Many coaches do not spend enough time in developing the necessary skills needed by linebackers. A few extra minutes of practice each day on these skills can be extremely beneficial.

To be a good linebacker, the player should do everything possible to develop his agility and quickness. Participation in other sports, such as basketball, handball, or tennis, can be very helpful to him in developing his coordination and footwork.

Most of the opportunities that a linebacker has of intercepting a pass involve moving laterally backward or cutting in toward the ball. Therefore, a linebacker should have someone pass the ball just above his head and run directly at the passer to intercept.

For the deep back the secret of good pass defense is always to have proper position on the receiver.

10

With the great emphasis on passing today and the pressing need for a stubborn defensive secondary, the deep backs are now being recognized as some of football's most exciting performers. Indeed, this recognition is highly justified when one realizes that pass defense is the most difficult assignment in Pro football. Therefore, the defensive backs, those who specialize in pass defense, have the most difficult positions to play. They stand back there and must compete with the fastest, most agile men in the game.

As a coach, I like to have four complete sets of deep backs in training camp. Sixteen deep backs allow me to organize our entire offensive and defensive practice program. I prefer to work them in units and have them always going at top speed.

For a collegiate player coming into professional football, pass defense is one of the hardest adjustments to make, primarily because now he will be playing man-to-man defense. Most college teams, in the past, have played a zone-type defense, so

now, the young pro has to pit his individual talents against another individual. My method of testing a rookie is to place him in a one-on-one situation, and then I'll know in a hurry what he can or cannot do.

Those who play in the defensive secondary do not become proficient at pass defense overnight. The rookie defensive back has never covered a receiver who possesses the moves and speed of NFL receivers. No matter how fast or how big he is, he must gain the necessary experience to effectively cover these skilled performers.

A defensive back, generally, will keep his job much longer than an offensive back simply because it is far more difficult for any young player to step in and take his job. Every year, an offensive player comes in and plays well, and he is a star, but not many times does a young deep back make the Pro Bowl. Len Barney of the Detroit Lions is one exception who became a star in his rookie year and has played in two consecutive Pro Bowls.

Fig. 10-2. TO COVER, THE DEEP BACK has to have speed. When the ball is in the air, he should play the ball, not the receiver, and play it aggressively. He should be rough and make an opponent respect him. On the right, Clarence Williams (24) and Ron Smith (41) exert close coverage on John David Crow of the 49ers.

Fig. 10-3. A DEEP BACK'S TYPICAL STANCE Irv Cross (27) demonstrates. The back's leg are flexed so he can react quickly in any direc tion to the moves of flanker back Clifton McNe (85) of the 49ers. Above, the Rams go into "revolve."

Star pass defenders are not born. Essentially, they are developed by a step-by-step process of teaching and practice. While some deep backs are gifted with speed and exceptional agility, everyone playing in the defensive secondary can improve by constant drilling.

Every deep back must take pride in his coverage and other defensive skills. They should realize that a good defense will keep any game respectable. There is always hope for a victory when there is confidence in the defense, even when your team is behind by a close score.

Remember, the defense can score five ways, while the offense has only three ways.

DEFENSE CAN SCORE
1. Blocked punt
2. Fumble
3. Pass Interception
4. Safety
5. Punt return

OFFENSE CAN SCORE
1. Pass
2. Run
3. Field Goal

Qualifications

The first thing I look for in a deep back is speed. Speed is the name of the game in Pro football and a defensive back has to have speed to cover. Secondly, he must have the ability to react. The ability to react involves quickness. Quickness is more important on pass defense than speed.

There are some deep backs who have speed, but if they don't have quickness, they cannot play in our league. By quickness, I mean the ability to move the hands and feet in a limited area. There are many good backs who are not exceptionally fast but they are quick. I like our corner backs to be able to run a 4.6 forty yards. Ron Smith, our strong safety, can run a 4.5 forty yards.

Quick hands and feet, good peripheral vision, timing, and body balance are reaction qualities that are necessary for deep backs. On pass defense, the defensive back's reaction ability will determine whether he will succeed or fail. The only way he will improve and develop is through constant drilling.

The deep back has to be tough because those big backs are going to break loose occasionally and run over him, and he will have to bring one down. The defensive back who can "put the leather to someone" will find a place on any football team.

Balance is another important qualification of a defensive back. Whether he is running, jumping, or diving, the player must keep his head and hands in position to see and catch the ball. If a defensive back should slip, he must regain his balance as quickly as possible and continue on to the ball or an area.

The outstanding deep back is an opportunist, taking advantage of every break or miscue by the opposition and making it pay off. When the opportunity presents itself, the "head-up," alert player is ready to make his move, with aggressive action. A deep back must have a strong desire to want to play pass defense. He should want to be the best pass defensive player on the squad.

Stance

A proper stance will help the defensive back be physically and mentally alert. A deep back must not become careless in taking his stance. He should work for "cat-like" reflexes. He has to be alert, but relaxed.

The deep back should line up with his outside foot up in a heel-toe relationship, with his knees and hips bent slightly. The feet are about the width of the shoulders. The outside foot is staggered to form a brace for a quick start.

The back is straight with the buttocks low to allow the weight to be on the balls of the feet. His arms hang loosely down at the side of his body, and the toes and shoulders are squared to the line of scrimmage. The legs are flexed so he can react as quickly as possible in any direction.

In the man-for-man coverage, the eyes of the deep back are focused through the receiver and on the quarterback. His head is held erect with the shoulders bent slightly forward. When it is time for a play to begin, the defensive back should get on his toes and lower himself. He must never fail to do this!

The outside or corner defensive backs must take advantage of the side lines. If the ball is on the hashmark and he is covering a receiver who is positioned near the sideline, the deep back should face *inward* with his inside foot back. In this way, he can view the entire offense and still see his man.

Footwork

No matter how much speed he has, a defensive back still needs drills to develop and improve his footwork. Footwork is a vital skill that every good pass defender must master. Fortunately, it is a fundamental that can be improved considerably through proper teaching.

In covering a receiver, the deep back uses every type of footwork he can possibly come up with. We try to teach our people to back peddle, to run backwards,

A. Eddie Meador

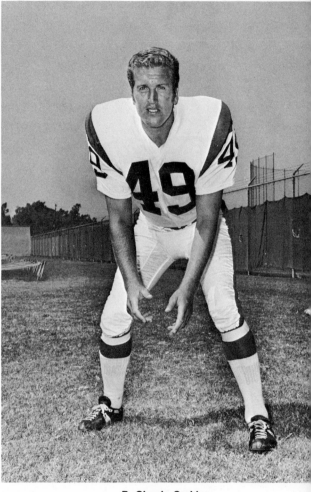

B. Claude Crabbe

C. Willie Daniel

Fig. 10-4. STANCE. Defensive backs have to be alert, but relaxed. Their knees are flexed, the shoulders are over their shoe tops, and the weight is forward over the balls of their feet. They are concentrating on their coverage. Note the arm action of Meador and Daniel as they backpedal.

B

C

A

Fig. 10-5. BACKPEDALING. (and breaking right or left). A deep back must develop his footwork to perfection and always be on balance. When backpedaling, it is essential that the defensive back plant the correct foot whenever possible. If he takes an extra step he will lose ground. This is the difference between completion and an incompletion.

Here, Eddie Meador plants his right foot and pushes off to his left. Notice that he keeps his head and eyes on the passer. When he plants his right foot, observe the good lean body and the angle, both of which facilitate quickness.

while facing the receiver. Defensive backs must be able to shuffle their feet. They have to be able to slide laterally, crossover, and then come out of a cross-over. Occasionally, they even have to turn their back on the passer and recover in the manner just described. When covering an

D   E

out pattern, the proper footwork is particularly important, in order to stay tight with the receiver.

Our deep backs work on running backwards every day. We cannot give them enough of it. In fact, we time our players in running backwards. We clock them for the 15 yard dash, and if a boy can run 2.5, that's excellent.

Most defensive backs will run backwards in starting off. When back pedaling, they must lean forward so that their shoulders are over their feet. We never want them to lean backward because they cannot stop or turn quick enough.

We believe a "deek" has to be able to carry a man about 10 to 15 yards backpedaling. He must keep the receiver a distance of three yards from him until he makes his break. From there, he must turn his legs from one side or the other and run with him. If a deep back cannot backpedal, then he has to come at the snap of the ball. By learning to run and

move backwards, the defender will be able to cover a break by the receiver in either direction.

A defensive back must practice his shuffle and glide steps from side to side. He doesn't want to get turned too soon. Many backs make the error of turning on the first fake, rather than wait for a second or third fake and then breaking.

Naturally, the receiver is trying to get the defensive man to run, get his feet crossed, so that he can make a break. Conversely, the deep backs covering him are trying to prevent this from happening. Therefore, the deep back must avoid crossing his feet, stumbling, or taking extra steps. Usually, when a back falls or stumbles, it is the result of poor footwork.

Defensive backs must practice running with their knees inward and looking over the inside shoulder. This is similar to an outfielder when going after a long drive. The deep back has to develop the ability to sprint when running this way.

251

Fig. 10-6. TEAMWORK is the name of the game on defense. Below, even though the Rams' Irv Cross (27) cannot intercept the pass intended for Jim Kelly (84) of the Philadelphia Eagles, he is able to tip the ball back to the Rams' Eddie Meador (21) who carries it 25 yards to a Ram touchdown, right.

B

A

252

Mental Stance

"They should want to play pass defense" best describes the attitude and frame of mind we like our players to have. To play to the best of their ability, defensive backs should always be thinking on defense.

If a football player doesn't know the situation, then he is wasting his time out there. We try to alert our people in the huddle just what the situation is—3rd and 7 or 3rd and 25. If it is 3rd and 7, we don't want to allow a 7 yard pass. If it's 3rd and 25, 8 yards won't hurt us unless the ball is down real close to our own goal line.

So our deep backs have to be thinking about the particular situation. We try to alert the man calling the defensive signals in the huddle. Quite often, we will alert them to make certain he knows the situation.

A good defensive back must have confidence in himself and his teammates. A good pass defender has to feel he can dominate the receiver. He must believe that he cannot be thrown on. We realize he cannot do it every time, but we like for him always to be thinking: "I'm the master of this guy. Just try anything you want, and I'm going to be with you. I'll be breathing right down your neck. And I'm going to take that ball away from you when it comes out here."

Actually, the perfect pass is extremely hard to stop, but that's what we are shooting for—to break up the perfect pass. However, the defense can expect offensive errors and should be mentally alert and ready for them at all times.

Deep backs should not worry about pass completions, but think only of stopping or intercepting the next one. They must not lose their poise if a pass is completed on them. They should hope they try another so they can intercept it. If they must give ground, they should allow it between the 20 yard lines. Actually, interceptions are mostly a matter of setting the mind to do it.

Approach and Position

The position the deep back maintains on the receiver must always allow him to maintain vision on the passer. The defender must never let the receiver get closer then three yards. He must remember that he can get too close as well as he can get too far.

Of course, the distance the defender plays from his man varies with the respective abilities, plus the down and yardage. Those receivers who don't have great speed and depend upon faking to get open are generally bothered by being played close. A deep back should get in the habit of covering his receiver closely and staying tight on him. He should hound him all over the field. He will find that it is actually easier to cover this way once he gets the practice. If he practices playing him loose, he will play that way in the game.

Proper position on the receiver allows the pass defender to do three things:

1. Intercept.
2. Break up the pass.
3. Tackle the receiver.

When a receiver fakes, the defender should merely drop back another step, but he must not decrease his speed or get turned. He should try to keep an outside angle on the receiver. If he does get caught out of position, he must learn to get into a favorable position quickly.

Occasionally, the defensive back will find it effective to bounce the receiver to make him aware of what is coming next. But, if he decides to cut him down, he should make sure he doesn't miss.

If a receiver is coming at him at full steam, the deep back must give ground rapidly. He doesn't want to let him catch him waiting for a move. He must learn to judge his approaching speed.

Once he starts up to stop a play, the defensive back must be aggressive and not hesitant. When going after the ball

Fig. 10-7. COVERAGE AND OTHER DEFENSIVE SKILLS. This group of defensive backs played together almost every minute in both 1966 and 1967. They are, left to right, Eddie Meador (captain), Chuck Lamson, Irv Cross, and Clancy Williams. They knew where their help was coming from, and communication was one of their strong points. In 1967, the Rams intercepted 32 passes.

and he has the receiver covered, but is directly behind him, he should try to keep one arm on each side of the receiver as he goes through his shoulders to the ball. Since almost anything is allowed if he plays the ball, the defender should go through the receiver's shoulders and go for the ball rather than the arms, or try to make the tackle.

When playing an OUT, IN and OUT, OUT and IN, CURL, STOP, and a HITCH from the inside, a deep back must remember he can reach across farther by using his inside arm. In addition, he has more force to knock the ball downward.

When a corner deep back is playing a HITCH, he should force the outside receiver inside. He shouldn't go for the inside fake and have him turn outside of him where there is no help.

The quarterback should not be allowed to complete the short passes. Our defensive backs have been guilty of lining up too deep and then retreating.

When covering the split or slot receiver on a fast "down and in," the defensive back must narrow his angle. He may have him covered, but he will be two yards away with the same alignment unless he can get in his path and narrow his angle. He then forces the receiver to shorten his course and, as a result, present the quarterback with a different picture. In addition, he is in a better position to cover his man.

Alerts

To improve their coverage and make possible a cohesive type of defense, the deep backs must do considerable talking with each other. Communication among pass defenders is a must for success. They must repeat everything three times and loudly so that it can be heard. The following are some of the alerts which the Rams use in communicating with each other:

1. *"Pass, pass, pass"* should be yelled as soon as anyone on defense recognizes that a pass play is on.
2. As soon as anyone on defense recognizes that a screen pass is on, he should yell *"Screen, screen, screen."*
3. Remember to yell *"plaster"* when the quarterback is scrambling.
4. Yell *"powder"* on crack back blocks on the weak side and on the strong side.
5. *"Ball, ball, ball"* should be yelled when a teammate is going after a long pass and his back is turned.

This alerts him that the man he is covering is the intended receiver and that the *ball is in flight.*

6. The linebackers should be directed by yelling *"In, in, in,"* or "out, out, out," when covering curls and hooks. Deep backs must communicate with the linebackers to improve their coverage.
7. The preliminary call for a switch is *far* and *near.* The call on the strong side is *switch, switch, switch,* and this must be answered by the strong safety before the switch is on. The call on the weak side is *"take, take, take,"* and again must be repeated by the weak safety.
8. The deep back plays everything as a pass until he is positive it is a run. Then, he should yell *"run, run, run."*

If he is talking, a player is thinking. And I firmly believe that talking takes a great deal of "pressure" off any player. To me, talking is second only to moving the feet as an essential fundamental in good defense. Without talking, it is impossible to be a good defensive team.

Tackling

No deep back ever has achieved greatness unless he has combined tackling ability with covering ability. Tackling is the backbone of defense. It is the "blood and guts" of defensive team play.

"You have got to keep your head up!" says Eddie Meador, the Rams' outstanding safety man and one of the surest tacklers in the NFL. "Be on balance and drive

A

B

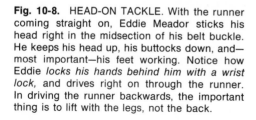

Fig. 10-8. HEAD-ON TACKLE. With the runner coming straight on, Eddie Meador sticks his head right in the midsection of his belt buckle. He keeps his head up, his buttocks down, and—most important—his feet working. Notice how Eddie *locks his hands behind him with a wrist lock,* and drives right on through the runner. In driving the runner backwards, the important thing is to lift with the legs, not the back.

C

A

B

D

C

Fig. 10-9. SIDE TACKLE. In making a side tackle, the defender must take the correct angle of pursuit. He must have good body control and must not allow the runner to cut back inside. In this series, Eddie Meador gets his head, shoulders and left arm in front of the ball carrier and makes a hard-driving shoulder tackle. He hits the runner hip high. After contact is made, the feet should continue to move in a driving motion through the target. The defender should always lock his hands and arms and drive the runner into the ground.

257

Fig. 10-10. HIGH AND LOW. The Rams' Maxie Baughan (55) and Irv Cross (27) demonstrate the correct execution of high and low tackling. Offensive back Doug Cunningham of the San Francisco 49ers has no place to go but down. After wrapping his arms around the runner, Cross locks his hands behind him and drives right on through him.

Fig. 10-11. THE BEST WAY to develop tackling technique is to begin on a dummy, so that a player can gain confidence. Above, a lively session takes place among the deep backs, as Coach Allen closely observes the technique and offers appropriate comments.

through your opponent," says Eddie. "With the big boys, you cannot hit them high. You've got to hit them low!"

While there are various theories on tackling technique, we teach our men to place the helmet in front of the ball carrier. If they miss, the runner is turned back into the playing field where there is some help. Generally, if the tackler places his helmet in back of the runner, if he should miss, the man probably is able to get out to the outside, and any pursuit that is coming either doesn't get there or he has a farther distance to go.

When tackling on defense, a defensive back must make sure! Sureness is better than how hard he can hit them. In no other phase of football can one mistake be so costly. There is nothing more discouraging to our rushmen and the entire team than to have a hard earned point margin wiped out because of a missed tackle.

Courage is no substitute for technique. No matter how much courage a player has, he must be taught the proper fundamentals of tackling. The best way to develop tackling technique is to begin on a dummy, so that a player can gain confidence.

Everyone appreciates a good tackler, and players, fans, and coaches all have the highest respect for the good "hitters."

Diagnosing Running Situations

The deep back must diagnose the play as soon as he can as to whether it is a run or pass. He should meet running plays as close to the line of scrimmage as possible and make the tackle from the outside in. The deep back must know which side is strong at all times. He watches the flow of the backs.

Prior to the snap, all defensive backs have a key that they try to play. This key will be determined by the type of pattern that will develop, or if it is a run. The key is really their play record.

The deep back should play the area and a man. He must see the men as they come into his area with peripheral vision, watching the passer and playing the ball tough from the outside.

First, the defensive back has to cover his man in his area. Then, he can move up to stop a run, but first, he has to stop the pass. After making a tackle on the line of scrimmage, a deep back can look for a pass behind him on the next play.

Perhaps, the only running play the deep backs can really key for is a sweep. They have to pick up interior running plays by the action of the linemen. "I key through the guard and tackle into the halfback," said Meador. "The linemen tell you if it's

a running play if they release across the line of scrimmage to block on us. If you see the end is definitely blocking down hard, you can get in there, but again you cannot commit yourself too fast."

If the ball carrier is able to get past the line of scrimmage and into the secondary, somebody has to bring him down. And, of course, before deep backs release their receivers to come up, the play must be a run.

Pass Defense

With nearly everyone throwing the ball today, the problems of pass defense have become just about the most important part of the game. The secret of good pass defense is for the deep back to always have proper position on the receiver. The defensive back must not let the receiver get him turned until his final move. There is an exact position for each defender to assume on each type of pass thrown.

The deep back must backpedal, shuffle, and glide before he ever turns. He must develop this at top speed. To remain sharp and improved, he must practice this every day. I want our pass defense to practice the way we want to play on Sunday. We practice at top speed only.

Great pass defenders are a combination of the following qualities:

1. Aggressiveness
2. Quick reactions
3. Alertness

4. Looking through the receiver into the passer
5. Always hustling when the ball is in the air
6. Determination to get the football

Confidence is also essential for good pass defense. When the ball is in the air, the defense must feel it belongs to them. By having a positive frame of mind, the deep back can help give his teammates confidence.

Many teams use both zone and man-for-man pass coverage in the defensive secondary. The Trojans of Southern California, for example, use at least five zone coverages and two-man-for-man coverages.

The most difficult situation for a defensive back to cope with is for a receiver to spread himself out about 16 or 20 yards. Now, a zone pass defense can't be used because the defensive man has gone too wide, and it's strictly a one-on-one situation. Any mistake can mean an easy touchdown.

A football team should have a strong pass defense if it has the following four elements:

1. *Recognition* of the formation and where to line up.
2. Knowing the individual *Responsibilities* or the zone responsibility.
3. Getting into *Position* on the *Receiver.*
4. Moving in to *Intercept* the football.

The deep back should not have any doubt that he can cover a receiver, even though his job is more difficult than his. He must hound him unmercifully until he knows who is the better man and who is the toughest.

Diagnosing passing situations

On passing situations, there are different theories on what the deep back should look for, who he should keep his eyes on. Some coaches like their defensive backs to keep their eyes glued on the passer, while others have their deep backs look for the receivers to come down. Both require good peripheral vision.

Personally, I think the ideal situation is to be able to see both, so that they can see the ball release and also see their receiver. Early in the season, we look at a lot of young players. Invariably, their eyes are fixed on the quarterback, and as a result, they are late in getting started, after a man makes his break.

Quite often, when a defensive back is having a problem reacting quickly enough, we will tell him to forget about the ball. We have this rule: "In terms of thinking, you can lose the ball but don't lose the receiver." But again the ideal situation is for the defender to be able to look through the receiver to the quarterback so that he knows when the ball is coming, and when there is an interception that we can take it. We are on the football field to play the ball, not to play three downs and walk off. We are there to get the ball on the first down.

If he is having trouble covering a receiver, a pass defender should concentrate on the receiver and nothing else, until he breaks. He should concentrate on his belt buckle, not his feet or head.

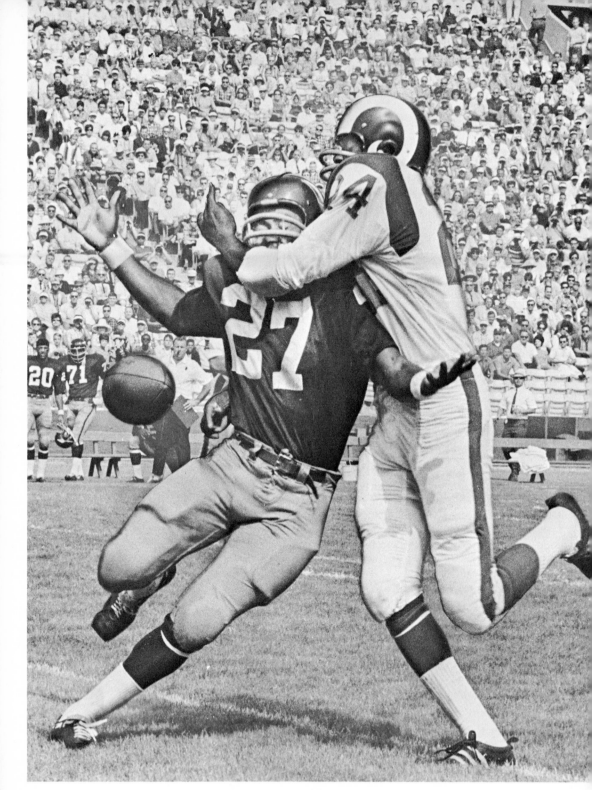

Fig. 10-12. BREAKING UP THE PASS. Rams defensive back Clancy Williams drives hard and clean on John Love of the Redskins to break up the intended pass. Clancy "played the ball," which is what we insist our defenders do.

Quite often, a defender is beaten and faked because he is attempting to cover too much with his eyes, for example, the quarterback, offensive lineman, and the receiver.

After the receiver breaks and *only* after the pass defender gets in stride with him, should the defender look back for the ball. His teammate will help him by yelling *ball!* If young defensive backs will try this in practice, they will see how it affects their coverage, particularly for the corner backs.

Tact position

In running with the receiver, our pass defenders use a TACT position, where they can see through the receiver to the quarterback at all times. I like this terminology to describe the exact position I want our defenders on the receiver. For certain patterns, it is often impossible, but for the major percentage of situations, we would like to have him assume a proper tact position.

The tact position is where the deep back can look through the offensive man into the quarterback. It is the correct position a defender should have on a receiver. If he is in an improper position, then he cannot see the ball leave the

passer's hand, and he doesn't have a chance to get an interception.

The defensive back cannot allow the receiver to run right on top of him, or he will run right by him before he can recover. So, he has to keep some vertical depth, and in addition, he must keep good lateral position on the man. In short, we like our people to employ tight coverage but not to gamble!

The most difficult position to maintain is the vertical position. More defenders are beaten because of this than as a result of any other factor.

The flight position is the position of the defensive back on the receiver while he is covering, and the ball is in the air.

Again, the deep back should read the receiver's belt buckle area. As the receiver breaks off the line of scrimmage, the deep back should glue his eyes on the receiver's belt buckle area. As a result, the deep back is less apt to look at the faking actions of the receiver.

Playing the ball

When the ball is in the air, the deep back should play the ball, not the receiver, and play it aggressively. Aggressiveness is one of the hardest things to teach on pass defense. It starts in practice against his own teammates and with helmets. Since many receivers are inclined to be timid, the deep back should be rough and aggressive and make an opponent respect him.

Playing the ball is not something to be taken for granted. It can be taught, however. Proper drilling can teach a man to play the ball while he is covering a receiver. The instant the passer throws the ball, the defensive backs must converge on the receiver. They must not just stand there and look!

In breaking up a pass, the defensive back goes up with two hands because two hands are better than one. He must remember he has equal rights for the ball once it is in the air. He plays rough and always plays the ball, not the man. Of course, there will be times when he can not get two hands on the ball, and he will be forced to use one hand. When using one hand, however, there is a tendency to tip the ball, so he should make sure he knocks it down toward the ground.

Once the ball is in the air, the defensive backs must converge on the ball. They must knock it down toward the ground, not up in the air. A pass defender should practice developing a "burst of speed" to the ball once it is in the air. Five or six strides with quick recovery at near top speed can be a tremendous advantage. Although he can gamble a little, he should know when to gamble.

When a teammate is covering on long passes and has his back turned, the defensive back should yell: "Ball, ball, ball!" He shouldn't yell too soon, because his teammate will turn to look, and this will slow him down.

There are times when a deep back has his man covered, but due to the type of pass thrown, it will be completed. An effective technique in this situation is to slap at the ball before the receiver can put it away. In most instances, he will drop the ball, but the defender is still in position to make the tackle if he holds ball.

Reaction to a deflected pass is something that must be practiced because it is not a natural type of movement. Deep backs, as well as linebackers, need this training so they can react correctly when there is a deflected pass, even when they least expect it. Each year, a significant portion of a team's interceptions result from deflected passes. This indicates the value of devoting some practice time to the playing of deflected forward passes.

Defending against the short button hook pass

If the deep back is screened out completely from the ball he will have to go straight through to the receiver and punish him. If the hook is thrown a little bit high and the receiver has his hands in the air, he can punish a man pretty well by hitting him in the ribs.

If the ball is thrown where the receiver catches it in his stomach, the defender possibly will try to get his arm around and in going for the ball get one hand in. Maybe, he can kick the ball out.

If the ball is caught just before the defensive back gets there, it leaves an

Fig. 10-13. PLAYING THE BALL. Defensive back Lee Calland, photographed here with the Atlanta Falcons, shows the importance of "playing the ball at its highest point" as he intercepts in the end zone. Bernie Casey (25) of the Rams had no chance to break up the interception.

unprotected ball. Consequently, there is the possibility of stripping the man, in other words, coming down hard on him over his limbs, hands, and primarily his arms. It is a hard "pulling down and out" motion, in the hopes that he will flip the ball loose. This may cause either an incompletion or a fumble.

We like our defense men to tackle high on the man who has caught the ball. Some defenders grab the receiver's arms, placing their arms completely around his body, thus preventing a possible lateral. If he gets there simultaneously with the ball, he can punish the receiver, but if he gets there after the ball is caught, he has to make sure he makes the tackle because the defense has eliminated their pursuit down to two or three men who are in the vicinity of the ball. If the first man does not get him down or get him slowed down, the pursuit may not get there.

Defending against the long bomb

The defensive back must always be conscious of the threat of a long pass, in which the receiver goes down, slows, and then sprints down field. The quarterback tries to hit him on the dead run. On this play, the deep back must maintain vertical depth until the receiver has made his positive break. Then, it is usually a matter of a foot race. He cannot always keep the perfect position; in fact, there are some receivers who are difficult to keep up with, stride for stride, in the correct position. However, if the defender can stay stride for stride with his man,

at the very last second, he can either get the ball or break up the pass.

The defensive back cannot afford to misjudge deep passes. This is an art and must be practiced. "A good rule to follow is to take one extra step before you commit yourself to go for the ball," said Meador. "Watch the ball all the way and only play the ball."

Above all, a deep back must *never* let anyone get behind him. This is the *worst* mistake he can make.

Intercepting a pass

The pass interception is one of the greatest and most spectacular plays in football. Intercepting a forward pass is a specialized skill consisting of perfect timing, coordination, relaxed hands, and footwork ability. Unquestionably, it is one of the most difficult skills in football to master. A pass defender running backward is required to cover a lightning fast receiver running forward. In addition, the receiver has the advantage of knowing where he is going.

A forward pass in the air is a free ball and belongs to the defensive team as well as the offensive team. Therefore, all defensive men should go after each ball in the air to intercept it, unless in special circumstances.

Deep backs should practice making interceptions above the head. If they take it lower and wait, the receiver will usually get it. The defensive back should watch the interception into his hands and then put it away. He can be rough as long as

B

A

C

D

Fig. 10-14. RECOVERING A FUMBLE. The player must fall on the ball, instead of trying to pick it up. In this series, defensive back Irv Cross falls on the ball, and while rolling over on his side, he draws the ball into the pocket.

It is not advantageous for the defender to roll because he leaves his body exposed to possible injury and loss of the ball.

Irv has both hands on the ball as he rolls. He draws up his knees to protect himself and the ball. "A fumbled football draws flies."

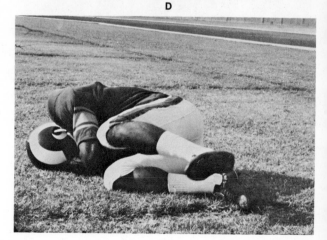

E

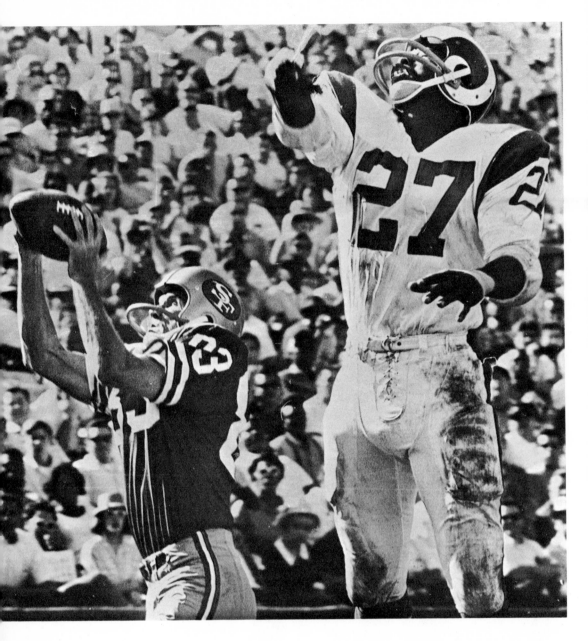

Fig. 10-15. JUDGING THE LONG BALL IN FLIGHT is one of the most difficult phases of pass defense. Much practice is required. Here, Sonny Randle of the 49ers makes a great catch of a perfect pass, despite the efforts of defensive back Irv Cross of the Rams. Irv took a swipe at the ball but just missed.

Fig. 10-16. TIMING OF THE BALL IN FLIGHT can pay off in interceptions. Rams defensive back Eddie Meador (21) is on the way down as receiver Aaron Thomas (88) of the Giants is at the "apex" of his jump. Luckily for the Rams, Eddie was able to get one hand up for a deflection. This skill can pay off in interceptions.

269

Fig. 10-17. TWO MEN ON ONE doesn't mean a thing unless proper teamwork is developed. On this play, we had double coverage on Charley Taylor of the Redskins, but he took a 14 yard pass and went the remaining 70 yards for a touchdown. Claude Crabbe and Clancy Williams are the defensive backs for the Rams.

he reaches for the ball with two hands. On long passes, he should watch the nose of the ball to improve his judgment as to timing for an interception or to break up a pass.

When there are two defenders covering one receiver, the one who is in position to intercept should yell "my, my," meaning his ball. The other defender stays right there and does not let up, but he is ready for a deflected ball, to block or to help in any way. As a result, the pass defenders will not be knocking each other off, besides increasing their interception chances.

When making an interception in a crowd, the pass defender should be sure to twist at the same time his opponent is attempting to get it away from him. He will get the ball every time.

Man-for-Man Coverage

With the forward pass becoming such a potent offensive weapon, more pressure is being placed on the defensive secondary to use man-for-man coverage or work in some combination with the zone coverage. Certainly, the principles employed in the zone coverage cannot be used in man-for-man coverage. Therefore, a set of rules must be developed which can be used in using the more difficult man-for-man coverage.

When using man-for-man coverage, the defense has more difficulty getting interceptions. However, pass defenders must use point vision on the receiver and peripheral vision on the quarterback. Some defensive backs make the mistake of focusing so much attention on the receiver that they are never in position for an interception, or they never see the ball in flight until it is too late.

When playing man-for-man coverage, it is better to play too loose than too tight, because it is easier for the quarterback to throw the "home run" pass. Actually, man-for-man coverage is no stronger than its weakest link—a deep back. This is why we devote a great amount of time to perfecting our coverage.

Since it is easier to fool the defender, a deep back must develop his footwork to perfection and always be on balance. I might say that if he can cover a man in our "one-on-one" drills, he can certainly cover him in the game. In this type of drill, he needn't be concerned about pass completions, but work for position on the receiver.

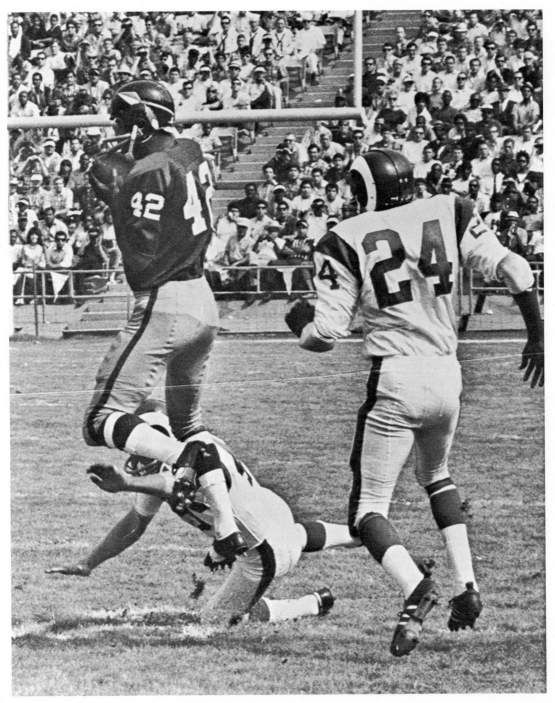

271

During a game, a pass defender never has time to really think out an offensive pattern. Instant reaction is demanded, and this will only occur by constant drilling and is a must with individual coverage. If he finds that a receiver is continually getting too close and is upon him before he can react, more than likely the deep back is watching the action of the backfield. He must never be fooled by play-action passes. With man-for-man coverage, he must remember to use point vision on the receiver and peripheral vision on the ball.

When using man-for-man coverage, it is essential that the deep backs talk to each other. Each defender needs all the help he can get, and it is absolutely necessary to work as a four man unit. They are like the outfield in baseball. *They must develop teamwork!*

Zone Coverage

The Cardinal Rule of a zone defense is to never let a receiver get behind the defender. This helps stop the long TD pass. The drop-back action of zone defenders makes it less possible than in other types of coverage.

A zone coverage should be as deep as the deepest and as wide as the widest man in the zone. The defender should always keep his receiver far enough in front so he can see through to the passer. On any zone defense, the defensive back wants to look through the receiver into

the passer. He knows there is no need to switch in a zone, and he never makes his break until the ball is thrown.

The pass defender should carry a receiver approximately 5 yards and do so cautiously. He must watch for a crossing man into his zone. If two men come into one man's zone, the defender is responsible for the deeper man of the two. If he sees two men coming into his zone, he should yell "Help, help, help!"

TALK-TALK-TALK is the key to good pass coverage, allowing for the necessary cohesion among the deep backs. Pass defenders should repeat everything three times—loudly—so that it can be heard.

The zone is also simple to learn because the defender has an area to cover rather than an individual, and he plays the ball from the time it leaves the passer's hand. The defender in the zone also has a clear picture up front which allows him to better diagnose running plays from pass plays, and vice versa. In addition, less speed is required by defenders in the zone because they are covering an area rather than an individual and play him loose.

Deep backs shouldn't worry about short passes being completed in front of them. They may bring first downs, but the long ones will bring the touchdowns. The "Home Run" pass must be stopped. There is no reason for this type of pass being completed against a zone defense.

There are a number of disadvantages in the zone defense. First, short zones are usually open for the passer to complete all types of short passes. As a result, an area is left between the linebackers and secondary when the deep backs start retreating immediately because the linebackers cannot drop back fast enough.

Delayed passes, hook passes, and flood passes are all effective against a zone. All types of screeners, running passes, and drains prove effective against this defense. Unless they are experienced, the deep backs may have problems trying to cover the width of the field.

The Weak Safety (Jill)

The weak safety, or "Jill" as we call him, should be the "spark plug" of the pass defense. He should be the leader in encouraging others to talk. He should call out the down and distance so that the other deep backs can hear him. Since he is a roamer, he has to have some speed to cover the ground.

When "Jill" is free, he should see the ball leave the passer's hand, enabling him to get more interceptions and increase the distance he can cover. He should also increase his depth, so that he can extend his coverage. By watching his eyes, he can study the actions of the passer to know quickly where he will throw.

His approach and responsibility on wide plays to the weak side is very important. His approach must be made to the outside of the "O" man on his side. The side back will always turn the runner inside to him because his approach is outside. Therefore, "Jill" must always keep

an inside angle on the runner so that he cannot cut back inside of him. He must not overrun the play.

The weak safety must take extra practice on playing the ball so that he will increase his interception distance. He should leave an instant before the ball is thrown and go to the intended receiver.

The Strong Safety (Sam)

The strong safety's approach and responsibility on runs to the strong side is most important. "Sam," as we call the strong safety, should always make his approach slightly to the outside of the offensive back when he blocks. He must play everything as a pass first. However, when he recognizes a run, he should "fly up" but be under control to make the tackle.

The side back will turn the play inside to Sam; therefore, he must approach from an inside angle on the ball carrier. He shouldn't come up too wide and overrun the play. When a ball carrier doesn't have the necessary speed to sweep wide, he will probably rely on setting up a cutback.

Sam will key the halfback looking through the offensive tackle and guard. This enables him to quickly diagnose the run from the pass and lets him know whether to expect help from Jill, as he also is keying the same back.

Sometimes the strong safety finds the receiver is continually getting too close and is almost past him before he reacts. When this happens, Sam is probably watching the backfield action. *Never be fooled by play action passes!*

Talking to the linebackers is a good habit for Sam to develop. They can help so much on curls, hooks, etc., if the deep backs will let them know where the receiver is.

When the tight end or slot back blocks and no back releases, Sam is free to read the quarterback and play the ball. However, he should be sure he has communicated with the strong side linebacker before he does this.

The safety man should perfect his footwork for the Drag pass, Cross pass, and the Lookie inside and outside. These are the ones he will face most frequently.

Since Sam usually covers the biggest and strongest receivers, he must hit them low to bring them down. We have learned from experience that the best of the tight ends cannot be wrestled to the ground effectively, because they usually carry their tacklers.

Since the offense sends blockers out after the safety men on just about every running play, they have to be able to fake and bounce away from them, and still stay between the ball carrier and the goal line. "You try to keep them from getting into your body," explained Meador. "Most of the time the tackle comes out from the side opposite where the play is coming off, and he is coming fast and hard. You should come up, stop for a split-second, and make your move away from him."

Ten Commandments of Pass Defense

1. *Watching the team while in the huddle* and as they break from the huddle.
2. *Calling Formation* (Sam's responsibility) and its direction.
3. Lining up in the *correct* place with the proper alignment.
4. Calling the individual responsibility or the zone responsibility, *knowing when you have help* and how to use assistance.
5. Indicating, when called upon by the coach, *your play responsibility,* whether pass or run.
6. *Recognizing and calling out* the pass pattern. Yell "Drag," "China," etc.
7. Getting correct *position on the receiver* and maintaining that position.
8. Moving in for the pass *interception* and playing *only* the ball.
9. Yelling *"Fire"* for the *interception.*
10. *Blocking for the interception.* Don't look back for someone to block, but knock down the nearest opponent.

Films

Play recognition can be taught when viewing films by running the play back and forth before its completion. The deep backs can call out "Run" or "Pass" which will help them get more out of the film.

Defensive backs must know the receiver they are covering. They should study him in all the films to know his strengths and weaknesses.

Everytime a pass is completed, someone is at fault. So, defensive backs must determine the reasons and study the footwork in the film.

A projector is always available whenever a Rams player wishes to devote extra time to view himself and others. Deep backs should analyze film the same as a quarterback. They should check their footwork to see if they made any false steps in covering.

Grading

The main purpose of grading is to recognize errors and eliminate them. By grading all phases of the game, careful attention is paid to each movement.

Pass defense men are graded mainly for positioning, as follows:

1. How *close* he allows a receiver to get to him.
2. Playing the receiver *too loose* so that it is impossible to break up the pass.
3. His *position on the receiver* when covering a "Goal," "Drag," "Cross," etc.
4. Whether the receiver got to his *outside.*
5. Whether the receiver got to his *inside.*

Drills

In developing our deep backs, we employ a countless number of drills, most of which stress proper footwork. It is not unusual for our defensive backs to stay after practice and work on their weakness. Defensive backs should try to improve their peripheral vision in practice. All good defenders have this. One of the most important is the "burst" drill, which is actually an acceleration drill. We try to simulate any break a receiver might make, whether he might be coming back for the ball, breaking at an 90 degree angle to the inside, or 90 degrees to the outside, the deeper angle, which we call a goal or post pattern.

We try to simulate any break a receiver might make and have the defender counter that break. In other words, he is coming out of either a backward run, backpedal, a shuffle or slide, or whatever he happens to be using at the time. He has to get into the proper angle of coverage and employ the type of break that he can cover and accelerate. In other words, he must make a complete change of direction and move quickly at full speed again in a new direction.

"One-on-one" (1 on 1) is still the best single coverage drill in football. Regardless of the type of pass defense, and even in a zone, it still involves man-for-man coverage. If a defensive back does not get enough 1 on 1, he should stay after practice. A deep back must remain sharp, and he needs this

Fig. 10-18. ONE-ON-ONE DRILL (defensive backs vs. defensive backs). Eddie Meador shows good form in playing the ball at the highest point with two hands and in catching the ball well out in front of his body. Note the head and eyes looking the ball into his hands, as he takes it away from the intended receiver Chuck Lamson.

276

C	B	A
D	E	F

Fig. 10-19. COVERING THE RECEIVER. This drill involves one-on-one defensive backs covering defensive backs on the flag pattern. Eddie Meador (21) demonstrates a complete turn, taking his eyes off the receiver and the quarterback while covering Clancy Williams (24). After making a complete change of direction, Eddie moves quickly at full speed again in a new direction. This maneuver takes considerable practice to develop the necessary footwork. With it, the deep back actually gains a step, rather than using an open pivot.

Fig. 10-20. PASS COVERAGE DRILL. It is through drill and through drill alone that the coach can be reasonably sure of good performance under game pressure. Here, Coach Allen drills deep backs Claude Crabbe and Chuck Lamson on their footwork coming into the ball.

every day, especially early in the week. However, his work must be against a receiver.

Defensive backs must drill on interceptions just as the offensive ends work on receiving. Statistics indicate that most interceptions are made while a defender is coming forward into the football. Unless the defender has sufficient training, there is often a clash of hand and ball.

If a deep back finds that he is just missing an interception or arriving a step late, he can improve his interception distance by asking one of the quarterbacks to throw him a few long passes after practice each day. He can leave an instant before the ball is thrown and go to the intended receiver. Five minutes a day will increase his chances for an interception. In practice, the back should return the ball at least 20 yards.

Deep backs and defensive backs should practice running backward every day, in order to improve their footwork and coverage. Defensive backs will be amazed at how fast they can run backward and still cut.

When our backs practice running backward we increase the distance from 10 yards to 20, 30 and even 40 yards. We even have them race going backward without turning.

7 on 7

The best and fastest way to teach pass defense is by the use of sectional drills. After the season starts, the Rams place more emphasis on 7 on 7 drills and less on individual drills. The deep backs, generally, team up on defense with the linebackers against an offensive team consisting of at least a center, quarterback, and two pass receivers.

One at a time, the deep backs communicate with the linebackers, which is essential in good pass coverage.

Pre-game drills

The primary purpose of pre-game drills is to warm up all the pass defenders. Deep backs must be loose and supple on the first play of the game. Quite often on the first play of a game, a long pass is completed because the defender was a step slow.

Fig. 10-21. PASS DEFENSE INTERCEPTION DRILL. The coach throws a line drive interception—high, wide, and low—to deep back Irv Cross. The purpose of the drill is to give the pass defender practice intercepting the three types of passes, while running forward and catching the ball at various angles. This is one of our favorite game warm-up drills.

Pre-game drills give the deep backs an opportunity to get the feel of the ball and the turf. Since the purpose of the drills is psychological in part, they should make the players look good.

Team Defensive Grading

The most difficult positions to grade, with the sole exception of the quarterback, are those in the defensive secondary, the reason being that there are so many variables as to why a pass was complete or incomplete or whether the defender had his man covered. One also needs to know whether he failed to cover his man when he was away from the point of attack. The secret of pass defense is for the defensive back to always have proper position on the receiver. There is an exact position for each defender on each type of pass thrown. The defense must be taught the correct position on the receiver for the curl, slant, out, etc.

We have used the grading chart to evaluate the entire team for the last six

years. It is a very fair way of grading, in that the defensive men are graded only when they are at the point of attack. However, they can pick up additional grade points if they perform their responsibilities and pursue and hustle, even though they may be on the off side. Since every man cannot be graded the same, this chart is broken down into three separate areas: RUSHMEN (defensive linemen), BU's (linebackers), and DEEKS (defensive backs).

Grading Symbols

S	Spot (initial location)
P	Point (destination of charge)
T	Tackles
MT	Missed tackles
A	Assists
SQ	Sack QB (tackle passer)
HP	Hurry Passer
EE	Extra effort
NE	No effort
OR	Obstructing the receiver
BB	Batted balls

DEFENSIVE GRADING REPORT

RAMS vs. VIKINGS   Date: _____   Coach: George Allen

Name	S.	P.	T.	MT	A	SQ	All Players HP	All Players EE	NE	OR	BB	AX	Blk	RF	Rushmen CT	Rushmen CE	Rushmen RA	Backers R	Backers PR	INT	Deeks R	Deeks PR	Deeks INT	PP	PE	Final Grade
Olsen	−1	−2	8	1	5	2	3	1	X	X	1	X	1	1	−1	−3	−1							67	56	84%
Williams	X	X	5	1	2	X	X	X	X	X	X	2	1	X								+6 / −2	+5 / −1 1	43	37	86%
Baughan	−1	X	9	2	3	X	1	1	X	X	1	1	1	X								+5 / −1	+3 / −1 1	62	53	85%

The secret of good performance at critical moments is found in drill.

AX   Axing
BLK Block
RF   Recover fumble

Rushmen
CT   Timing of charge
CE   Elevation of charge
RA   Recovery angle

BU's
R   Reaction (run or pass)
PR   Position on receiver
INT Interception

DEEKS
R   Reaction (run or pass)
PR   Position on receiver
INT Interception
PP   Possible points
PE   Points earned

This grading chart is an off-season project. It is too time-consuming to keep up during the season, unless the head coach has enough assistant coaches to be able to assign one of them to work on it several days a week. It serves as a guide for estimating improvement as well as for grading, because the coach is grading strength as well as weaknesses. The best way is for one coach to grade the entire defensive team; in that way they are all being evaluated the same way. Every coach on the staff will come up with a different grade if asked to check the film. It is a big project for one man and at times it is advantageous to have the defensive line coach grade the rushmen and have the defensive back coach grade the backers and secondary.

POINT STRUCTURE

S	1	*Rushmen*	
P	1	CT	1
T	+3	CE	1
MT	−3	RA	1
A	1		
		Linebackers	
SQ	6		
		R	1
HP	3		
		PR	1
EE	+3		
		INT	+6 (TD pass allowed −6)
NE	−3		
OR	1	*Deeks*	
BB	1	R	1
AX	1	PR	1
BLK	1	INT	+6 (TD pass allowed − 6)
RF	6		

Still another way is for the line coach to grade everyone with respect to runs and the secondary coach to grade all eleven men with respect to passes.

Grading points

The team defensive grading form has a sample of player grading for each of the defensive areas. The manner of grading and the points awarded (or penalties given out) are presented above.

Point Structure

Since we want our defensive unit to attack and get the ball, we have structured our point system to reward positive efforts to get back the football. Sacking the quarterback, pass interceptions, and fumble recoveries are all supreme efforts which can earn a man a maximum of 6 points.

Because the pass rush is the name of the game on defense, we award 3 points to those who hurry the passer. By hurrying the passer and forcing the issue, they can cause an interception, a big factor in getting the ball back.

Notice that extra effort by a player will award him 3 points whereas no effort will penalize him 3 points.

The plus-minus system also works well in grading the individual's tackling skill. Each tackle earns a player 3 points, a missed tackle costs him 3 points.

Awarding (or penalizing) points

To show how individual grading works out, let us take the case of Clancy Williams, our defensive back (DEEK). Note that

ALL PLAYERS

Column		Points
T	Player made 5 tackles	+15
MT	Player missed 1 tackle	−3
A	Player had 2 assists	+2
AX	Player executed 2 Axes	+2
BLK	Player executed 1 block	+1
	Deeks	
R	Player reacted well (6 times)	+6
	Player reacted poorly (2 times)	−2
PR	Player has good position on receiver (5 times)	+5
	Player had poor position (1 time)	−1
INT	Player had 1 interception	+6

when there is a box with an X inserted, this shows that no grade was given in that area.

All possible points are added, the total here being 43, and the figure is placed in the PP column. Now all minus numbers are subtracted from the possible points and this remainder will give the coach the players' points earned. This figure (the total here being −6) is placed in the PE column. Now the percentage grade can be arrived at by dividing the possible points earned (the percentage here being 86 percent).

If a deep back or linebacker allows a touchdown pass, it counts minus 6 (−6) points. If he intercepts, it counts plus 6 (+6) points. If a long pass is completed for a TD, everyone is penalized one point and the particular defensive back is penalized six points. The coach cannot blame just one player. If the line had rushed better, perhaps the quarterback would not have had the time to get the pass off.

Conditioning

*Good physical condition is the most important
factor in competitive sports.*

11

I believe that conditioning and training play a large part in the success of any football team. No one can play the game of football well unless he is in top condition. Quite often, a player is called upon to use every muscle in his body, and unless his muscles are properly conditioned, he will not be able to do an efficient job. Moreover, by being in good condition, the chances of getting hurt are considerably less. I always tell our players that being in good condition is like taking out an extra insurance policy.

I really believe in our physical conditioning. We feel that the Rams can wear teams down. If someone scores on us quickly or the breaks go against us early, we do not panic. We feel it is just a matter of time before things start going our way. Our players have a great love for the game of football. They are willing to make the physical sacrifices that are so necessary for success. Conditioning can be a constant problem unless the players have the right attitude about the team, the organization, and their physical condition.

To All Young Athletes

A young player must lead the kind of life that is expected of an athlete, starting back in junior high school. It actually starts in Little League, in Pop Warner football. He must keep himself in top condition, working very hard, and even going into weight training and isometric programs which are so beneficial for the young men today. He must develop good health habits, getting to bed early at night, and also learning to eat the proper foods, meat and potatoes, vegetables and fruits, for proper vitamins, nutrients, and minerals.

If an athlete works, really drives himself to the limit, he will accomplish things he never thought possible. Moreover, a player must learn to respect the judgment of all of his coaches, both on and off the field.

The Rams' Success Formula

The Los Angeles Rams have earned a good reputation for remaining strong throughout the entire 60 minutes of play. The Rams' success, particularly our strong second-half performance, can be attributed to the following areas:

1. *Conditioning.* If a team doesn't have conditioning, it will not be able to stay in there—blocking, running, and tackling for 60 minutes.
2. *Half-time Organization.* This involves making the necessary adjustments for effective performance in the second half.
3. *Morale.* A team that has morale and enthusiasm is always going to look good the second half.
4. *The Big Play.* A championship team must have the ability to make the big play and take advantage of the breaks. A team usually makes its own breaks.

The Untapped 25 Percent

No matter how strong, how big or how fast an athlete is, he is not going to succeed or be consistent unless he is in excellent physical condition.

God has given each of us a wonderful body. This is a fact that almost every athlete will accept without question. However, an equally accurate statement, but one which most athletes fail to wholeheartedly believe, is that this wonderful body, this great creation, can never be developed to its capacity. Persons who make their living in the field of physical development realize the truth of this statement, but they pinpoint the reluctance of athletes to accept it by citing the following figures: most persons develop their bodies to approximately 20 percent of capacity, some to 50 percent, a very few to 75 percent, and only the champions to a higher degree. If we can prove to our players the importance of surpassing the 75 percent mark, and help them to reach that goal, we will have achieved our purpose.

The conclusion is only this. If a man takes care of himself, whether he is a high school, college, or professional player, or whether he has a weight problem or not, *he would be a much more effective football player.* I might add that coaches will sometimes assign a weight to a player without proper research. This can be dangerous. Coaches should always check first with the team doctor, then the trainer.

This brings up another point: physical condition is a relative matter. It is important to be in good physical condition, but it is even more important to be in better condition than your opponent.

In short, there are no easy ways to attain this good conditioning, but one can take heart by recalling that only a few

Fig. 11-2. MAKING ATHLETES RUN Is the best way to condition them. Coach George Allen puts the Rams through the "Striders" at the conclusion of practice. This is Coach Allen's favorite team drill.

athletes develop the body to the 75 percent mark. There is plenty of room for an athlete to be in better physical condition than his opponent. All he has to do is *PAY THE PRICE.*

Running

Running is the greatest conditioner, so we do run a lot. If a team can run in practice more than it has to run in a game, the football game becomes easy.

If a player runs only enough to go half a game, then the second half is going to seem very tough.

We urge our players to develop their endurance. To become champions, they must be stronger in the fourth quarter than their opponent. If they are not getting enough running, they should stay after practice and run on their own. "Your body is your best friend," they are told. "Don't abuse it and shorten your playing career."

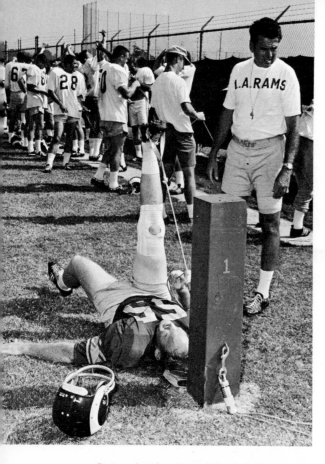

Fig. 11-3. MENTAL ATTITUDE AND CONDITIONING go hand in hand. The players must have the right attitude about their physical condition. Fortunately, men like Maxie Baughan, in lying position, are sold on such conditioning periods as the Exer-genie stations. Coach Allen, right, observes the workout.

Determination to get the job done

When a player starts a conditioning program, he must stick with it. He shouldn't expect results in a day or two. It will take one month at least to see and feel the results. After his first workout or two, naturally, he is going to be stiff, but he must have the determination to continue. He must assign a time every day for exercise and adhere faithfully to his schedule.

Six Qualities of A Good Athlete

There are six qualities of any good athlete in any sport. They are as follows:

1. Willingness to take coaching and study football.
2. A spirit of competition in practice and in games.
3. An intense desire to win and accept nothing less than victory.
4. Willingness to practice hard at all times.
5. Willingness to make sacrifices for the team.
6. A desire to improve himself on and off the field.

Personal appearance

All athletes should try to be neat. The present trend is long hair, long sideburns, etc. During my coaching years on the campus, though I always urged my athletes to dress conservatively, with clean shoes, short haircuts, shirt tails in, and socks on. What they do on and off the field reflects on their parents, teammates, and school. They should be a credit to each of them.

I have had the privilege of coaching in three Pro Bowls and I have observed that all the biggest stars in all sports and the NFL have a great deal of class. They are gentlemen off the field and are not troublemakers. They do not expect special favors because they are athletes.

Game experience

While everybody today is going by stopwatches, building for foot speed and fast reactions, there is nothing like game experience. Jimmy Orr of the Colts could not beat many outside receivers in a foot race, but he is as difficult to cover as anyone we face. The Rams have won many big games because we had experienced men who could quickly understand a complicated game plan and execute it without error.

The majority of our games are close in scoring, three to 13 or 14 points, and they are decided by a few plays which come up suddenly. This is where the ability of a veteran to "read" and anticipate and make exactly the right move is so important. By wasting no motion, he compensates for any slowness on his part. The poised experienced players do the right thing at the right time.

Proper Diet

A well-rounded diet plays a vital role in the physical fitness of an athlete. A person today has the benefit of good food, and good food supplements, and he should take advantage of them. Three meals a day, with as little eating as possible between meals (especially after the evening meal) is the best plan.

Pre-game meal

The last regular meal should be eaten at least three to four hours before game time. Physiologists recommend such non-greasy, non-gas-forming foods as bread, honey, broiled steak, baked potato, green peas, ice cream, and either fruit juice, vegetable juice, or tea.

Weight

The common mistake a rookie makes is to come in too heavy. Most players in our league would perform better if they lost weight. Certainly, a regular check on the weight of each player should be kept. As a person grows older, this becomes even more important. Nothing destroys conditioning or causes an athlete to become ineffective faster than being overweight.

Large fluctuations in weight can also be harmful to good conditioning. A great loss of weight may be necessary for an athlete to become a champion, but this tends to reduce strength and speed until the desired weight has been reached and the body has had time to revitalize itself.

We feel so strongly about this matter of weight that we give each Rams player a weight to maintain during the off-season. We ask him to report at this weight at the beginning of each season. We also check our players periodically during the season to see if they are keeping their proper weight.

Fig. 11-4. A PLEASANT ENVIRONMENT at meal time is important to morale. The Rams have a beautiful modern dining hall on the campus of California State College at Fullerton. It is spacious, air-conditioned, and conducive to the type of eating facilities that help build morale during summer training.

Drinking and smoking

Many of the top stars in the NFL do not drink or smoke. There is no place in the athletic program for an athlete who drinks or smokes to excess. Both are harmful and are very detrimental to an athlete.

Warming-up

No athlete should ever begin competition without a period of preliminary warm-up activity. Before he starts going at full speed, the player must get blood flowing into his muscles at a faster rate. We feel all our Rams need a minimum of seven to 10 minutes of stretching and loosening up exercises. We have our players warm-up until the muscles in their arms and legs feel loose, and they have begun to perspire a little. Otherwise, they are asking for pulled and strained muscles.

Staleness

The common causes of staleness are overwork, monotony and, occasionally, dietary deficiencies. Rest or change of activity, and a revised diet is the surest cure for staleness. However, prevention is better than the cure.

Players shouldn't be overworked. The daily practice sessions should be made interesting and the practice routine should vary somewhat from day to day.

Plenty of sleep and rest

It is best to have a regular pattern of sleep. An athlete should try to get eight hours or more each night, not four tonight and twelve tomorrow. At training camp, our players are in bed by 11:00 p.m. each night. When we are on a "two-a-day" workout schedule, almost

Fig. 11-5. THE NEED FOR DAILY CON-
DITIONING can be emphasized when a good
example is set for the players. Members of the
Rams' coaching staff run laps before and after
each workout. "This helps me relieve the daily
tension and helps me relax," says Coach Allen,
shown here completing his daily 880 run.
"Running also gives me important strength
and stamina to go through a long and rigorous
season."

all of them spend at least one hour in
bed following a light noontime lunch. On
Saturdays (pre-game day) throughout the
season, we encourage a three-hour siesta
period.

Injuries

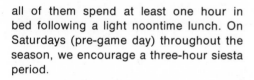

Serious injuries can occur in such a
rough-and-tumble sport as football without proper physical conditioning. Before
an athlete is allowed to play, he must receive a complete physical check-up by a
physician. (It is also recommended that a
full coverage insurance program be ob-
tained for every athlete.) Again, the best
insurance policy against injuries is a
strong, well-conditioned body.

Rehabilitation

In 1967 we hired a full-time off-season
trainer for rehabilitation. We now have
two full-time trainers. An athlete with an
injured knee should begin his rehabilitation program as soon as his physician
permits it. The athlete with a sound knee
should begin his conditioning program as
soon after the season as possible, and
should continue it right up to the beginning of the next season.

Resistance exercise should never be
taken just before game time, since the
resulting fatigue in the exercised muscles
may dull protective reflexes. The exercise
should be scheduled after practice sessions or an off day so that full recovery
can take place before the next day of
play or practice.

291

B

A

Fig. 11-6. THE STOP WATCH and the chart combine to provide the spark of competition that is much needed in programs involving running. Clocking the players is Coach Tom Catlin, left.

Speed Improvement

Many football players fail to realize their maximum running potential. While speed cannot be created beyond an athlete's potential, a highly competitive program in sprinting can be followed. The prime objective is to get the player's running muscles and wind in shape and to improve his starting and sprinting ability.

The sprinting program should start from 4 to 6 weeks before the opening practice and should continue on a three workouts per week basis. The sprinting distances are 10, 20, 30, and 40 yards, with the emphasis on the 10 and 40 yard sprints. The most important distance in football is the first 10 yards, whether the athlete be a back or a lineman.

The player should practice and be tested on the ability to move from his stance to the 10 yard mark. The 40 yard sprint is felt to be the best indicator of starting and sprinting ability. A good time for a college lineman is 5.2 seconds for the 40 yard sprint, while a back with good speed should do it in 4.8 seconds. It is essential to keep a chart each day, as well as a file of the daily charts for reference use.

By adding the stop watch to the running program, the competitive factor is added. Besides achieving good conditioning, the player will be running for the sake of "beating" the stop watch. The competitive factor will make him push to greater heights.

The proper techniques of the sprint include four components: the stance, the start, the run, and the finish. The start is the key component for it can "make or break" the athlete. Some players lose as much as two-tenths of a second in the initial 10 yards due to an improper starting technique.

The following rules characterize the proper uses of the hands and arms:

1. Do not clench the fists.
2. Keep the elbows in close to the body and swing them with a smooth pumping action.
3. Synchronize your arm action with that of your legs.
4. Keep relaxed.

We have continually consulted with track coaches for their advice. Jim Bush of UCLA and Payton Jordan of Stanford, also an Olympic track coach, have been helpful.

I have observed that every one of our players who participated in the sprint program has realized some degree of improvement.

The use of the stop watch and the chart combine to provide the spark of competition that is much needed in programs involving running.

Calisthenics

Before our players go to the Exer-genie stations, the entire team goes through a five minute warm-up period of calisthenics.

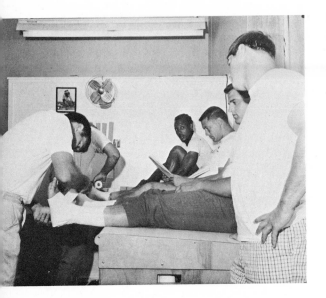

Fig. 11-7. TAPING. The Rams are required to have their ankles wrapped or taped prior to practice.

Here, trainers Jerry Rhea and George Menefee (behind Rhea) handle the daily taping chores.

Fig. 11-8. STRETCHING EXERCISES. At th beginning of every practice session, the Ram go through seven to ten minutes of stretchin exercises. Captain Eddie Meador provides constant flow of chatter.

We go through about five or six stretching exercises, taking from 7 to 10 minutes, making sure they cover every vital part of the body. We try not to overdo them at first, but build up gradually.

The purpose of exercise is to condition the entire body to the highest degree possible. In this way, quickness will increase with strength.

Calisthenics can become dull and monotonous unless everyone sees that plenty of enthusiasm and pep are put into each drill. We like our players to count cadence whenever possible. A constant flow of chatter should come from the coach leading the squad. He should always change from one exercise

to another without a waste of time. He must do everything possible to keep this period moving fast. Pep, enthusiasm, and spirit are the things we are looking for.

A strong stomach

The focal point of any body conditioning is the stomach or abdominal area. Almost any movement involves the stomach muscles. If they are soft and flabby, the efficiency of the entire body is impaired. Good muscle tone in the stomach helps keep an athlete's internal organs in proper alignment, aids his digestion, and even helps his outlook on life.

Developing the legs

An athlete is only as good as his legs. This is why it is so important for him to keep his legs in top-notch condition. Running builds the legs, heart, and lungs more than any other exercise.

Early season exercises

In the summer training season, our exercises are more strenuous than the loosening up type of calisthenics engaged in after the season begins. Our exercises include:

1. Back twister
2. Cross-over toe touch
3. Tail gunner
4. Quadricep exercise
5. Horizontal run
6. Prone side straddle
7. Side straddle hop
8. Alternate toe touch
9. Touch the ground
10. Arm swinging
11. Push-ups
12. Rock and roll
13. Running up and down
14. Jumping jack
15. Inguinal roll
16. The bridge

Fig. 11-9. FOOTWORK is nearly everything in football, whether in offense or defense. "This is why one of my favorite training camp drills is running through the ropes," said Coach Allen. "We use two complete sets of ropes in camp. The ropes help improve eye and foot coordination and strengthen ankles, knees, and legs. Many players are tight through their hips. The ropes will develop flexibility in this area. The ropes tell me a great deal about all my players, both rookies and veterans."

A

B

A

B

Fig. 11-10. BACK TWISTER. The back twister is a two-count exercise which loosens up and stretches the upper body. The player tries to throw the elbows as far as possible. On "one," he twists to his left, and on "two," he swings in a clock-wise direction back to the right. He must perform this exercise as quickly as possible (here, Dean Halverson demonstrates).

Fig. 11-11. QUADRICEPS EXERCISE. The player starts from a kneeling position, his hands on the insteps of both shoes. Sitting back on his haunches, he extends and pushes his pelvis as far forward as possible and then bounces. This exercise stretches the groin and quads.

A

B

Fig. 11-13. CROSS-OVER TOE TOUCH. The player will make five movements downward, each moving a little farther down until he has his palms flat on the ground. He should keep his back and legs straight. This is one of the better hamstring exercises.

C

Fig. 11-12. HORIZONTAL RUN. This four-count exercise strengthens the belly muscles and generally loosens up the entire body. From a forward sitting starting position with hands on helmet, the player runs in place, alternately touching his elbows with his knees. On "one," he touches his left knee with his right elbow. On "two," he returns to starting position. On "three," he touches his right knee with his left elbow. He returns to the starting position on "four."

A

B

A

B

Fig. 11-14. TAIL GUNNER. Starting from the squat position, the athlete straightens both legs. He comes up on "one," down on "two," up on "three," and down on "four." This exercise is excellent for the hamstring, groin, and quad muscles.

A

B

Fig. 11-15. PRONE SIDE STRADDLE HOP.
This four-count exercise loosens and strengthens
the groin muscles. The player begins by pointing
his fingers away from him, exerting good
pressure on the triceps muscle. On count "one,"
he hops to the spread position. On "two," he returns to the original position, and repeat.

Fig. 11-16. FOLLOWING CALISTHENICS, the players go through the Exer-genie stations involving 10 to 30 minutes of isometric-isotonic exercises, including the Big Four below. Each player has a partner. Three coaches superivse.

Exer-genie Program

The Exer-genie is a resistive exercise program that the entire team can use in a short period of time. Isometric contraction can develop strength faster than any other form of exercise. Moreover, it can be maintained with relatively short workouts that won't leave the player unduly fatigued. By starting each exercise isometrically, the athlete can obtain exceptional strength benefits, and by combining it with isotonic movement, he can build much needed endurance and flexibility. This is highly important in preventing muscle pulls and sprains. After all the players complete the sets of Exergenie exercises, they begin their drills.

Exer-genie has been enthusiastically adopted by many high school, college, and pro squads throughout the country. Devised by Dean Miller, the Exer-genie consists of an engineered cylinder and a nylon rope that can be pulled back and forth through the cylinder with equal resistance in either direction. It permits an individual or a squad to perform the equivalent of an hour of weight-lifting in just six minutes, and the equivalent of 60 sit-ups in just 35 seconds.

The Los Angeles Rams was one of the first professional teams to utilize the Exer-genie as an integral part of its training program. Our program is mandatory for every player and is carefully supervised. We warm-up before every practice with the Exer-genie. We even take it with us on trips. We have been pleased with this program and recommend it as an ideal method of body development and conditioning.

Our players come out to practice feeling stiff and sore, but a short workout with the Exer-genie relieves all their soreness and gets them ready to go. They no longer require half a practice to get ready. A regular program of exercises on the Exer-genie reduces both injuries and the recuperative period following injuries.

Procedure

We always begin each exercise period with easy bending and stretching. The Exer-genie period usually takes from 10 to 30 minutes. All exercises should be done using one repetition and should be continued throughout the season.

There is a right way and a wrong way of using the Exer-genie. We have our players work in pairs. By working in pairs, one player can exercise and his partner can handle the trailing rope controlling the amount of resistance needed to make him work at his capacity. Resistance can be set at 10 pounds for high school, and 20 pounds for college and professional.

On all exercises, the trail line should be controlled with the index finger so the line will not move during the ten-second isometric contraction. It should not take more than 22 seconds to complete the exercise. The player starts each exercise with a ten-second isometric contraction and then moves through a full range of motion within twelve seconds.

Breathing is very important in performing the Exer-genie. The athlete should not hold his breath, but should breathe normally.

A typical Rams' Exer-genie period

Phase I For six minutes, the entire squad will start off performing three "Big Fours." With two men per station, the squad of 36 men will utilize the 18 stations. The "Big 4" consists of four weight lifting exercises: 1. dead lift; 2. shrug; 3. clean; 4. press.

Phase II All players will then move over to a 10 pole area which can accommodate 40 men (2 Exer-genie units per pole).

Actually, we do not include running except for the members of the defensive line. Normally, a player will do two upper body exercises, such as the lats pulley and bench press. After doing another Big Four, he will work on his lower body by rowing, leg extension, and leg drive. The leg drive involves working with the quadriceps muscles at a 90 degree angle. Then, he finishes with a "Big Four."

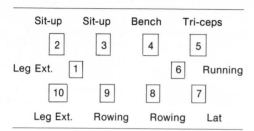

Illustration 3. Rams' Exer-genie course. Phase II takes place on a 10 pole area which can handle 40 men (two Exer-genie units per pole).

Exer-genie exercises

1. *BIG FOUR* After holding a ten second isometric contraction from a dead-lift position, the player pulls straight up with maximum effort, keeping his arms straight until his legs have raised the body to an erect position. He releases the trail line slowly for maximum resistance while straightening his legs (dead lift—4 seconds).

   Without relaxing, he releases the trail line, moving his hands to his chin (clean—4 seconds). Without relaxing, he rotates his hands,

palms outward, moving the handle above his head as far as possible, while stretching and rising to a toe raise as he competes the military press (4 seconds).

2. *LATS PULLEY* The exerciser stands facing the post, arms fully extended, elbows locked. Grasping the handle, he exerts a maximum downward isometric contraction for 10 seconds. Without relaxing, he releases the trail line and moves the handle down across and in front of body to the waist position. He keeps his arms fully extended, body erect (12 seconds).

3. *TWO ARM TRICEP PULL* Grasping the handle above head level, elbows in tight, the athlete exerts maximum isometric contraction for 10 seconds. As the trail line is released, he keeps his elbows at a 45 degree angle and moves immediately through a range of motion until the elbows are at his sides. From this position, he extends his arms out straight and then down to the waist position. This routine is an excellent exercise for quarterbacks.

4. *REPEAT BIG FOUR*

5. *BENCH PRESS* Grasping the handle, his elbows are in a Bench Press position. He holds a 10 second isometric contraction, then pushes to a maximum against the handle. Releasing the trail line and without relaxing, he pushes the handle forward, as he extends his arms away from his body (12 seconds).

6. *ROWING* Sitting with the feet against the wall, his knees are bent in a

B

C

D

A

Fig. 11-17. THE BIG FOUR: 22 SECONDS (Dean Miller demonstrates). "The Big Four is the heart of our Exer-genie program. Even if we are short on time, this is one exercise we don't eliminate," said Coach Allen.

A

B

Fig. 11-18. LATS PULLEY: 22 SECONDS. The lats pulley must be performed correctly or the athlete can injure his back. The important thing in this exercise is to keep the arms straight; do not stand too far away from the bar where you have to bend your back.

C

A

B

Fig. 11-19. TWO ARM TRICEP PULL: 22 SECONDS. The triceps are among the weakest muscles in the body, but are vital in football. This is one of the very best exercises to strengthen the triceps and is a must for all defensive players.

C

A

B

Fig. 11-21. ROWING: 22 SECONDS. This is a combination exercise of the triceps, latissimus, and all the posterior muscles.

If performed with the legs extended, it stretches the hamstrings and builds flexibility.

C

C

Fig. 11-20. BENCH PRESS: 22 SECONDS. The purpose of the bench press is to develop and strengthen the pectoral muscles. The Rams have two poles for the bench press.

B

A

A   B

rowing position. He pulls with
maximum effort for the 10 second
isometric contraction. Without relaxing, he pulls through with a complete rowing motion and continues
to pull the handle to his chest.

7. *LEG EXTENSION* Lying on his back,
head toward the unit, the player
places one leg in an upright position while the other leg is in an
extended position. He keeps his
toes pointed, legs extended and
knees locked. He brings one leg
upward and over his body as far
as possible. With pressure on the
trail line from the opposite leg, he
does a 10 second isometric and
then moves with a straight downward sweep. He keeps his knee
locked through the range of motion.

While maintaining resistance, his
opposite leg moves upward to the

exercise position and the exercised
leg assumes control of resistance to
repeat the exercise (12 seconds,
each leg).

8. *LEG DRIVE* Lying on his back with
his head toward the unit, he fully
extends one leg, parallel to the
ground, and controlling the trail
line. He brings the other thigh as
close to the body as possible and
bends the knee. He then drives the
bent leg against the resistance, iso-
lating and working the quadricep
muscles. He holds this position for
a 10 second isometric contraction.

Without relaxing, he presses the
bent leg straight out, maintaining
maximum resistance through the
range of motion. While maintaining
resistance, the opposite leg moves
into a bent position and the opposite
leg assumes control of resistance

C

Fig. 11-22. LEG EXTENSION: 22 SECONDS. Performed with the legs extended, this is an excellent groin exercise and one of the best in the Exer-genie program. The athlete can exert as much resistance as he desires.

to repeat the exercise (12 seconds each leg).

9. *SIT-UP* Using the rowing handle, he bends the knees, keeping his feet flat on the floor. He holds the handle at the base of the neck with an overhand grip. He holds a 10 second isometric contraction with his body at a 45 degree angle, his shoulders off the floor. Without relaxing, the trail line is released, and the player moves forward until his elbows touch the knees (12 seconds).

10. *LATERAL LEG PULL* From a standing position, the athlete has his exercising leg extended and his knee locked. Lifting his leg in a lateral direction, he does a 10 second isometric and continues upward in a lateral movement. His knee is kept locked through the range of motion.

11. *RUNNING DRILL* In using the "buddy system," a harness is placed around the midsection of the participants. One player runs forward to the end of the line while his partner in harness walks back to the point of anchor. The returning player then runs forward, alternating three trips forward, three trips backward, three trips both to the left and right sides.

The player maintains a 30 second count for each trip. If he reaches the end of the line before the 30 seconds, he should run in place. Proper form and running technique can be easily corrected in this drill.

A

B

Fig. 11-24. SIT-UP: 22 SECONDS. This is the best abdominal exercise that we know. It is a difficult exercise if performed correctly. Many athletes cannot do one properly. We feel three sit-ups properly performed in the Exer-genie are equivalent to 42 without resistance.

A

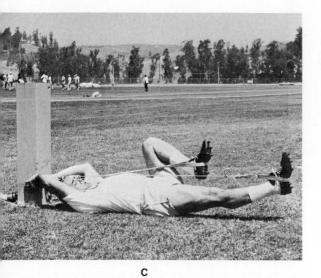

C

Fig. 11-23. LEG DRIVE: 22 SECONDS. This is another exercise to strengthen the groin and abdominal regions. The athlete can exert as much resistance as he wishes.

B

C

A

B

Fig. 11-25. LATERAL LEG PULL: 22 SECONDS. We are always trying to loosen up and stretch the inguinal area of the body to prevent those troublesome groin pulls from occurring.

C

Fig. 11-26. RUNNING DRILL: 30 SECONDS. Sometimes we substitute this drill for wind sprints. It is designed to develop leg power. This is an excellent drill for offensive and defensive linemen.

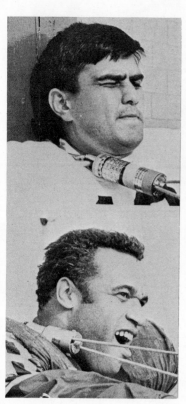

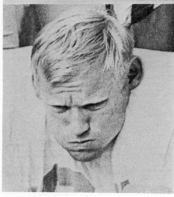

Fig. 11-27. EVERYBODY PUTS OUT. Facial expressions mirror the determination of these Rams as they engage in the various Exer-genie stations in preparation for a big game. Even Coach Allen, center, tones himself for the conflict. The players are Roman Gabriel (top left), Roger Brown (bottom left), Deacon Jones (top right), and Les Josephson (bottom right).

Fig. 11-28. WEIGHTS. Heavy resistance exercise with weights is just as important for restoring strength as it is for preventing injury. Exercising their injured knees on the Universal machine are George Burman and Les Josephson.

Weight Training

A weight training program can be of tremendous help in developing strength in the muscles used in playing football. The prime objective of a weight program is to help the athlete become larger in

Fig. 11-29. VICTORY is often the result of a tough program of conditioning and fitness.

muscular development and body size, and a great deal stronger, while improving upon his agility.

The key areas needing muscular development are the calf and thigh muscles of the legs, the lower back for explosion, and the neck, shoulder and tricep muscles. Our weight-training program is designed to develop these areas of the body. Much loss of time and general muscular soreness could be avoided if the players devoted some of the late summer time to weight training.

The basis of weight training as a conditioner deals with the principle of overload. The use of weights during exercise speeds up the conditioning program by making the muscles do an above-normal amount of work in a short period of time. The athlete performs several repetitions with weights that can be handled with relative ease, rather than attempting to lift maximum load. By working with increasing load, he gradually builds up to heavier drills. Remember, the repetitions that hurt are the ones that build.

Prior to reporting to summer training, we encourage our players to participate in the weight program three days a week, and do their running two days a week. Regularity is a very important part of this theory. They must *never miss a workout.* We want them to be proud of their consistency.

Competition is the basic motivation for the lifter, and the athlete will generally be competing against himself. He must constantly shoot for a goal. As he achieves that goal, he can set a new and higher standard.

For every minute of weight conditioning, an equal amount of time, or even more, should be given to the development of agility. This time should be devoted to

enjoyable, competitive athletic activity, such as basketball, handball, volleyball, and tennis.

Hand-in-hand with the Exer-genie and weight training for strength and flexibility, we stress rope jumping and short sprints for quickness of hands, eyes, and body. We feel that these two also strengthen those parts of the body most susceptible to football injury—the knees and the ankles.

After a player has worked for a long period of time, he will attain a state of peak conditioning that will give him new and greater confidence.

If, in his heart, the player knows that he has paid the price to attain top conditioning, he will be a confident and greater athlete. He will become the top man in the stretch run, in the fourth quarter or in the final set. He will know that he is able to handle any physical challenge that might confront him. Peak physical conditioning will not make all men world champions, but it will insure something else—a championship with respect to his own heart, mind, and soul. This is more important than any medal, trophy or any other material reward.

Mental attitude and team morale are 90 percent of football. This game is 90 percent mental and 10 percent physical.

12

A football coach, a player, and a team must have a strong will to win. I am convinced that on gridirons of all levels of play, the will to win has made the difference between mediocre athletes and outstanding performers. To be a good football player, an athlete has to have something deep down inside.

I like emotional football players—I want them to put forth so much of themselves that after a game they are drained emotionally. No matter what the situation may be, they must have a mental attitude that NEVER gives up. They will keep going. They will give the very best they have, battling the opposition all the way. When we lose, I want everyone to feel miserable. I want to see a few players crying because they have failed, but only as a team. They have not failed as an individual.

The greater will to win is often the deciding factor in a close game, and we always strive to send our men into the game determined to win. I'm very proud to say that the Los Angeles Rams have developed a distinct identity—a tough, disciplined group that never quits in the face of adversity. The Los Angeles fans have become accustomed to expect a last-minute Rams victory charge when defeat seems just around the corner.

The past greats of professional football were driven by a burning desire to win. Winning was a way of life, a passion to them. They didn't know the meaning of "quit" even when the odds seemed insurmountable. The Rams' coaching staff look for men with this spirit and attitude. We want men who have the desire to do their best at all times.

Fig. 12-2. MENTAL TOUGHNESS. The football team that never quits in the face of adversity is a potential champion. This has been the Rams' forte for the past three years.

Most successful football coaches instilled in their players a burning desire to win. They were able to drill into their men the will to excel—to be the best. WINNING was their prime goal. Fritz Crisler was that way. The University of Michigan is a great institution, but I went there primarily because of coach Crisler. I wanted to study his type of football program.

I once heard an assistant coach say that if he had to work "this hard to win," it wasn't worth it. He would rather be 7 and 7 and have more fun. When you have coached as long as I have, you know that winning is the most important thing.

A Game of Emotions

Football is a game of emotions, a vigorous, highly competitive contact sport involving desire, discipline, and drive. It is the popping sound of pad against pad. The tenseness and nervousness of the pre-game wait in the locker room is followed by the thrill of charging out onto the field.

Victory is often highlighted by the beauty of an electrifying broken field run or the precision of a long pass. Defeat is marked by the frustration of missing the winning field goal or dropping a touchdown pass.

I'm an emotional coach and I'm proud to be that way because I put every fiber in my body into every practice and every game. I'm sometimes ill after a bad practice. I just can't help myself.

Proper mental attitude

Mental attitude, therefore, plays a tremendous role in the success of a football player. An athlete can have great

B

A

Fig. 12-3. THE GREATER WILL TO WIN is often the deciding factor in a close game. Above, "extra effort" pays off for the Rams' Ron Smith who goes all the way against Pittsburgh.

natural ability but will never reach his potential unless he can develop a proper mental attitude. The athlete with the right frame of mind will make his natural ability work. I would rather have a player on the Rams with the proper mental attitude and less ability than a player who has more ability and a bad attitude.

When he takes the field, a football player's thoughts should be strictly football. He can groove his mind and body in performing a skill, by concentration. He must be alert and thinking EVERY MINUTE.

Relaxation is also highly essential in acquiring skill and perfection. Actually, concentration and relaxation go together, whether it is catching a touchdown pass or kicking a winning field goal. By concentrating on what he is doing, an athlete can remove tension and fear from the

mind, and replace them with a confident mind and relaxed body.

I try to make our players realize that one of the great things in life is to take an ordinary job and make something out of it. We all have ordinary jobs. Whether a man be a coach or a player, a musician, or anything, he should want to do something in life and make a contribution. He should be proud of himself, not just go through life and eat, watch TV, sleep, drink, and drive a car.

I urge any young athlete to try to get the very best out of what they have within themselves. Not too many people do this, in any walk of life. If a player will play as well as he is capable, using all the resources that God gave him, I feel he will have done an excellent job.

We tell our Rams that "Every play is a big play"—never let down! A player must

Fig. 12-4. ON THE BENCH. When a player is not in the ball game, he still is thinking football, always trying to beat his opponent.

Even though he may not be playing, he can help his teammates with his moral support. Here, Jack Snow intently watches game action.

be inspired never to let "cannot" come into his mind. Even when he may believe he is outweighed and outmanned across the line, he must have a WILL TO WIN and the confidence that he can get the job done.

Morale

After the players learn the fundamentals and plays, it is morale that makes the team. To win a football game, there must be a strong mental togetherness on the part of every player. Each player must have the same purpose and goal, and it is this kind of group feeling or team spirit that wins games. We urge our squad to always have one common goal in mind—to win that next ball game. Without a burning ambition to gain victory, there would be little spirit.

We try to make everyone feel that there is no number one man on the Los Angeles

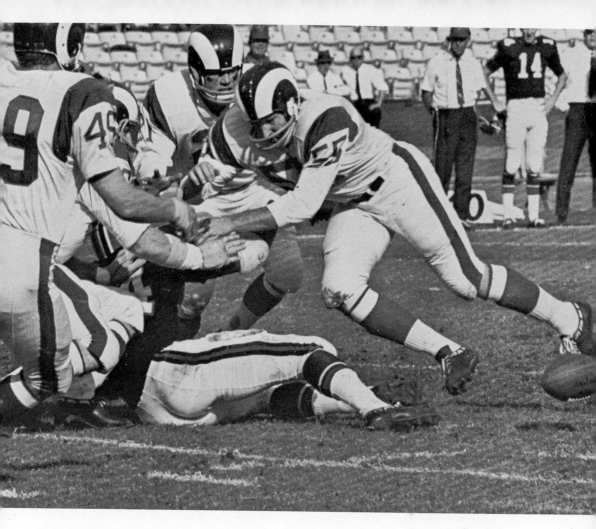

Fig. 12-5. ONE HUNDRED PERCENT IS NOT ENOUGH! One hundred and ten percent is needed. Victory can come if a group of players would really go to work together, as a team. Above, Atlanta's Junior Coffey is mobbed by Maxie Baughan, Jack Pardee, Eddie Meador, and Claude Crabbe of the Rams. The Rams also came up with the football (lower right corner). Nothing is more demoralizing to the offense than gang tackling by the defense.

Rams, no number 40 man. The team is everything! Any success we have had is the result of team play, not some individual. We can have six all-pro's on our team, but if we don't win the championship, it doesn't mean a thing. I would rather have a team that is balanced and not have any all-pro's and win.

Morale is a mental condition and attitude. It is characterized by a never failing ability to "come back." Time after time, our ball club has demonstrated this important quality. We have tried to create in our men a real love for the game and a spirit of work, determination, and loyalty. Convincing a whole squad of players to become "one team," to forget any jealousies or animosities, cannot be done 15 minutes before game time. The coach must start getting the team ready in the off-season.

This may appear corny to many, but we want emotion and enthusiasm. To

Fig. 12-6. TO IMPRESS THE TEAM with the importance of all-out effort and self-sacrifice, the Rams place slogan signs like these on the walls of the locker rooms: WINNING IS A WAY OF LIFE.

Fig. 12-7. KEYING UP THE TEAM. The players are continually reminded what effort and desire can accomplish.

impress the team with the importance of a particular game or all-out effort and self-sacrifice on their part, we make it a practice to post various slogans on the walls of the locker room. Most young people will accept challenges, and quite often, we will challenge them with slogans and posters.

The squad meetings throughout the week, particularly the one the night before the game, provide the best times for establishing a proper mental attitude for everyone.

With the Rams, we try to create an atmosphere of discipline and good humor. The coaching staff tries to subscribe to the old cliche, "firm, fair, and friendly." The office doors of our staff are always open to members of the team. If a coach is genuinely interested in his boys, they will know it and believe in him.

We try to have the players respect each other and help each other. In other words,

a general feeling of mutual admiration and warmth is an important quality of a team. We have not always succeeded in this aspect but we have tried.

Each player deserves to be treated with equality and fairness and nothing will ruin a player's morale quicker than his feeling that he is not getting a fair chance.

We do not like to hear any excuses and alibis. If we lose, we lose. We do not want to complain about the breaks of the game, the officiating, and all that.

We urge our players to be highly aggressive, with a degree of meanness in them. A player should be determined to dominate his opponent. He must hit him with reckless abandon. This is why a wise coach will withhold judgment on a promising newcomer until he gets a taste of scrimmage, some hard contact. "Let's see what he does when he gets knocked down a few times," is the feeling of most coaches.

Fig. 12-8. A GREAT CATCH is the result of extra effort by the receiver and is often the difference between winning and losing. Above, Pat Studstill's diving catch was the big play in defeating the Cleveland Browns, even though it was a pre-season game.

Self-discipline

If he wants to win and play his best, a football player must discipline his life—lay off smoking, drinking, over-eating, or anything that keeps him from doing his best.

To be mentally tough, an athlete must show a tremendous amount of self-discipline. He must NEVER break the discipline of his mind. There have been athletes with great physical qualities, but they couldn't control their temper.

Football demands stern self-discipline. Each player must do the things which he feels are the very best for the team. He must accept responsibility and carry out his assignment to the best of his ability.

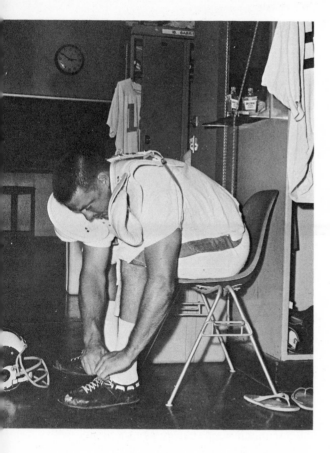

Fig. 12-9. SELF DISCIPLINE. Every time a player puts on his uniform, he should have the desire to play his best. Every practice, every chalk talk, every player meeting will test his self-discipline. Ken Iman, left, prepares himself for a practice session.

This conformity to rules and regulations, personal sacrifice, and individual discipline will be of great value to the individual throughout his life.

Outstanding athletes have the mental discipline to control their moods. "I'm not happy to lose," says Johnny Unitas. "Who would be? Sure, I'm upset. It happened, so forget it and go on to something else."

It takes heart

It takes a lot of heart to continue playing football in the face of defeat. Some players are front runners and excel only when they are ahead. The real mark of a champion lies in his ability to come back— to come from behind.

If a player makes an error, he should hold his head high and not get down on himself. When the breaks are going against him, he must always maintain his poise. He must *STAY IN THERE* and *NEVER GIVE UP!*

There are always pitfalls or obstacles along the way. Many athletes are made champions by setbacks. A setback often brings out the fighting spirit in an athlete.

Courage

Football demands courage. A player must possess the courage to throw his body around with reckless abandon on the field of play.

Every football team needs a team leader who can go up to his teammates and say:

Fig. 12-10. A LITTLE EXTRA EFFORT can make the difference.

"We can beat them!" This is the kind of will power that can make champions, a will to conquer and to go to the top.

There has never been a great athlete who quit when he was beaten. An athlete must have a fighting spirit that will take him through difficulty and discouragement. They refuse to go down, but can bounce back to an even greater victory. Combined with their spirit, however, is their dedication and desire to perfect their skills, spending countless hours and hours of practice, always striving for perfection.

Extra-effort

A man must be willing to put out just a little bit more. We expect each member of the Los Angeles Rams to contribute just a little more than his ability indicates. That is the true test of a champion. No matter what happens, if an athlete will do his level best, his coach cannot ask anything more.

Clutch player

The clutch player has an overpowering team spirit and prefers team victory rather than personal glory. The player who sees defeat and victory in a proper perspective is cool under fire. This is one secret of relaxation.

Clutch players are scarce only because most athletes refuse to believe the clutch player possesses a combination of qualities that they could have if they were only willing to work for them.

Inspiration

A football player has to be inspired. There must be a challenge, a goal, a person or something that pulls or drives him along. Without this powerful inner motivation, he will always remain a mediocre ball player.

Once a player gets a vision or an idea of what he can become, he will be on the right road. With disciplined training and

Fig. 12-11. HUSTLE. Football players should hustle at all times. An enthusiastic Rams team leaves the field after a big effort.

hard work, and a strong will to win, he will have taken a giant step toward becoming a champion.

Confidence

The great athletes have confidence in themselves, a will or positive attitude which says, "I know I can do it!" If an offensive receiver, for example, loses his confidence in catching a touchdown pass, he will never catch the ball. The only way to really build confidence is through practice, practice, and more practice. It doesn't come any other way.

Competition

A good football player welcomes competition. Most people do not compete enough—they give up too easily. They never press on. If a player is to play to his true potential, he must be willing to put out just a little more. This willingness to put out a little more than your opponent often makes the difference.

Intelligence

All football today requires a considerable amount of intelligence—smartness, the ability to learn plays well and then apply this knowledge to the proper situation. A player must study hard, not only football knowledge but in the school classrooms as well.

So, an athlete must keep up his grades. He should remember that his primary interest is education and football is sec-

Fig. 12-12. A RAMS LEGEND. Here, Dick Bass, Rams fullback, is being congratulated by teammate Eddie Meador after surpassing 10,000 yards by rushing during his career.

"The quality I am most pleased about in our 40 man team is their unselfishness," says Coach Allen.

ondary. Besides, a college scholarship or a lucrative professional contract might be at stake. Players who let down in their studies are usually the ones who will let down in a game.

The Rams have won many big games because we had experienced men who could quickly understand a complicated game plan and execute it without error. The ability of a player to "read" and anticipate and make exactly the right move is so important. The well trained, experienced players do the right thing automatically.

Loyalty

Loyalty is essential to a winning football team. The TEAM PLAYER never says anything bad about his teammates or his coaches behind their backs. The TEAM PLAYER never second guesses the quarterback, a teammate or a coach. Regarding the clubhouse, we urge all players to "Let what you hear there, see there, and say there . . . STAY THERE!"

We try to discourage arguments and hard feelings between team members. The Los Angeles Rams have a feeling of love, pride, and respect for each other.

Discipline

The discipline the Rams' coaching staff tries to get revolves around four basic points:

1. Making players work hard without having to scream and yell at them.
2. Making them stay at a certain weight.
3. Making them prepare mentally at meetings.
4. Making them be proud to be part of an organization.

We do not believe in chewing out and getting on the players in front of the whole squad. There are not many people who enjoy being criticized in front of 50 or 60 people. It is much better to talk to them alone. Everybody should be treated as a man.

331

Fig. 12-13. WORDS OF ENCOURAGEMENT. Football players can be encouraged to give greater performance. If they are going to fight for him, the coach must let them know he is willing to fight for them.

So, we will not criticize them for a mistake they made while trying. The only mistakes that we will criticize are mistakes of omission or let down, allowing something to happen because they did not give 100 percent to prevent it from happening.

I like to be rational with them and explain to them what the problem is. I make it clear that I will apply whatever punishment is necessary. However, the matter is strictly between the player and me. If disciplinary action is taken, no one else should have to know about it.

Encouragement

Every coach has to be himself and not try to imitate someone else. However, I firmly believe a player can be encouraged to greater performance. The more athletes are encouraged, the more a coach will get out of them and the better they will play.

Then, each player will have a better relationship with his teammates.

So, we do not "brow-beat" our players or chastise them for their mistakes. Basically, these things are stored for the next time we get to talk to him, when we can lay it on the line with him. However, there are corrections made on pass patterns or other plays on the field, but these are helpful corrections. They are not intended as, nor do they have the effect of, "browbeating."

Pride

The great athletes have a tremendous desire to excel, the urge to be the best. They take pride in their play. They hurt when they lose. Too many athletes are satisfied with fair or good performances, when they could do better with more effort. An athlete should always be striving for perfection. He must never be content with mediocrity.

Fig. 12-14. PRE-GAME SQUAD HUDDLE. Moments before kick-off time, the Rams gather around Coach Allen for last-minute tactical instructions.

When a coach has players who have a real pride in being champions, his team will always be tough to beat. They will never fold. Their opponents will have to kill them inch by inch.

We want our players to think in terms of winning championships. Any player who loses and is satisfied could never play for me.

The Psychological Profile of A Champion

While in training camp, we usually outline the "Psychological Profile of a Champion" and also the profile of an "Also-Ran."

When things go wrong, we sometimes call in a player and mention one of these characteristics. I'm pleased to say we have not had to be very negative in the past three years.

AMBITION Desire for high goals. Hates to lose. Cannot stand failure. Puts goals above ability.

COACHABLENESS Takes advice and is easy to coach. Eager to learn. Easy to approach. Follows rules and directions.

AGGRESSION A tiger! First-place-belongs-to-me-type. Asserts himself.

LEADERSHIP Shows the way and sets a good example. Respected by team members. Mixes well. Others follow his example and take his advice.

Fig. 12-15. PAY THE PRICE. Many athletes would like to be outstanding players but they don't want to work at it. They don't want to "pay the price!"

In the off-season, Roman Gabriel runs as much as 10 miles in a single day to improve his stamina.

You have to sacrifice to win! That's my philosophy in six words.

TAKE-CHARGE GUY Will take over when things go wrong. Under pressure, he does something about the problem. Often a hero.

HARD WORKER One of the first to practice—the last to leave. Does extra work. Never misses practice and follows instructions.

PHYSICAL TOUGHNESS Develops toughness by hard work. In great condition. Keeps training rules and trains year around.

MENTAL TOUGHNESS Never gives in to his feelings. Has never-give-up attitude. Ignores heat, cold, pain.

PSYCHOLOGICAL ENDURANCE Stays with job until the end. Will do his best against top competition. High endurance all season. Reliable.

Psychological Profile of An Also-Ran

NO DRIVE Does not care whether he wins or loses. Goes with the tide.

KNOW-IT-ALL Never listens and will not accept new ideas. Rebel, griper. Works by himself.

MOUSE Never talks back. High on self-abasement. Always kicking himself. Introvert, generally.

FOLLOWER Will go with crowd and generally behind them. Never tries to lead.

A WATCHER Joe Milktoast. If there is an accident, he watches or runs away. Worried about what people think.

CORNER CUTTER Ducks practice. Cuts out tough practice. Always has excuses. Lots of absences from practice.

HYPOCHONDRIAC A muscle grabber—always has an injury. Never works out consistently.

COMPLAINER Gives up easily, and is easily distracted from the job at hand. Will look good when competition is not of high caliber and will look bad in the big game.

QUITTER Cannot stick to the end. Easily distracted. Starts many jobs, finishes few. Unreliable.

Professional Organization 13

Football is a game of detail.

13

First rate organization—along with superior personnel—is the surest way to achieve team success. Many coaches do not know what the word organization means. Careful attention to the details of organization is a must for any football team. Since the beginning of the National Football League in 1920, the most successful coaches were men who excelled in organization, like my former boss, George Halas, Vince Lombardi, and Paul Brown.

The story of the NFL has shown that no team of individual stars has ever won a championship. The team has to be a 40 man unit! I have found from past experience in college and Pro that the only way we can win is to play together as a team.

Perhaps, the most important thing on a football team is the exact timing that comes from playing together week after

week. Injuries, whether in the line or backfield, can wreck this timing and precision. We went through this in 1968 when we lost Les Josephson, Dick Bass, and Tommy Mason. For instance, all backs run differently. If he is a reserve fullback, he will hit the hole differently than the No. 1 fullback.

Our practice program is set up to accomplish basic objectives. We do not go out just to have a one and a half or two hour practice. We go out on the field to accomplish something, and we will give as much time as is necessary to accomplish a goal. The time element does not bother us too much. If it's five minutes, it is five minutes. If it is 20 minutes or an hour and it takes that much to do it, that's what we will do. We have found that if we just go out to practice and warm-up, we

Fig. 13-2. ORGANIZATION. Pro football is a nervous, pressure-packed, highly complicated game which requires outstanding organization. Coach Allen carefully views play during the Pittsburgh game.

gain nothing. The players, as well as the coaches, understand this. We probably have longer practices than most teams.

Organization involves more than the scheduling of available practice time so that every minute is used to the best advantage. It includes game plans and evaluations, staff assignments, and the utilization of scouting reports. Certainly, a carefully planned schedule is necessary if the practice program is to be successfully adopted to the needs of the squad, such as previous games, player grading, and film studies of future opponents.

Any Game Can Become A Season

The season: a period of time that becomes one big game—or where any game can become a season; where any minute can produce a game winning play—and any play a winning season.

840 minutes of anxiety, elation, frustration, satisfaction, anger, desire, hope, confidence, and unyielding tension.

This is one look—at one game—in one season.

Fig. 13-3. ORGANIZED PRACTICE. The back-bone of any football operation is a well organized program of practice. The Rams go through a Saturday light work-out. Here, everybody is all business!

Practice

The backbone of any football operation is a well organized program of practice. I have always felt that tough practices will lead to winning football. A good practice is highly important. Your team plays the way it practices.

The Rams have two types of football practice schedules. The game plan schedule is designed for a specific opponent, Whereas early in the summer, we concentrate on teaching techniques.

If a team practices sloppy, they are going to play sloppy and make mistakes.

The coach that allows his practice to get out of hand, to get loose, will find that his players will continue to practice that way. It becomes a matter of habit. Every practice is a game, so to speak. I'm so upset after a bad practice that I have difficulty eating at night.

We like our players to be punctual, even early, for all practices, games, and departures. We urge them to use the time after practice to improve themselves. "Stay out after practice and work on your weakness" they are told by the coaching staff. Each player is given an improvement sheet, and we like him to use it.

Fig. 13-4. THE COACHING PROFESSION takes long hours, and we may well have the longest hours in the business.

The 1969 Rams coaching staff. First row (left to right) Ted Marchibroda, offensive backs; Dick Vermeil, special teams; George Allen, head coach; Ray Prochaska, offensive line; Tom Catlin, defensive backs. Back row (left to right) LaVern Targeson, defensive line; Howard Schnellenberger, offensive ends; Joe Sullivan, special assignments.

If the practice is not up to the standards the coaching staff believe it should be, we will go over a 15 minute period, if necessary. Time is just a guide for us, a working time. We do not live by it if we have not got the job done.

The coaching business takes long hours, and we may have the longest hours in the business. The coaches arrive at 8:30 in the morning, and we finish up anywhere from midnight to 1:00 o-clock the next morning. Charles Maher of the *Los Angeles Times* did a series of articles on our program and followed us around. I didn't realize it, but we had put in over a 40 hour week by Wednesday. This did not include Sunday because we play on Sunday, just three days—Monday, Tuesday, and Wednesday.

Our practice sessions are always busy. The players move from drill to drill, area to area. They are always moving. Again, we believe a team plays like they practice, and if the players are allowed to practice sloppily, they are going to play a sloppy game.

The coaching staff can tell half way through the week pretty much what kind of frame of mind the team is going to be in for the game on Sunday and what has to be done to get them going. We often have to shock them, and many times we will handle them softly. Coach Al Sherman of the New York Giants has done a good job of getting his club ready mentally, in spite of inexperienced personnel.

Drill

The secret of good performance at critical moments is found in drill. However, I have found drills are not as important in Pro football as in college or high school. It is through drill and drill only that the coach can be reasonably sure of good

340

Fig. 13-5. CALISTHENICS can become dull and monotonous unless everyone sees that plenty of enthusiasm and pep are put into each drill.

performance under game pressure. There is one caution, however, that should be followed to keep player interest. The individuality or initiative should not be drilled out of the players. The player should be encouraged to control the drill himself. In Pro ball, we feature more team drills than in high school and college ball.

Coach's whistle

On the whistle, every player must come "on the double!" We like them to always run when going from one area of the field to another. We tell them: "Don't be the last one!" When the coaches are talking, they must have the individual attention of the players.

Football practice might seem tiresome and monotonous at times, and a practice can be rough and tough and fatiguing, too. However, for success, it is a must. If a team is to perfect the fundamentals of

the game and the execution of the plays, constant drilling must be a daily ritual. The execution of a perfect play requires the teamwork of eleven men.

There are seven check points that every practice or training program should stress:

1. Aggressiveness (mental as well as physical)
2. Conditioning or stretching
3. Alertness
4. Discipline of some form
5. Team work
6. Toughness (mental or physical)
7. Quickness improvement

Squad meetings

A team has to have meetings to be prepared (Fig. 13-6). Players have to study off the field in order to be champions. There is not enough time to do it on the

341

Fig. 13-6. SQUAD MEETINGS. The best time to establish a proper mental attitude for every- one is during the squad meetings. Here, Coach Allen is shown supervising a squad meeting.

field. During the summer training program, the coaches hold nightly meetings with the players, dividing up according to position.

Personally, I am a great believer in constant meetings with players, getting a group of one to three players together and talking things over. This is the time when we can get their ideas on things and can instill in them our basic ideas on football and get them to believe in them.

We have tried to prove to our players that by following what we are telling them to do, they will improve. The coaching staff believes that if our players will follow what we have told them to do, they will win. *In 1966, our major job was to get a team that had not won to believe that they could win.* In our first year here, we won eight games, followed by eleven victories in 1967 before losing out to the Packers. We have been able to convince the players that by working hard and playing as a team, they can win! "The only way we can lose is to beat ourselves."

Summer Training Camp

Opening day normally is a day for physical exams. Each player is given a complete exam of the upper and lower body, including the complete muscular and bone system of each man. All of these things are checked to be certain if each player is in good enough shape to play this game. They have to pass a very stringent physical examination. Various aptitude tests are taken by the rookies that give us an idea of their potential. We also believe in a complete eye examination, and we bring in Dr. George Jesson from Chicago.

During rookie week, any players who come to us by trades must report with the rookies, and there are usually some veterans who would like to get into camp early and start working on a heavy conditioning program.

Basically, we will run 15 days of two- a-day practices which is what we strive

342

Fig. 13-7. ROOKIE WEEK. Before the veterans arrive, the Rams hold one week of workouts, strictly for rookies and players who have come to the Rams through trades. Since the group is small, the coaches are able to give individual attention to the young players. Coach Allen, right, explains a point to Don Martin, rookie from Washington.

for, and there are occasions when we just have one drill, for instance, when we have a closed scrimmage with another NFL team.

Typical Rams daily practice session

Wake-up call is given at 7 a.m., followed by breakfast from 7:30 to 8:00. Breakfast is mandatory, as is the bed check at night. After breakfast, the players go to the locker rooms and start to get taped and ready for practice.

Warm-up Everyone must be on the field dressed by 9:30 a.m. However, prior to this time, the quarterbacks have their regular early drill supervised by Coach Marchibroda. We scrimmage the Dallas Cowboys twice every year, and I like Tom Landry's warm-up program because it contains much breakdown work by positions.

Rams drill At 9:30 a.m., we have the Rams Drill, a passing drill to warm up the

quarterback's arms and get the receivers to run a little. We have two quarterbacks, one at the goal line and the 40, and they will throw to the receiver on their right running up field.

Calisthenics and Exer-genie We will go directly to the calisthenics period which consists of about seven minutes of warm-up exercises. Then, we go to our Exer-genie stations program where we engage in a variety of isometric routines. We can put the entire team through the Exer-genie program in approximately 15 minutes.

Cadence drill The offense will huddle, call a play, come out and run 12 yards with the ball across the goal line. Each of our three offensive teams will run through this drill. I got this idea from Coach Lombardi when he was at Green Bay, and we like it as a team drill to further the warm-up.

Then, the defense will come up to the defensive spot and will call a defense in the huddle. They will come out and run a defense for those 12 yards. Again, this is

Fig. 13-8. BLAIR FIELD. During the league season, the Rams hold all of their practices at Blair Field in Long Beach. The excellent facilities include the clubhouse, meeting rooms, training room, weight room, and a complete layout of Exer-genie stations.

a team warm-up and get together type of thing lasting for three or four minutes.

Agility and fundamental period Early in camp, we will start with 25 minutes of individual breakdown work. Later, we cut it down to 15 minutes, and after the season begins, we may only devote 10 minutes to this portion of our practice session. Early in camp, it is necessary to give it considerable emphasis.

Basically, there will be five groups. The fifth group, though, consisting of the deep backs and linebackers is often split up. I will take either the deep backs of the linebackers, and they will do different drills. The offensive backs, offensive line, receivers, and defensive line make up the other groups.

The offensive backs will work on such fundamentals as stance, where we want them spotted, hand-offs from the quarterbacks, and pass receiving.

The receivers often work in front of a net. During this session, they receive at least 20 balls in front of the big net. This is an area where they get a lot of balls thrown to them which means considerable ball handling.

7 on 7 Following these warm-up drills, we go into a period we call 7 on 7. It gets its name because there are seven defensive people, 4 deep backs and 3 linebackers, against the passing game. They will defend against the offensive backs and receivers. There are no linemen in this group.

The offense will perfect its timing, its passes, and pass patterns against the defense. Both units get considerable work this way because it is up to the defense to cover the offense, and the offense is perfecting its plays. We feel this is a very good drill.

Lineman's 7 on 7 While the 7 on 7 is going on, the defensive and offensive lines are working against each other on another area of the field. The offensive line will be working on their blocking against the defensive line.

Fig. 13-9. RAMS' OFFENSE. This period consists of plays run against the type of defense our opponent for the week is expected to run. The manager records the plays on a portable blackboard and makes them available to the extra players.

Separate period Then, we go to the separate period where the defense will be working on new defenses put in the meeting the night before. The offense works on its new plays, too, but against no opposition. The whole offensive team and defensive team work separately.

Rams offense This is an area where the Rams' defense will primarily be working on plays that their opponents will run. These plays are taken from films, put on cards, and are run by the offense which emulate the team we are playing.

The Rams' offensive period consists of plays run against the type of defense that our opponent for the week is going to run. These will vary but it gives the offense a good picture of what they are going to face that week.

Kicking Each day we work on one phase of our kicking game. We have it broken down into five phases: punt, punt return, kick-off, kick-off return, and the field goal which includes the extra point team.

Conditioning period After the kicking program, we get into the conditioning portion of our daily practice session. We will run striders, interception drills for the defense, or perfect plays for the offense. All of these are designed to gain conditioning and to get some extra skill work.

During the Season

Monday

Following the ball game on Sunday, the players have a day off, except for those

Fig. 13-10. FILM BREAKDOWN. Special assistant Joe Sullivan, left, prepares a film for showing to a group of players.

Essentially, Monday is a film breakdown day in preparation for the next opponent.

players who have to report to the training room for bumps and bruises. These can range from a major to a minor injury that needs treatment by the trainers.

Although Monday is a day off for the players, there is no rest for the coaching staff. Essentially, Monday is a film breakdown day in preparation for the next opponent. We are at our coaching offices by 9 a.m. with movies of Sunday's game. We run the films back and forth, back and forth, and we all make notes. This goes on until early afternoon. I try to view all the film of the previous game but many times, due to press commitments and other time-consuming details, it is not possible to do this on Monday.

Around 4 p.m. the movies of our next opponent are delivered by Mickey Dukich, our film expert, and the coaches are finished with our films. We sit down and look at the team we are playing next

Sunday. It is more back and forth with the projector. I like a lot of projectors around because we usually have one or two in the repair shop.

Tuesday

The coaches look at movies of the team we are going to play until the players start coming. When the players arrive, we go over the game film of the previous game with them. The offense, as a group, will look at the offensive pictures, while the defense will see the defensive pictures. Then, the whole team will look at the kicking game, as a total team. Mistakes are pointed out or great plays are noted on how we did things, how the offense and defense went, and what improvements we must make for the next game.

After this film session, we go out to practice, basically a "get over the aches

Fig. 13-11. VISUAL DISPLAYS. These are used to familiarize players with personnel of the opposing team.

and pains'' session. Normally, it is a little bit shorter than the other ones. It is largely conditioning and going over basic mistakes, game mistakes, and also preparation for the next team. We will start to run some plays that we are going to use, defensively and offensively.

Wednesday, Thursday, and Friday

This is preparation day for the opponent, and we will go over offense and defense every day. We begin by discussing personnel of the team we are going to play. While we run the films back and forth, the players sit with the coaches and we point out the opponent's strengths and weaknesses. Some teams just have an offense or defense stress day, but we go over the same type practice Wednesday, Thursday, and Friday.

The physical session begins with a workout on the Exer-genie machines, then

pads are downed for formal practice. We end this offensive session with a ten minute ''down and distance'' drill, a simulated scrimmage with the defensive team giving us the other team's defense.

Once the season starts, there is no scrimmage. The only hitting we might get would be a five or ten minute area on something we might need, such as a goal line defense or goal line offense. Basically, however, the heavy hitting is over.

Saturday

When playing at home, our Saturday practice will be pretty much a loosening up hour affair. We report about 10:30 a.m., and the session is devoted to a review of the specialty teams—punt protection and coverage, field goals, kick-off returns, punt returns, and kick-off coverage. We also cover our offense and defense goal line defenses and our two minute offense, which we use when we are in the last two minutes of a half. Again, we work on our special two minute offense to stop the clock and to move the ball. This is done with the offense going up and down the field against the defense. Actually, they have two minutes to score from their own 20 yard line. This Saturday practice lasts about 45 minutes.

If it is a home game, the players will go home after the Saturday practice and report to our hotel at night at 7:30 p.m., at which time we hold a meeting. Then, there will be a bed check.

After checking the mail, making a few phone calls, and any other final details, I will join the coaches at the Plush Horse Motel where the Rams will stay that night.

Sunday

There will be a wake-up call and a pre-game meal about four hours before the game. Then, the players will take off on their own and report to the Coliseum for the game. We will arrive at the stadium about two hours before game time.

The team will take the field about 45 minutes before the game and go through a series of warm-up drills. The kickers come out early, and then the passers come out to get loosened up. Some of the receivers like to come out early and get some running on their own and do some loosening up themselves.

After the whole team has their calisthenics, we will break into two areas. The linemen will run down to cover punts, while the punt receivers will catch the punts. The linemen will take striders down

field after the punts, while the receivers and passers will work on our Ram Drill which is the same that we use in practice.

Then we will break up into individual groups of the offense, running patterns for the quarterback, the defense working on agility, and the linemen working on protection and rush. These are principally done to get loosened up. We will get together in our 7 on 7 period, throwing passes in the patterns they have worked on during the week. Then, we will go into a full group running plays, 11 on 11, for a certain segment of time. The defense will go in first, while the offense continues to end up with perfect plays, at which time everybody goes in.

Pre-game meeting

I do not believe in a frenzy type of meeting, but we will go over things that we must accomplish that day. We will cover the frame of mind we have to be in to win. We will discuss the basic things that we have gone over during the week, mainly repetition of the points we brought up during the week at meetings. I will remind the players about how I want to kick-off, what defense we want to open with, and make a few remarks before I leave them alone.

As for a pep talk, no, I wouldn't classify my remarks as being a pep talk. These are mature men, not kids. In fact, the actual mental conditioning starts on Tuesday. If we cannot get started on Tuesday, then we will have trouble on Sunday.

And there is no rah-rah at the halftime either. We will divide the team into groups,

Fig. 13-12. LEAVING THE FIELD for the pre-game meeting in the clubhouse are Offensive Line Coach Ray Prochaska, Head Coach George Allen, and Quarterback Coach Ted Marchibroda.

like we do during the week in practice, and discuss and analyze the situation as it involves each group. The coaches who view the game from high above the stands make their recommendations, correct mistakes, and we revise our game plans if necessary. I try to be with both the offensive and defensive teams, but for three years, I have devoted most of my time to defense. I talk to some of the players and to the doctors to learn about the injury situation.

About five minutes before we are due back on the field, I pull everybody together again, tell them about the second half plan. After the game, the first thing I do is talk to the players. Before the press is admitted, I like to have something to say to some players, something personal but general and brief.

When things have calmed down a bit, I check with our team physicians on the injury situation. Then the coaches get together and rehash the game a little. Another game has gone into the books, but the cycle starts all over again. It's back to work. If we win, I have trouble sleeping, and if we lose I have trouble sleeping.

Preparing For A Game

The first thing we do is to look at the films of the opponents. We try not to let anything slide by. We want to cover each and everything as well as we possibly can, offensively and defensively.

While looking at these films, we chart the opponent's defenses, and on Monday, we put them into a computer system. This comes back early Tuesday morning from the Computer Company. The defenses of the opponents that week will be broken down in many categories, by down and distance, position on the field, the hash marks, and how they defense certain sets.

Fig. 13-13. TRADES. A major part of organization in professional football is making trades. A series of shrewd trades helped bring the Rams into title contention. Above, Coach Allen, center in front row, poses with 19 of his 40 Rams footballers, some of whom didn't get their professional start in Los Angeles. They hold cards designating teams from which they came to the Rams.

Any set that we might want to run, we will know basically what defense they like to use from looking at the films.

Defensively, I do not use the Computer at all. I have many reasons, but will not go into them now. We will chart complete offensive programs for two games, which is what our league allows. What passes do they like to throw? What do they do by down and distance? Everything is broken down by hand. It's a little slower, but we feel we can get a little more out of it ourselves breaking it down this way.

From this extensive amount of information, we will come up with a GAME PLAN, which is designed to work against this particular ball club. How should we handle this team?

Scouting

Scouting a future opponent is an important phase of football coaching. Motion picture films actually provide the most accurate report of the offensive and defensive tactics of a team. However, some NFL clubs have a scout who covers as many games of future opponents as possible. Some clubs have two or three scouts working for them. We put out a scout report each week which is given to each player.

A good scout should have on hand the necessary forms and be ready to jot down as much pertinent information as he can. He shouldn't trust his observations to memory.

A

B

Fig. 13-14. COMMUNICATION. Quarterback Milt Plum listens to instructions from coaches high above the stands, while down on the field, Coach Allen explains defensive tactics to Eddie Meador.

Offensive Philosophy

The Rams' style of offense is simple. We employ an uncomplicated and balanced offense which excels in execution and ball control. We are constantly striving for a contrived, well conceived offense, with as few mistakes as possible. Everything we do is done on timing, timing and assignments. This is why we practice a little longer than most teams. We don't believe in the gimmick offense, in doing a lot of things where we have a chance of fumbling the ball or losing our timing.

Our passing attack revolves around the concept of simplicity and timing, running the patterns the way they are supposed to be run so that the quarterback knows exactly where they are. After this is completed, the personal adjustment area must be considered, what a defensive back is doing to a receiver. For example, if the receiver runs an 8 yard slant and a linebacker comes right into the area, maybe he has to take a 10 or 12 yard pattern. Or, he may have to adjust his pattern into a different area.

These are things the quarterback and the receivers have to work on during training periods after they have the basic concept of what will happen. If Gabe sees the defense is strong where he is going to throw, the first thing he will look for is the receiver to adjust his pattern. If it's Bernie Casey, he should know how Bernie

351

Fig. 13-15. SEVENTY-FOUR YEARS OF EXPERIENCE. In 1966, Coach Allen (kneeling) said, "It is nice to see a few bald heads and some grey hair on the Rams. A good defense needs good linebackers, and one of my favorite 'indulgences' is having plenty of experienced linebackers around." From left to right, Doug Woodlief, Cliff Livingston, Tony Guillory, Jack Pardee, Dan Currie, Bill George, Maxie Baughan, and Myron Pottius.

likes to adjust his routes. If he feels there is no possibility of having the adjustment work, Gabriel will go to a different area to throw to. So, working together constantly is most essential.

Defensive Philosophy

Successful defense in football depends on the individual skills of all eleven players. Good defensive play is a coordinated effort on the part of the deep backs, linebackers, and linemen. Teamwork is essential.

Defense, to me, is the most interesting science in the world. One of the Rams' most satisfying defensive efforts was achieved on December 17, 1967 before 77,277 fans in the Coliseum. On this memorable afternoon, the Rams defeated Johnny Unitas and the Colts 34 to 10 on the forward passes of Gabriel, who completed 18 of 22 and three touchdown strikes.

Attack

My philosophy about football defense can be summed up in one word: ATTACK. We believe in attacking an offense and manhandling it. Constant drive must be exerted by the defense, never letting the offense get the upper hand. The defense has to take over the game and make the

352

Fig. 13-16. THE MEDICAL STAFF plays a vital role in the success of a professional football team. Injuries must be kept to a minimum.

Dr. J. Victor Rasinski, Jr., Team Physician, and Trainers Jerry Rhea (now with Atlanta) and George Menefee (left to right) are shown on the job in the Rams' fine training room facility.

offense play their game. It must never give them the strong suit to work with. Make them work from their weak suit.

We like our defensive players to have the attitude there is nobody better than we are. They can handle anybody. "I don't care who they are, we will take them on!" is the mental attitude we like them to have.

Player leadership is all important. Veteran end Doug Atkins was able to perform well for the Atlanta Falcons and still give leadership to a young club. Tommy Nobis is an excellent leader, despite being young, for Coach Norm Van Brocklin's Falcons. A coach must be able to get his players to do things that they are not aware they are doing. He must prepare his team to be able to combat what the offense is going to throw at them, and overcome any shortcomings they may have. We have six excellent leaders on the Rams' defensive unit.

Members of the defensive platoon must go out on the field and not kill, but *hurt* their opponent. They must let them know that they are there. PUNISH THEM!

A sound multiple defense requires two or three basic defenses with stunts and a sound goal line defense. We like a quick and resourceful defense with few blitzes and little risks involved.

Training Room

The Training Room is for taping, first aid, and the treatment of injuries. It is a place of business and is not to be used as a lounge. Absolutely no horseplay is tolerated in the Rams' training facilities.

We are constantly striving to keep these facilities "Big League." Players are told: "Don't throw old tape, soiled white goods, equipment or any other articles on the floor." We have provided disposal containers for refuse. So, we want our players to use them and keep this area clean and sanitary.

It is the responsibility of each player to report injuries to the trainers immediately. On the morning following the game, it is their responsibility to report for treatment to get all the "bumps and bruises" taken care of.

353

Fig. 13-17. THE TRAINER. Reporting to Coach Allen during noon hour on the condition of the players is the trainer, discussing minor as well as serious injuries.

Treatments are given before and after practice and immediately after the evening meeting. We have two full-time trainers, George Menefee and Cash Birdwell.

"Never miss a treatment period!", the players are told. "You must be able to go full speed to help yourself and the Rams. By observing training rules, an athlete will be a better football player.

When one takes a look at the expenses and items used by a typical NFL team, it is quite evident that Pro football is an expensive sport. For instance, in one season, a trainer will spend 300 hours taping ankles, which involves about 46 miles of tape. Cost of the tape amounts to over $5,000. An average annual cost of equipment is $14,000, including $4,000 for 19 dozen footballs at $19 each.

Dining Hall

Our grocery bill at training camp comes to around $20,000, including $7,000 for meat alone and as high as $300 per meal.

A pro team will drink 1,440 gallons of fruit juice after practices. Other expenditures are:

$2,500 in fruit
300 gallons of ice cream
600 pounds of cheese
500 loaves of bread
350 dozen rolls

Films

Over 40,000 feet of film are used in filming exhibitions and regular season games. The total cost of all films amounts to over $20,000, for three prints of each contest.

Equipment

Proper equipment should always be worn when playing such a highly competitive

354

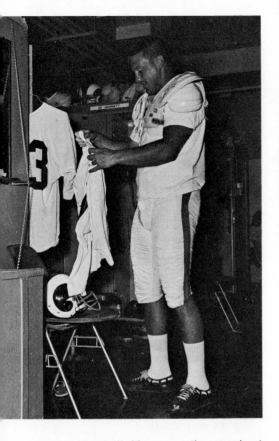

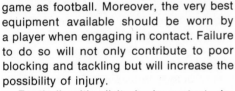

game as football. Moreover, the very best
equipment available should be worn by
a player when engaging in contact. Failure
to do so will not only contribute to poor
blocking and tackling but will increase the
possibility of injury.

Football, with all its body contact, demands that properly fitted shoulder pads
and helmets be worn, together with snug
fitting pants that keep the tight guards
and hip pads properly positioned. Backfield men and receivers, as a rule, wear
only shoulder pads and helmets, modified
hip, thigh, and knee pads, plus the usual
tape on their ankles. Such protective
equipment is necessary to any NFL club
not only to prevent injury but to provide
added protection in case an injury has
already been sustained.

Proper shoes

A very important piece of equipment is
the shoe. The shoes must be comfortable,
and they must support the joints of the
foot and ankle. The shoe cleats should
always be checked before every game
and practice to make sure they are the
proper type for the condition of the field.

We urge our players to take care of
their equipment and not to throw it
around. We do not like to see our men
dress sloppily for practice, just because
it is practice. Instead, they should have
pride in their appearance every time they
go on the field with their team.

Indeed, it costs a lot of money to outfit
a professional football player. Locker room
costs, such as training devices, medical,

tape, and just the maintenance of equipment, can be a sizeable sum for a squad of 40 players, averaging well over $20,000 annually.

The Off-Season

Our off-season isn't an off-season at all for the coaching staff, contrary to what most people may think. In January at the completion of the season, I give each of our coaches a list of jobs, maybe 10 or 15, which they must accomplish during the off-season.

Each coach must write up a report on his area of the team and submit his recommendations for improvements for the next year. This goes into a booklet which the entire staff receives.

Film breakdown

The first area we get into is a comprehensive breakdown of all game films for the season just completed.

Offensively, all passes are broken down into patterns, while all runs are broken down according to holes. On the hole breakdown, the plays are categorized by 0 and 1 hole, 21 Trap, 40 Trap, etc. All plays are broken down according to the times used and the success of each.

A general overall review of our defensive films is made at the close of each season, at which time we detect the most repeated errors. We then try to correct these mistakes in order to make us a better football team. As an example, the films often show that we lose a lot of yardage by arm tackling, not getting that shoulder into the blow.

Most of the film watching is done individually because it takes a long time to do it. However, the offensive coaches do get together because they are working on the same plays.

Manuals

During the off-season, we make up the manuals. Again, this is a coaching staff cooperation program. From the offensive standpoint, we weed out plays which have not worked well and the blocking assignments might be revised to make the play go. Of course, most NFL teams run about the same plays; the difference is in the talent they have to make them go.

Forms and charts

Most charts and forms require constant revision if a coach is to keep up with the constant changes in offensive and defensive trends. The purpose of these charts is to assist both the coach and player before the game. The forms and charts are intended to make the players more conscious of vital statistics. In addition, they serve as a motivation to the players.

A wall chart, for example, is very useful in providing pass defenders with a visual aid to assess their performance. Pass training cards illustrate every pass pattern that the opponents could employ.

Off-season training programs

To keep a close check on the condition of our players during the off-season,

Fig. 13-20. THE WEIGHT OF EACH PLAYER is of vital concern to the coaching staff. Excess weight can hinder the performance of an athlete. During early season training, every player goes on the scales before and after each work out. (Tom Mack is shown here.)

trainer Birdwell is sent to the home of every player. We believe the year around condition of our players is so important that we want to be certain they will come into summer camp in shape to play the game.

A trainer will visit a player, put him on the scale, and go over an individual workout program with him. He will find out if there are any major or minor injuries the season before. He will check them out and file a complete report on each player, weight, running report, etc., which goes to each coach.

An off-season gym for players living in the Los Angeles area is another innovation we have added. Under the supervision of Menefee and Birdwell, the facilities include Universal weight machines, sauna, a field for running, and football for those requesting them.

We assign a reporting weight for all heavy players. During the season, we will weight these people every Thursday under a fine system. The coaches have set a fine of $100 per pound overweight.

Rules and Club Policy

At the start of the summer training season, members of the Los Angeles Rams are given a printed copy of the General Rules and Club Policies which are applicable for the entire season. The copy reads: "You are expected to conduct yourselves as gentlemen at all times and in a manner that will reflect credit upon you, your teammates, the Los Angeles Rams, and the National Football League.

1. Keep yourself neat and clean-shaven at all times.
2. Team members will eat all meals at the prescribed time. It is mandatory that you attend the *Breakfast* period each morning.
3. It is YOUR responsibility to be on time for all practices, meetings, and other appointments. Do not rely on someone else. Excuses will NOT be accepted.
4. Drinking of *Hard Liquor* will not be tolerated.

357

5. *Curfew* for all players is 10:45 P.M., unless told otherwise by the Head Coach. *Lights out* is at 11:00 P.M. in training camp and this means that each man must be in his own room and bed.

6. The volume of radios, TVs, phonographs, or musical instruments must be kept low in the dormitory area.

7. Every player must weigh IN and OUT every day. A fine of $100.00 per pound will be assessed for overweight players.

8. Every player will wear prescribed uniform and there will be no exceptions. A protective face guard will be worn by all personnel unless permission has been secured from the Head Coach. While on the field of play, or practice, the helmet will be worn or carried at all times.

9. All players must have their ankles taped before every practice and game.

10. The club reserves the rights to impose and require observance by the players of *reasonable* standard of personal conduct. Players must conform to, and abide by, the rules and restrictions established by the Club to protect and safeguard the game of Professional Football.

If a team has the proper mental attitude to begin with, training rules take care of themselves. I like to think we have fair training rules, but at the same time, I think they are as strict as necessary. We have a bed check at 11 o'clock every night during training camp, as well as every night we are on the road. During the three years I have been in Los Angeles, I have only had to fine two ball players for missing curfew. I don't like to fine a player, but if I have to, generally, the fine is not a token one.

Publicity

We remind our players that they are engaged in Professional Football and that our success is not only dependent on how many games we win, but also how many fans attend our games. Therefore, publicity and promotion play an important and very large part in our program. When not actually engaged in a team function, their first responsibility will be to the publicity department. They are expected to perform these duties with the same enthusiasm as those which are directed by the coaches.

Our relationship with the press, radio and television people, and others of the publicity field is extremely important and at our training camp and in our clubhouse these people are our guests and should be treated accordingly.

Traveling

While on the road, our players are required to wear a coat and tie at all times, unless they are instructed otherwise by the staff. They are required to take care of all their incidental hotel charges upon checking out of each individual hotel. The club will take care of their room charge only.

Gambling

Gambling is a very serious problem in all sports. Our players are explicitly told

Fig. 13-21. ATTENDANCE. The success of a professional football team is dependent not only on how many games it wins but also on how many fans attend the games. In 1965, the Rams drew 736,000 fans at home and away. In 1967, the George Allen-coached team drew a record 1,230,059, an increase of approximately one-half million fans in just two seasons.

to avoid any association with gamblers. In addition, they must be very careful of strangers who attempt to strike up a conversation. Under no circumstances are they to discuss the physical condition of members of our team, or any other subject that might give aid to gamblers.

I cannot completely express how important this is. We urge our players to always be on the alert regarding this problem. If they are approached by anyone, at any time, whom they feel is suspicious, they should report it to me or the management personnel.

Future Careers

Professional football has been a springboard to success for many former players of the Los Angeles Rams, as well as those throughout the NFL. Many NFL players have advanced quickly to important positions in industry, commerce, and the financial world. A player in the pro leagues can not only earn a sizeable income during a five month season, but he can employ himself in the off-season apprenticing in the field he has chosen for his long-range career. In addition to an attractive pension, he can retire from football with a substantial savings account.

League Growth

Indeed, professional football has come a long way since the first game was played on September 17, 1920 in Canton, Ohio, when the actual birth of the National Football League took place. Through the foresight, hard work, and organizational skills of league executives and club owners, combined with crowd-pleasing play and masterful coaching on the field, the league has grown to unprecedented proportions. Pro football today, under Commissioner Pete Rozelle, is regarded by many as the major sports attraction in the U.S.A.

High School and College 14 Organization

QUALITIES OF A GOOD
FOOTBALL PLAYER

1. Size, Speed, Agility
2. Development
3. Desire
4. Playing Experience
5. Coolness under Fire
6. Self-Discipline
7. Ability to Learn
8. Mental Attitude
9. Leadership
10. Courage (Guts)
11. Aggressiveness
12. Loyalty

14

Organization is the foundation of all successful football coaching. This is just as true in the handling of high school and college teams as it is in coaching play-for-pay professional squads. Organization is the basis of the whole game.

Winning football depends not only on how well organized and co-ordinated the coaching staff is, but also on the efficiency of scouting, player assignments, and practice sessions. Checklists, forms, charts, schedules, scouting reports, drill diagrams should be available and ready for use. The practice schedule should be developed so that every minute pays off, and the coaching staff must make the best possible use of time all year long.

Since coaching football is a year-round job, a yearly organizational plan must be prepared and followed as closely as possible. An outlined plan of organization to be administered by the head coach should be prepared for the entire year. He must realize that no detail or technique is too small to be ignored.

Building a football program on the high school or college level is a cooperative effort and includes the school administration, faculty, community, and the news media. If the coaching staff does not have the support and cooperation of the school and community, it is not possible to produce a top caliber football program.

Practice

The caliber of a coach is not what he knows but what he can teach his players. *Teaching is most effective when it is done during practice, when there is time for both repetition and close supervision.* The

OFFICE OF THE FOOTBALL COACH

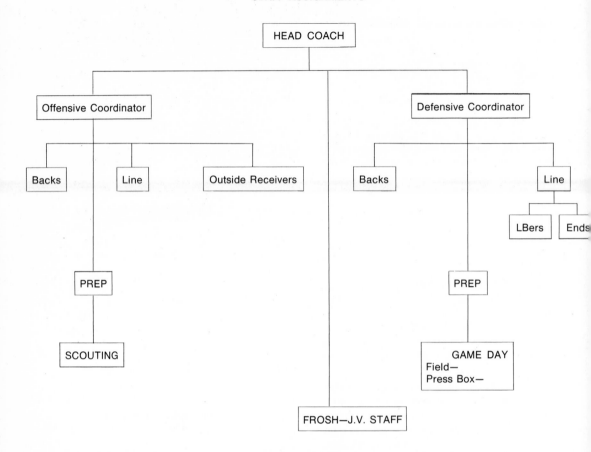

STAFF ASSIGNMENTS

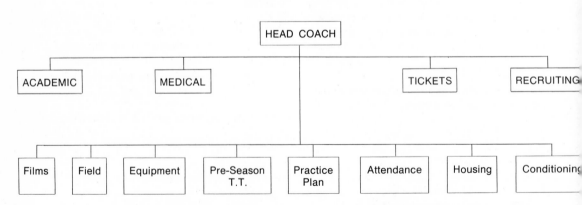

BASIC ASSIGNMENTS

Fig. 14-2. YEARLY FOOTBALL ORGANIZATIONAL PLAN

Fig. 14-3. KEEP THE DRILLS MOVING! Players must hustle from start to finish, whether in a game or during practice. On pass drills, patterns must be run at top speed.

best drilled team usually makes the fewest mistakes and manages to win the close games.

During the first two weeks of practice, usually before school begins, two drills are held, the first at 8:00 o'clock and the second at 3:30.

Most high school and college coaches prefer one and a half and two hour practice sessions. Once the season gets underway, they will hold practice two days for two hours a couple of days a week and possibly for a half hour less on the other days. The final workout on the day before the game is usually never more than 30 to 45 minutes, in addition to a squad meeting.

The practice plan

The following general segments make up the daily practice plan:

1. Meetings.
2. Calisthenics.
3. Specialty period.
4. Group drills.
5. Individual drills.
6. Team development period.
7. Kicking.

PRE-SEASON PRACTICE PLAN

Morning *(Concentration on Offensive Football)*

8:00–9:00	Tape and dress
9:00–9:10	Specialty period
9:10–9:20	Calisthenics, cadence, and agility drills
9:20–9:25	Bertha (offensive fire-out)
9:25–9:30	Perfect tackle technique
9:30–9:50	Individual offense
	A. Fundamentals of the play-of-the-day.
	B. Review past fundamentals.
	C. Coordinate line and backs.
9:50–10:20	Half-line (offense vs. defense)
10:20–10:40	Pass offense (individual and team)
10:40–10:50	Team offense
10:50–11:00	Conditioning period
11:00	To the showers

365

Fig. 14-4. SUPERB PHYSICAL CONDITIONING is essential in championship football. Plenty of enthusiasm and pep should be put into each drill. Count cadence whenever possible.

Afternoon *(Concentration on Defensive football)*

3:30–4:30	Tape and dress
4:30–4:40	Specialty period
4:40–4:50	Calisthenics and cadence and agility drills
4:50–4:55	Bertha (defensive pursuit)
4:55–5:05	Perfect tackle technique
5:05–5:25	Individual defense (fundamentals such as key, movement, blow, pressure, and pursue.)
5:25–5:35	Group defense
5:35–5:55	Half-line
5:55–6:10	Unit defense
6:10–6:20	Punt returns
6:20–6:30	Conditioning period
6:30	To the showers

Game Preparation

Sunday

This is the important study and strategy day for the coaching staff. Scouting reports are broken down, as the coaches analyze the strength and weaknesses of opposing personnel. Then the game films are shown; they are studied and graded quite extensively.

Following this study, the staff starts making up the game plan. The passing patterns and strategy along with the running attack are devised according to the opposing defense.

The staff also discuss the best methods of getting the team mentally ready for the next opponent. To key the players into the game plan, the bulletin board, signs, and banners are prepared.

Monday

Before the team takes the field, a squad meeting is held, at which time the players

TYPICAL GAME DAY SCHEDULE

3:00–3:30	Student body, pep rally
3:30–4:30	Training room: tape ankles, draw game equipment, check equipment.
4:45–5:30	Suggested pre-game meal: lean beef (fish), baked potato, fruit, vegetable, dry toast, tea with sugar.
5:30–6:30	At the school: movie room (30 minutes) viewing movies of tonight's opponent; gym (30 minutes): walk through various defensive adjustments.
6:30–6:45	Free time, relax.
6:45–7:15	Dress for game and final taping.
7:15–7:35	Pre-game warm-up.
7:35–7:55	Pre-game instructions
7:55–8:00	Loosening up and National Anthem
8:00–10:00	Game time
10:00–10:30	Post game talk, showers

receive a preliminary game sheet, plus a grade from the previous game. After the squad takes the field and has their stretching and warm-up exercises, each group—seven or eight players—is assigned to come in and view the films individually with their coach. This film schedule by group will go on all week.

Tuesday

This is the heavy work day, about two hours of practice at a fast pace. A thorough review is devoted to offense and defense fundamentals. Then an hour of offense and defense drill, featuring recognition exercises with the game plan in mind. A short scrimmage is held, matching the first and second teams. Important stress is placed on the defense's ability to read tendencies and formations.

Wednesday

An offense and defense dummy scrimmage and emphasis on the kicking game

Fig. 14-5. A PRE-SEASON INTRASQUAD SCRIMMAGE under game conditions is necessary to sharpen up the offensive and defensive systems. A crew of officials give the scrimmage a realistic touch.

take up one hour of this practice session. The line spends 20 minutes in the chute for offensive take-off, plus work on the seven-man, two-man, and one-man sleds. While the line is hard at work at their end of the field, the backs are working on offensive execution.

Later, the squad goes through all phases of pass protection, screens, and draw blocking, but with a minimum of contact. The ends and backs are given 10 minutes of work to perfect their patterns and technique.

Defensive recognition and the defensive kicking game are carefully reviewed. Then the offensive teams run through their perfect plays, moving up and down the field, calling out the down and distance.

Thursday

After a good loosening-up period, the approaching game is reviewed for approximately 45 minutes. The squad then works on punt returns and kickoff coverage and returns. Both the punters and the place

kickers sharpen up their skills. The major portion of this workout is devoted to warm-up, running plays, reviewing the game plan, and some jogging. However, the chief concern is that the game plan be fully understood by everyone on the team.

If the game is slated for Friday, the game captains lead the squad in a short meeting.

Friday

On game day, high school players usually are requested to wear their blazers, or sweaters, and ties to school. After the completion of classes, the weekly pep rally is held.

The players arrive in the dressing room, where a quiet atmosphere prevails. They are given an opportunity to think of the game coming up.

Several meetings are held by members of the coaching staff. The backfield coach meets with the defensive secondary and reviews coverage and various adjustments. The line coach checks his players

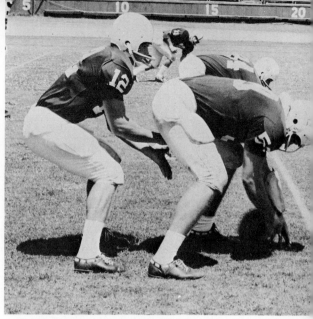

Fig. 14-6. THE SELECTION AND DEVELOPMENT of a quarterback should receive full attention. He must develop a mastery of mechanical details, such as the exchange from the center, various pivots, ball handling and fakes, and perfection of passing and running techniques.

on their blocking assignments. The defensive line have a meeting with their coach, while the offense and defense signal callers go over the game plans.

As the players begin to dress, taping takes place in the training room. After the warm-up session on the field, the players are given an opportunity to concentrate on their game thoughts. Many football squads have a team prayer before they leave for the field.

Game plan

A football team, particularly the quarterback, should be fully prepared each week against the defenses to be seen. After viewing game films and listening to scouting reports, the coaching staff on Sunday formulates the weekly game plan which appears on a 4" by 6" easy-to-carry card inside a transparent plastic folder.

The quarterback should master the following:

1. Defensive alignment and stunts
2. a. zone coverage (rotation, inversion, revolve)
   b. man coverage
   c. semi-zone and man
   d. free safety
3. The scheme of opponent's up-front defense

4. Strengths and weaknesses
5. Exact system of secondary coverage to be used and how to identify spefic coverage
6. Individual characteristics of opponents
7. Expected tendencies
8. Overall plan of attack
9. Specific formations and plays available

In addition to the game plan for the offensive quarterback, the defensive captains should receive a similar tactical plan in line with the offensive strategy expected from the opponents.

Press box coaching

Press box-to-field cooperation is vital to football success. In this era of multiple offenses and defenses, effective communication is a must. Getting proper information from the press box can prove extremely valuable in making tactical decisions during a game.

Training rules

To be successful, a football team must have discipline. Discipline cannot be enforced if punishment is varied. There cannot be a double standard. To have a well-disciplined team, training rules must apply for one and all.

If rules are broken, the football coach must take action or face a breakdown in morale and a loss of respect of his players for him and the program. Above all, when rules are broken, the same justice should be rendered the "star" as the substitute.

A "training pledge" signed by both parents and high school prospects will likely provide better results than with a mere statement. Generally, parents will cooperate quickly when telephoned about disciplinary action by the coaching staff.

The following are training rules commonly practiced by high school and college football teams:

1. Drinking and smoking are not allowed at any time. You will hurt yourself and your team.

2. Be neat around school. Dress conservatively, with clean shaves, short haircuts, shirttail in, socks and shoes on.

3. Attend classes regularly and on time. Class cuts are not tolerated.

4. Use only good language on and off the field.

5. Report to practice on time and know your assignments.

6. Try to get nine hours of sleep.

7. Do not expect favors and special treatment from your instructors.

8. Watch your weight. Your coach can recommend your best playing weight.

9. Helmets should be worn at all times on the practice field; they are not to be thrown.

10. Hustle from start to finish, whether in a game or during practice.

11. Wear ankle wraps or tape during practice and games.

12. Show respect to the managers, who have an important job to perform.

13. Cooperate in the huddle.

14. Accept the official's decisions without question.

15. Wait for the coach to call upon you to play when he sees fit. Never ask him!

The psychological approach

To get the most from his players, the football coach should use the psychological approach whenever possible. He must try to get them "up", to get boys to play with emotion, heart, desire, and determination. Tradition and pride can be key factors which can be utilized in turning out championship football teams.

Effective techniques for psychological motivation could be to:

1. Dedicate games to a special cause.
2. Change routine—have fun!
3. "POINT" for an opponent.
4. Challenge the players.
5. Develop the art of needling.
6. Deflate the star.

Medical aspects

Mandatory medical examinations and medical history should be taken at the beginning of each season. Physical conditioning should be proper, gradual, and complete. A physician should be present

Fig. 14-7. WINNING TRADITION. A tradition which makes each athlete play with tremendous pride and a "burning desire" to surpass previous individuals and teams at the school.

at all games and practice sessions. The team trainer, whether he is a coach or non-coach, should be adequately prepared and qualified. Insurance plans should be made available to squad members.

There should be strict enforcement of games rules. Above all, the technique of "spearing" or "goring" must be eliminated from the game of football.

Since statistics show that the majority of player injuries occur during the first 10 days of practice, extra precaution should be taken in an effort to keep injuries to a minimum. The players can help considerably by being in top condition when they report, but the coaching staff must make sure the practice field and all player protective equipment meet high standards.

Selecting talent

Classifying the talents and shortcomings of the players is one of the most important phases of organization.

Qualities to be considered include relative speed, tackling ability, range, passing talent, and blocking ability. Along with the physical qualities, *a burning desire to win* is a quality every coach is seeking in a player. Players with this will to win and competitive attitude are the players who will be at their best in the fourth quarter when a few plays will decide the outcome.

The shrewd and wise coach is able to make adjustments with his personnel to compensate for a deficiency in quality or numbers.

Fig. 14-8. FOOTBALL FILMS are essential. While college programs are able to utilize 16 mm equipment, high schools can save money by using an 8 mm camera.

Player notebook

The notebook covers the chief rules, field regulations, dressing room requirements, injury prevention, diet, daily fitness, and calisthenics. Play book material includes:

1. Formations
2. Hole-numbering
3. Pass and backfield patterns
4. Play diagrams
5. Signal calling and checking
6. Defensive manual

Pre-season team brochure

Each year on about August 1, a brochure can be sent each football candidate. This brochure is designed to acquaint everyone with the plans for the season. Some of the major things the brochure covers are:

1. Pre-exam schedule (physical exam, equipment, etc.)
2. Game and practice schedule
3. Training program, including proper diet, etc.

Program checklists

Checklists or outlines should be used in all phases of the football program. In addition to specific skills, drills, and techniques, the checklist can save valuable time in preparing daily and weekly practice schedules. Individual defensive and offensive line position lists are particularly valuable. As each assignment is accomplished, it should be checked off.

Analysis and grading

Written tests are often used by coaches in early two-a-day practice sessions, to enable the coaching staff to make sure the players understand all of their defensive assignments. The test may require a short written answer or a diagram of the correct defensive course of a given illustration.

Film grading

The most accurate method of evaluating football players, as well as coaching methods and techniques, is by grading the game films. The coach may grade the

Fig. 14-9. AN ACCURATE, up-to-date filing system, combined with an orderly, well-kept desk, can save many hours in the coach's schedule. Such aspects of coaching as scouting, film breakdown, and practice schedules can save hours of searching, rewriting, and duplicating information.

player or the player may grade himself. The film is run over and over until the coaches have graded and written down their players' scores.

Season report

The coaching staff must enjoy a friendly relationship with the administration and the faculty.

The administration should be provided with a complete report on the previous football season. The report should include:

1. Participation
2. Record
3. Success of the program
4. Failure of the program
5. Grades and attendance
6. Equipment and facilities
7. Physical condition
8. Needs
9. Comments
10. Outlook

Defensive and offensive ready sheets

After a careful study of the scouting reports and movie breakdowns, defensive ready sheets are written and diagrammed. A detailed written and illustrated defensive ready sheet is important for each defensive position.

The offensive sheets consist of a rushing sheet and a passing sheet. The coach in the press box uses his offensive ready sheet in calling down plays from the press box.

Travel policies

When traveling to out-of-town games, members of the football squad should keep in mind that they not only represent themselves but their school and community as well. Therefore, their standard of dress and appearance should be taken very seriously.

Fig. 14-10. ALL FOOTBALL STAFFS should have offensive and defensive personnel boards, with hooks and removable round tags for players' names.

Among the policies adopted by many school teams when traveling are:

1. Report ahead of scheduled time. The bus will not wait.
2. No gambling, whatsoever!
3. Do not take candy or food with you.
4. Wear a shirt and tie. Be neat, well-dressed.
5. Coaches will sit with their players on the bus.
6. Arrange in advance the meals at restaurants.
7. Members of the squad must eat and stay together.
8. Each player must take care of his own gear.
9. Be quiet on the bus going to the game.
10. Players must return with the team, unless excused by head coach.

Scouting

The more information a football team has about the opponent the greater chance there is for victory. This is why teams of all levels place considerable emphasis on the scouting phase of their organization.

When scouting a team, the individual scout must:

1. Take away the most important material he can obtain.
2. Exploit the weaknesses of the team scouted.
3. Above all, never guess.

Weekly scouting report

A scout must give a written report to the coaching staff. Normally, he will also give an oral report to the squad and an-

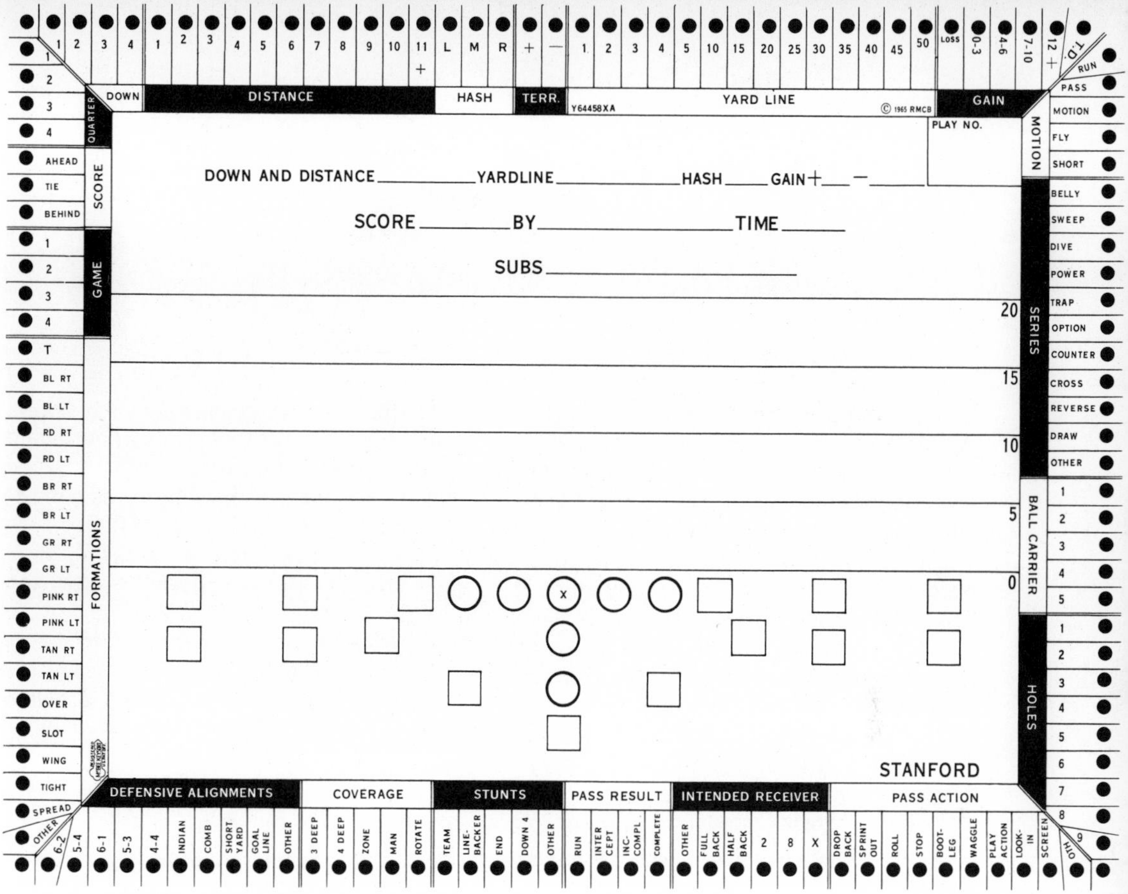

Fig. 14-11. SCOUTING CARD. This card contains the most important offensive information on one side and all defensive data on the other.

swer any questions the players may have.

The scout, if not the coach, is concerned with: transportation, film exchange, scouting materials, scouting techniques, and scouting schedules.

Movie analysis

Movie breakdowns are more accurate than scouting reports. Key-sort scouting cards are used both in film breakdowns and scouting reports.

Key-sort card scouting

This card contains all of the most important offensive information on one side and all of the defensive information on the other side. The card enables the coaching staff to gain the most important statistical tendencies of the opponent.

Fund raising

The success of football program in most high schools and colleges rests in large measure on gate receipts and money raising projects. The quality, as well as the quantity, of equipment, facilities, and program supplies is determined by how much revenue comes in. The work of booster groups, in particular, has been a huge source of income for high school and college football programs. The coaching staff can work closely with the booster club in raising money to purchase football equipment and to help pay for insurance.

Fund raising dinners have been big revenue producers for the football program. Candy sales and promotion of exhibition basketball games have also proven successful. An annual faculty-student basketball game proves a winner time after time. Many athletic booster clubs have annual membership drives which provide the club with the bulk of its revenue. Usually there is a $1.00 individual membership fee, and a minimum fee of $5.00 for commercial membership.

Weekly booster meetings during the football season prove highly popular to club members. The head coach or one of his assistants would be present to narrate the films.

Public relations

The news media provide the principal link between the football coach and the public. Therefore, it is in the best interest of the coach and his program to cooperate to the fullest extent when dealing with the press and with radio and television.

Team support, particularly of gate receipts, is directly related to the coverage of the team by the news media. Keeping the public informed and interested is the surest way to bring them out to the stadium.

In dealing with the press and radio-TV people, the football coach should:

1. Be honest, cooperative and fair.
2. Refrain from playing favorites with reporters.
3. Provide fair treatment to all media.

4. Request the availability of a sports information man who can coordinate the distribution of all news.
5. Never use the news media as a propaganda or psychological tool.
6. Admit newsmen to the dressing room just as soon as possible after the game.
7. Never expect a reporter to be a cheer leader.
8. Invite reporters to attend practice sessions and meet with them after practice.
9. Reserve the press box and camera locations for the working press.

Promoting the football program

Football organization, whether on the college or high school level, involves "selling" the values of football to the athlete, his parents, the faculty, the administration, the student body, and the community. The idea that "football is a very worthwhile endeavor" must be promoted to the fullest.

A football coach has to be a salesman. He must not only sell himself but the sport as well. Therefore, he should welcome the opportunity to speak to almost any group on his program.

The following techniques should be considered by the football coach in promoting his program:

1. Send out weekly news releases containing information on the progress of the team.
2. Information brochures should be distributed to the news media and to opposing schools.
3. Inform the parents about what their

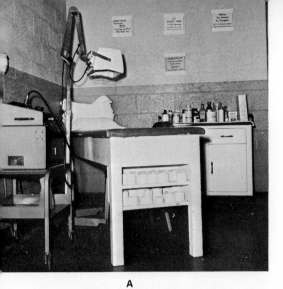

A

B

Fig. 14-12. THE TRAINING ROOM should be located near the locker room, but used only for treatment of injuries. Whirlpool baths, like those shown here, are excellent for heat and massage at the same time.

sons are doing. Write to the prospects and parents. Arrange home visitations.

4. Organize a booster organization. They can play a significant role in success of the football program.

5. Have the Quarterback Club meet at lunch every Monday during the season. They can hear a report from the coach and replay the football game. Invite members of the team to a post-season special luncheon.

6. *Encourage a strong contribution from the cheerleaders.* They have their own effective gimmicks for promoting team spirit and getting the team up for the game. Besides leading the cheers, the song girls spend considerable time painting pep signs and organizing the pep rallies.

7. Hold an annual awards banquet, highlighted by a presentation of a "hardnose" award to the most deserving player. In addition, awards can be given to seniors for the following honors: most improved, most spirited, most coachable, best offensive back, best defensive back, and best defensive lineman.

8. Have clinics conducted by college mentors. Clinics can be a key factor in improving the style of play.

9. Encourage the players to watch college and professional contests, either in person or via TV.

Facilities

Proper facilities should go along with a good football program. If the team is to play in big league fashion, the coaching staff should provide facilities that are as near top caliber as financial assets and ingenuity will allow. Office facilities should include a sound filming system and other administrative methods of procedure.

Football is such a complicated game that three or four different practice areas must be run at the same time. All in all, the practice site should be large enough to facilitate five large areas where the following groups drill:

1. Defensive backs
2. Offensive backs
3. Defensive linemen
4. Offensive linemen
5. Quarterbacks and receivers

377

A

Fig. 14-13. KEEP THE LOCKER ROOM NEAT! This is everyone's responsibility. Players should use the containers when removing tape and mud. There should be no fooling around in the locker room. Horseplay has caused many injuries.

The development and construction of a training room for the treatment of injuries, a weight training room and an Exer-Genie area will provide the physical conditioning necessary for championship play. Equipment and locker room facilities should meet good standards of operation.

Building a farm system

Winning high school teams, typically, are blessed with a successful feeder or farm system. To be successful, the high school program must have an organized feeder system. This applies to "Pop Warner" or a midget league, and touch or flag football programs at the lower levels.

Ideally, the entire football system of the city or community should be under the direction and leadership of the head football coach at the high school. This enables everyone to teach the same method. The junior high school players are oriented at an early age to the varsity system. The sophomore team plays a full schedule, and those junior and seniors who do not make the varsity play a full schedule against the smaller high schools.

A typical feeder program begins with touch football in the fifth and sixth grades. Tackle teams start with each seventh grade room and each eighth grade section. Pop Warner and other little league tackle football programs have accelerated rapidly across the nation.

Off-Season Programs

High school football players, generally, participate in other sports, depending on

Fig. 14-14. BUILDING A FEEDER SYSTEM. Almost all winning high school coaches have a successful feeder or farm system, whether it is "Pop Warner" or a midget league program at the lower levels.

the size of the school and the skills and talents of the players. Good track participation can be a major factor in the success of a high school football team. College players, though, usually confine their participation to just one sport.

The easiest way for a football player to cut short his gridiron career is to be lazy during the off-season and become soft and out of shape. The task of returning to tip-top condition is not always easy.

Most schools have some form of concentrated physical fitness program during the off-season (including summer months). Specific regulations, however, forbid the playing or coaching of football at any level of a school program. This does not mean

that squad members cannot get together for workouts, particularly the passing and receiving combinations. Players should be told what fundamentals, skills, and patterns to work on as a group during the off-season. Footballs should be issued to quarterbacks and kicking candidates for individual use.

Strength is a prime objective in any off-season conditioning program. The program usually consists of weight lifting, rope skipping, the Exer-Genie program, (which includes isometric exercises for the neck). The Exer-genie program has been of significant value in limiting the number of injuries and in keeping strength at a maximum, particularly during the third and fourth quarters of the game. Weights and the Exer-genie system are a great combination.

In addition to considerable running, good off-season activities are handball, basketball, badminton, paddleball, soccer, volleyball, and speedball.

A sound program of exercises could include:

1. Neck conditioning
2. Knee exercises
3. Regular push-ups
4. Mountain climber
5. Hurdler's spread position
6. Squat jump position
7. Sit-up position
8. Chin and record

A typical conditioning program

December 1   Team members are measured and tested.

January to April Weight training and Exer-genie exercises three times a week; conditioning and agility program twice a week.

April to July 15 In addition to the January to April program, running takes place two times per week.

July 15 to the start of season   Conduct isometrics, conditioning, agility drills, and running (five times a week.) Sprint for time (speed development): one 440 yard dash; sprint 20 yards, walk 20 yards for 100 yards (three times a week).

Physical fitness test

Prior to the first practice session, a test is conducted which consists of:

1. Sit-ups
2. Push-ups
3. Pull-ups
4. 40-yard dash
5. 100-yard dash
6. 440-yard dash

All candidates are checked on their ability with the weights, and comparison is made with their efforts in March. Isometric exercises with the Exer-genie are continued during the season.

Post-season brochure

A brochure made up by the staff can be distributed to all football candidates, and includes:

1. Statistics from the season just completed
2. Returnees for the upcoming football season
3. The upcoming schedule
4. Tips on growth and development
5. A three-part conditioning program

Study tips

Off-season preparation also involves checking on grades, hitting the books, and making certain that prospects are eligible for participation in football in the fall. Most low and failing grades are due to one or more of the following reasons:

1. Failure to study
2. Careless, sloppy, incomplete or late homework assignments

3. Goofing off, inattention in class
4. Failure to grasp or understand class material

Organizational Calendar

June

1. Check players' final grades
2. Write out and run off six-week weight and running exercises
3. Check the film trading agreements
4. Follow up on summer clinic reservations
5. Re-evaluate entire spring football program
6. Make out summer assignments for staff members

July

1. Attend football clinics (two weeks)
2. Send for college films
3. Review fall teaching schedule and organize office hours
4. Evaluate pass defense
5. Check with grounds keepers about new turf and plans for game and practice field

August

1. Finish running off defensive alignments and stunts
2. Re-evaluate and finish viewing various college films
3. Prepare checklist for basic attack and practice schedules
4. Work on players' notebooks and finalize basic offensive attack

5. Meet with student trainers and football managers
6. Request transportation for scouting
7. Check on pre-season football scrimmage date
8. Organize detailed practice schedules
9. Conduct pre-season staff meetings

September

1. During first week, evaluate, rate, and discuss football personnel
2. Formalize game plans for the first game
3. Obtain films of opponent's games
4. Keep master scouting plan up to date
5. Work on the kicking game

Offensive Football

The football coach should try to fit his system to his personnel. Ideally, the personnel should dictate the offense; during the pre-season training program, the coaching staff must find the basic offense the team is most capable of running. The type of quarterback will often determine the style of offense.

To be successful, an offensive attack must have balance and be able to run effectively, inside and outside. The quarterback must be capable of throwing short and long; if he can run, he will be an even greater asset to his team. The quarterback option, although risky and time consuming to train, is most difficult to defend against.

Current offenses feature wide flankers, split ends, slot backs, overloaded formations, and many other alignments. An offense may have their ends tight or split, or a combination of the two. In an effort to split the defense, a growing number of teams are employing multiple offenses, although the multiple theory has been more in use on the college level. Once the basic alignments and the main formation have been decided, the coaching staff should establish the sweeps, power plays, dives, counters, and traps of the running game. It should be kept in mind, though, that it is better to run a few plays well than to run many plays poorly.

High school

With the increasing popularity of Pro football, there is a trend among high school teams to employ wide-open formations which involve many passes. Many high school teams have been successful with the Pro-set and Pro-slot formations, with some modifications. The split wing-T formation has been bolstered by the use of split ends and flanker backs.

The Power "T" has been one of the most prominent offensive sets used by high schools in Ohio, relying heavily on power off-tackle and power sweep plays.

The Power "I" series of double-team blocking involving numerous pulling linemen and leading backs has become a popular offense in both high school and college football.

The "I" formation, with the single split end with the slot, or a wide flanker and split end, has been used successfully, also. While the "I" offense is simple and effective, it does require specific talent which

colleges can recruit but the high schools cannot. The "I" calls for a quarterback who has outstanding ability, running and passing.

Since few teams on the high school and college levels are blessed with the strong armed drop-back type passer, the sprint-out pass should be considered. A fair passer with some running ability can make the sprint-out a potent weapon of the offense. The sprint-out pass is particularly effective when used from the "I" formation.

College

The offensive system used most prominently on the college level in the 1960's was the "I" offense and its variations employed by U.S.C., Indiana, San Diego, Oklahoma, and others. The "I" has proven highly effective in attacking the odd-front, "monster"-type defense which has been so effective in college football. The "I" backfield alignment with a roving wing back offers a multitude of advantages.

San Diego took a single-wing type of football and made it "I" formation football. Their offense requires a tailback with great speed. Indiana has used the "I" offense exceptionally well, utilizing the quarterback run-out option, the off-tackle play, and sprint and roll. Their offense is geared to the outside. They run very few plays (about six running plays), but strive for flawless execution with these. The fullback's running play consists of a direct hand-off, and he "runs to daylight."

Michigan State also works from the "I" formation, featuring pitch sweeps and options. They also run a lot from the slot formation, featuring the lead dive and the sprint-out. A favorite play of the Spartans is a power draw. Their best counter is a fake option, slot counter. Teams pursue so quickly on defense today that the offense has to have counters to try to slow them down.

As an example of their highly diversified attack, MSU runs six types of passes: 1) fake option, 2) belly action, 3) bootleg action, 4) sprint-out option, 5) pitch sweep, 6) the drop-back.

More and more, the offensive thinking of college teams is becoming more aligned with the Pros. Such teams as Stanford, San Francisco State and Florida State have gone to the Pro style of attack. The offense gives three receivers to one side and two on the other side. In this way they are capable of getting five receivers out any time they want.

The Pros, having had such great success with the forward pass, have been largely influential in leading teams on the college and high school levels to become great advocates of the pass. As a note of caution, however, it must be realized that the college and high school offenses will never be able to do quite as much with their Pro offenses. During practice, if they cannot complete the pass 9 out of 10 times against no defense, they should not go into the drop-back passing game.

The Power I and Triangle I offenses used by Oregon State and Ohio State are all versions of the Full House which is coming back in popularity. More teams are beginning to run with tight lines again.

The Power "I" series has been as effective with colleges as it has with high schools. The Flip series has been designed to complement the Power "I" formation by adding much needed deception, thus destroying defensive pursuit.

The Power "T", with the off-tackle and sweep plays, has been a potent attack for many collegiate teams. The inside and outside belly series, traps and counters make a fine ball control offense.

Offensive Systems

The following systems have met with much success recently.

The "I" offense (Diagram 14-1).

While the "I" offense has many variations, the play which USC uses so effectively is the off-tackle play to the back going to one side or the other. This play has the quarterback executing a deep reverse pivot, and the tailback either takes one step or three steps, and he runs off-tackle. The fullback will block the end out. Also used successfully is the pitch to the tailback, or a fake of that play and the quarterback will run out.

San Diego runs well the old fashioned off-tackle single wing play where they pull the offensive guard and tackle. With the fullback leading, the quarterback hands off and he will run some type of fake. They will use the drop-back pass or they may fake the pass.

In running the power off-tackle play, the quarterback will fake, and he will run

SYMBOLS OF DEFENSIVE PERSONNEL

△ Rushmen or defensive men (in 3-point stance)

□ Linebackers

/S\ Deep Backs Inside (Safetys)

/C\ Corner Backs (H for halfbacks
is sometimes used)

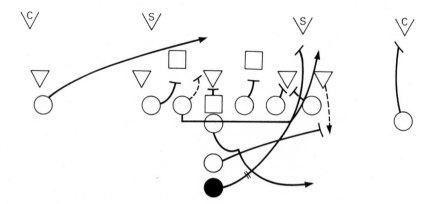

Diagram 14-1. The I Offense (power off-tackle
against Oklahoma defense).

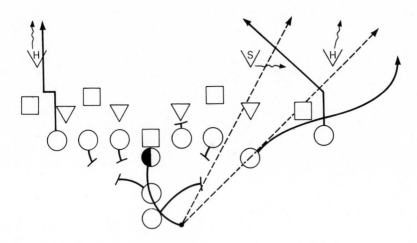

Diagram 14-2. Slot I Formation (hitting the split end and slot back). (Against 4-4 defense)

outside, giving an outside version of a belly fake. Placing strong pressure on the corner, he will either throw or run from that type of play.

The Power "I" series, involving pulling linemen and leading backs, includes the following plays:

1. Fullback trap up the middle
2. Tailback power off-tackle
3. Halfback pitch-out around end
4. Quarterback faking and varied pass patterns

The Slot "I" formation has proven to be an effective offense against the man-to-man defense (Diagram 14-2). Among the methods of attacking the defense are strong side patterns, isolation of line-backers, throwing to the weak side and

three-men combinations away from the split end. The quarterback should be taught to hit the split end and the slot back repeatedly with individual pass routes.

Triple option (Diagram 14-3).

The "Triple Option" used by Houston utilizes the split backs, with the backs stationed right behind the guards. The half-back, on the side the ball is going, will hit right outside or in the gap between the guard and the tackle. The offensive tackle will step down to the inside and block the linebacker. The guard will either help and double on the linebacker, or he will block the nose man to prevent the slant defense.

The quarterback tries to read the man outside the tackle. If the man's helmet comes inside, then he will fake the dive

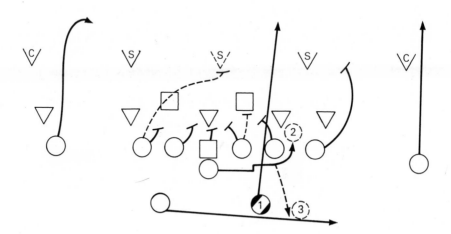

Diagram 14-3. Triple Option (against Oklahoma defense).

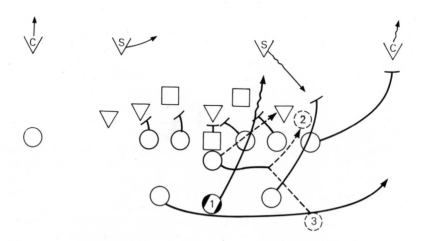

Diagram 14-4. Texas Option (from a "Y" formation). (Against Oklahoma defense)

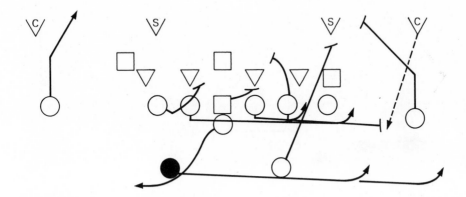

Diagram 14-5. Pro Offense (Green Bay Sweep).
(Against Pro 4-3 defense)

and run an option. If the man's helmet comes outside, then they will give the ball to the man running the dive. If the quarterback keeps the ball, he has the option to run or pitch to the trailing back.

An offensive force which has been infringing on the "I" is the "Triple option" used by Houston, utilizing the split backs. Although the Triple Option can fool a lot of people, it involves considerably more time to perfect than some people think. The quarterback must be able to read the tackle quickly and also pick the back up without fumbling. Texas has run the Triple Option from the "Y" or "Full House" backfield (Diagram 14-4).

Pro offense (Diagrams 14-5 and 14-6).

Pro type plays are run from the Pro-set. The backfield is split or divided with wide receivers out to both sides. The split end and flanker forces the defense to spread.

The conventional Pro plays can be run from the Pro-slot and Pro spread formations. The Pro slot formation has the split end still spread, and the flanker is in the wide slot position. The linemen are about two feet apart.

Basically, the Pro offense has the tight end split in order not to be pinched in when he wants to release for the forward pass. He can isolate the man defending against him so he can get a one-on-one block.

With the two wide outs, the Pro style offense can run such plays as the Green Bay Sweep (Diagram 14-5), the Isolation play, off-tackle play (Diagram 14-6), the quick trap (Diagram 14-7), and the quick toss to either side. The Pros' "bread and butter" play against the Pro defense, of course, is the Green Bay Sweep.

On the Green Bay sweep, the guards will pull, and the runner will cut off the

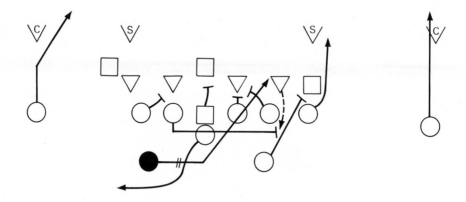

Diagram 14-6. Pro Offense (Off-tackle play).
(Against Pro 4-3 defense)

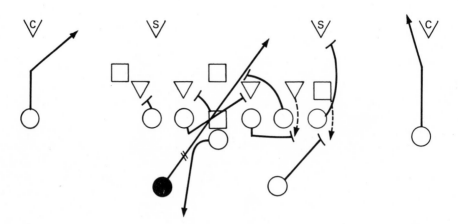

Diagram 14-7. Pro Offense (Quick Trap play).
(Against Pro 4-3 defense)

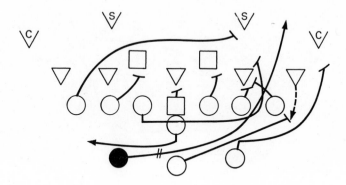

Diagram 14-8. Power T (Off-tackle play). (Against Oklahoma defense)

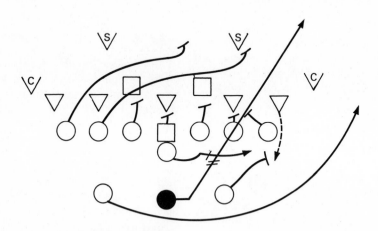

Diagram 14-9. Power T (Outside Belly series). (Against Oklahoma defense)

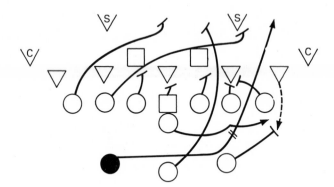

Diagram 14-10. Power T (Inside Belly series). (Against Oklahoma defense)

block of the tight end, a "Daylight Play". The split back to the tight end side will block the inside safety because the guard now is going to block the contained man.

The quarterback will give to his back and fake the bootleg action. This play is effective because the split end is able to release more effectively for the forward pass.

Full House (Diagram 14-13).

The Full House is coming back in full strength. Some teams really move the Full House around, with different offensive sets. Some will move one man and put him behind the fullback to a "Power I" set. They will place one of the ends and put him on the other side and have an unbalanced line.

Favorite plays off the Full House (meaning a full backfield) are the off-tackle plays, sweeping the wide side, bootleg into the wide side, quickie pass, and hook and flat pass.

Power "T" offense (Diagrams 14-8, 14-9, 14-10).

The Power T relies strongly on power off-tackle and power sweep plays. The inside and outside belly series, traps and counters makes it a good ground gaining attack.

The passing game features action passes, bootleg passes, sprint and rollouts, and pocket passes. A change-up in the backfield alignment, split end variations, and man-in-motion provide variety to the basic plays of the Power T.

Slot "T" offense (Diagram 14-14).

A power off-tackle play is a favorite play to the slot side of the Slot T. The offense

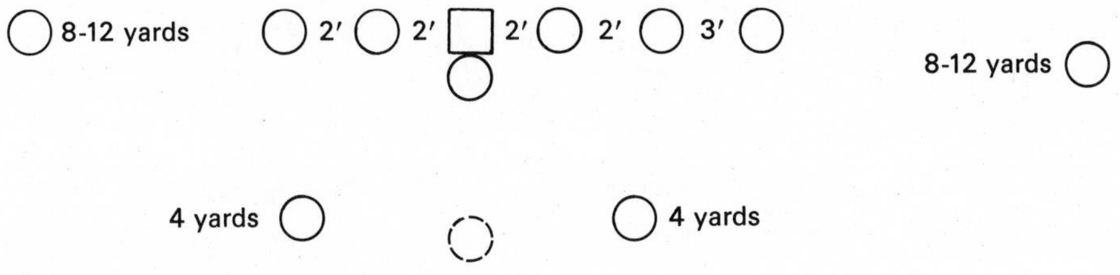

Diagram 14-11. Pro-Set.

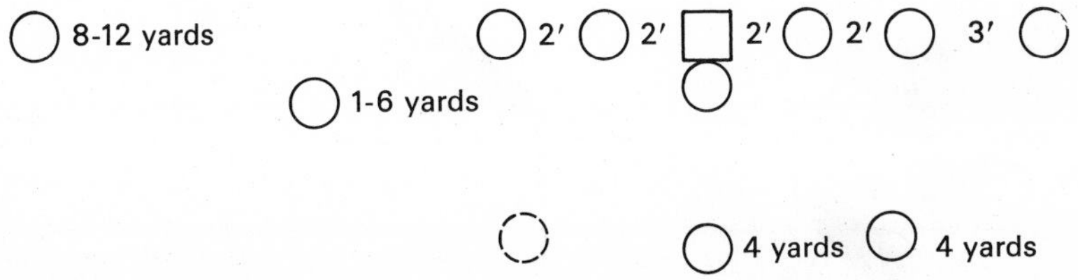

(diagram: 8-12 yards ○   ○ 2′ ○ 2′ □ 2′ ○ 2′ ○ 3′ ○   8-12 yards ○   4 yards ○   ○   ○ 4 yards)

Diagram 14-12. Pro-Slot.

(diagram: 8-12 yards ○   ○ 1-6 yards   ○ 2′ ○ 2′ □ 2′ ○ 2′ ○ 3′ ○   ○   ○ 4 yards ○ 4 yards)

can flip-flop either way. From the wide Slot T, three basic plays are utilized:

1. Sprint-out run or pass.
2. The belly series to the remaining back's side with the slot back in motion.
3. An off-tackle or sweep play off a split or cross-buck faking action in the backfield.

The double slot formation features wide flankers to each side and halfbacks in the slots on each side (Diagram 14-15). Either slot back can be in motion.

Passing Attack

With increased emphasis on the passing game, colleges and high schools now employ as many as 10 or 12 different pass patterns, in addition to their many variations (Diagram 14-16). To fully exploit all types of defensive secondaries, a short release man and a deep receiver are involved in all the patterns. The short release man can exploit the red dogging linebackers of the defense. They also leave vital short

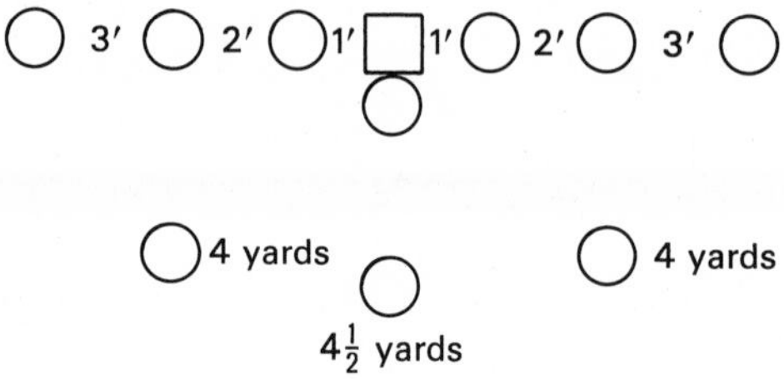

◯ 3' ◯ 2' ◯1'☐1' ◯ 2' ◯ 3' ◯
                   ◯

◯ 4 yards   ◯ 4 yards
        ◯
    4½ yards

Diagram 14-13. Full House Formation.

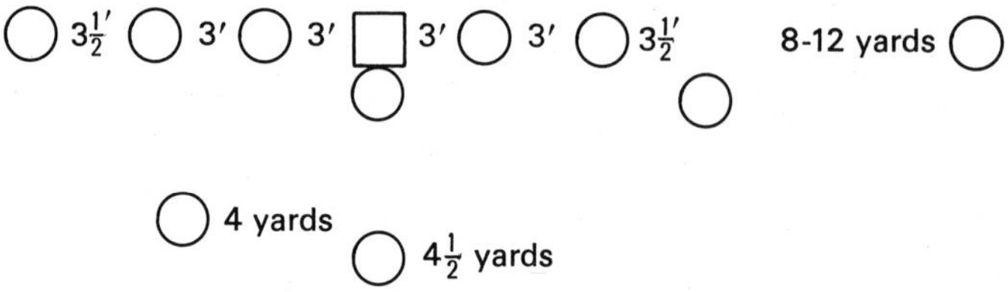

◯ 3½' ◯ 3' ◯ 3' ☐ 3' ◯ 3' ◯ 3½'   8-12 yards ◯
                    ◯

◯ 4 yards
          ◯ 4½ yards

Diagram 14-14. Slot T Formation.

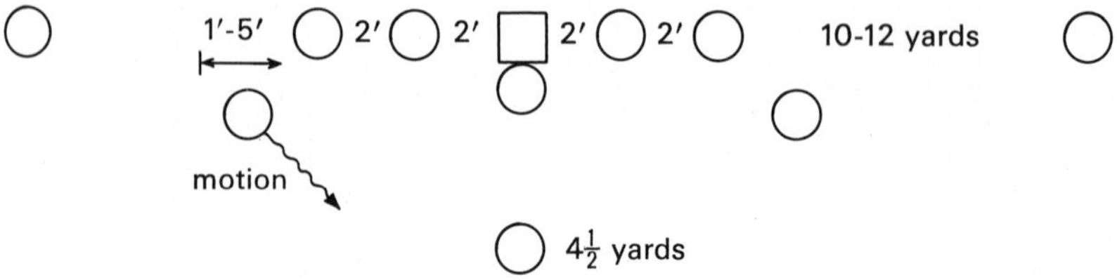

◯   1'-5' ◯ 2' ◯ 2' ☐ 2' ◯ 2' ◯   10-12 yards   ◯
        ├──→   ◯

◯
motion ⤳↘

                    ◯ 4½ yards

Diagram 14-15. Double Slot T formation.

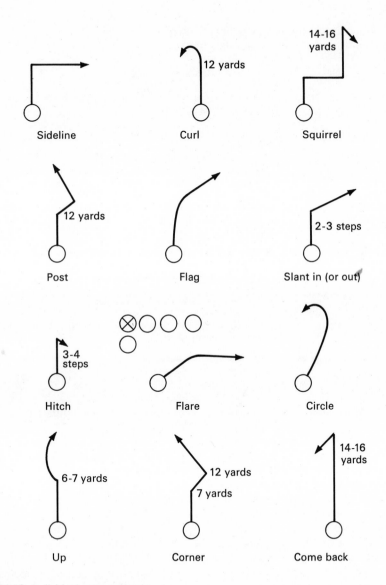

Diagram 14-16. Individual pass patterns.

Individual patterns run by most college
and high school teams (Diagram 14-16) are:

1. SIDELINE	an "out" pattern of 12 yards.
2. CURL (or Strike)	the receiver comes down hard, turns in on his curl and receives a bullet pass.
3. SQUIRREL	faking the quick "out" and breaking back up, and breaking out again at 15 yards.
4. POST	receiver breaks down for approximately 12 yards, fakes to the outside and breaks to the goal post.
5. FLAG	drives to inside of defensive man as if running "Deep Slant" or "Curl". Then drives off inside foot to corner.
6. SLANT (in or out)	cutting off the outside foot, the receiver makes his break quick and sharp, in a slanting angle.
7. HITCH	a quick pass to an outside receiver.
8. FLARE	a swing out by a back into the flat.
9. CIRCLE	breaking right off tackle and swinging back up into the linebacking area.
10. DOWN AND OUT	a pattern by the backs.

pass zones open, such as the flat, hook, and curl zones.

Most college patterns are built on the flood basis, primarily because most college teams are still predominately and primarily zone teams. The high schools employ pretty much the same tactics. By forcing the deep man to cover deep, they have the underneath man practically open.

Many teams have been successful in building a set of patterns for man-to-man and another set for the zone. They run a crossing pattern and a pick pattern against a man-to-man defense. Against a zone

operation, they will employ a flood kind of pattern.

The passing game is divided up into three areas:

1. *Drop-back action.* The quarterback moves straight back behind the guards. This action requires more protection.
2. *Half-roll action. The quarterback* simply rolls out to the position called, from the guard area to the end area. If the quarterback rolls out to the

"7" position, for example, the line will block to that.

3. *Full roll action.* The quarterback rolls out wide to the outside area.

Favorite patterns

Many coaches feel the curl is the best pattern a college team can run. The sideline also ranks high as an effective route for a receiver. The sideline and up, a deep pattern calling for tremendous speed, and the flag are also popular. Perhaps, the most successful pattern in the sprint-out pass is the halfback flare.

Combination routes can be worked successfully with the tight end. One man might be sent deep while the tight end is brought shallow across under him.

Defensive Football

No single type of defense in football can stop every running and passing play. This is particularly true in this present era of multiple offenses. Therefore, to cope with the multiple offense theory, the defense finds it necessary to adopt a basic multiple approach of their own, including several alignments and adjustments.

The multiple theory involves changing defensive fronts before the ball is snapped and after the ball is snapped. These moves are basic and the rules are simple enough so that high school teams as well as college elevens may apply the multiple theory to their defensive football system.

Actually, the basic alignment employed by the defense is secondary to the indi-

vidual qualities of the players. A group of smart, quick, tough, aggressive, determined football players can make any defense work.

College and high school coaches, like the professionals on Sunday, are teaching their people to ATTACK on defense, to force the issue and make something happen. We have been using this philosophy since 1948. They want their defensive team to think aggressively, to be savage and ruthless when tackling. They want them to attack by stunting, looping, and—on occasion—blitzing. The defense must always be thinking positive—to get that ball!

High school

High school teams can get the best results through simplicity, by avoiding highly involved combinations on slants, pinches, red dogs, loops, and other stunts. Assignments must be kept as simple as possible so that players have a complete understanding and can concentrate on coverage and interceptions.

Indecision must be eliminated from football! A player is more likely to react quickly if he has less thinking to do. Stunting, particularly, is a difficult phase to chart in advance. Keys and rotations require an enormous amount of time.

Against the Split "T", the Notre Dame defense is an excellent high school defense because its primary objective is to stop the run. Generally, high school teams have more kids who can run than can throw.

More and more high school teams are employing the professional 4-3 formation scaled to their personnel and requirements. The chief concern of the coaching staff is to make the 4-3 stronger against the running game. A secondary defender can be brought inside, changing the 4-3 to a split 6. A regular practice is to use 4-3 as a combination with many other defenses. This would be my recommendation.

The Monster 50 defense is still popular in some areas of the country, although the trend is moving away from it to the Notre Dame defense. The 50 defense is an unbalanced defense which is used against strong sets, unbalanced line or teams with unusually strong running tendencies. This defense has proven successful against the ''I'' formation, and it has been good as a short yardage defense. This defense involves a gap charge and may utilize a zone or man-for-man coverage.

The Split-6 type of defense has achieved much prominence with high school teams over the past five years. The alignment used most places the linebackers inside of, or stacked behind, the rushmen who are aligned in front of the offensive guards.

The Oklahoma defense is still one of the most popular types of defense employed on the high school and college levels. Perhaps, it is even more popular today because people can play 4 deep which makes it effective against the forward pass.

Since most high school teams do not have great big people, they must play a more diversified type of end play. While the play of the linebackers and the deep secondary is basically the same, the end and tackle play is changed in order to: 1) split the option; 2) stop the off-tackle play; 3) stop the ''sprint and roll''.

The most difficult play to defense is the option. Therefore, the defense must get

enough flexibility in their end play to be able to switch up and change their play at the corner.

College

The basic defenses commonly employed today on the college level are the Oklahoma 5-2, Monster 50, Pro defense, Notre Dame 4-4, and the Split-6. In this era of multiple offenses, many college defenses have adopted in one form or another a theory of multiplicity within a simple framework of defense.

Any defense can be given a basic multiple approach, either by stacking men in a gap, shifting and sliding them to one side or the other (Diagram 14-17). Basically, the linemen and linebackers are trying to do the same thing, except they are being moved around a little. Play after play, most coaches rarely set the same defense.

College and high school linemen are using various Pro techniques and maneuvers. Some linemen will vary the depth that the man will play off the ball, either playing tight on the ball and attacking or playing off the ball and reading.

Team stunts can be essential to a successful college defense. Stunts such as looping and slanting enable the defense to get an effective pass rush. Commonly used against bigger people, the stunts are very simple and can be implemented without changing from the regular defensive alignment. The slant, popular in the Arkansas kind of defense, involves running at an angle, while looping is stepping laterally.

If a team has big, strong defensive tackles, the Notre Dame defense can give good versatility. These two big tackles,

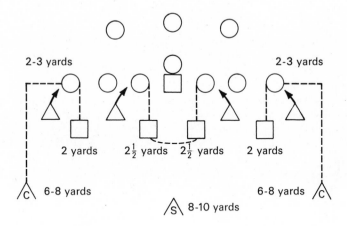

Diagram 14-17. Notre Dame 4-4 Defense.

from a pinched position, must come hard through the outside shoulder of the offensive guards. The ends play a crashing game, and a standard three-deep secondary may be used.

The Pro 4-3 formation, along with the 4-4 and 4-5 defensive alignments, has been gaining increased use throughout the country. Various college coaches have been able to adapt the Pro defenses effectively to their requirements, particularly to make it mutliple enough to attack the run and the pass.

Because of its flexibility and consistency, the Arkansas Monster 50 defense compares favorably with many other popular defenses. Because of this, it is regarded as an excellent field position defense.

The Oklahoma 5-2 defense, for years one of football's favorite defensive alignments, is still popular today because of its effectiveness against the forward pass. The 5-4 version of the Oklahoma defense is stronger against the running game.

Since many high school and college coaches feel they are not able to compete with their opponents on a man-to-man basis, they commit themselves to the zone defense. Even though a team may play a strictly zone defense, however, it should understand man-to-man techniques. As was noted previously, more high schools and colleges are employing man-for-man coverage in an effort to combat the growing versatility of the pass patterns and the spread alignments.

Defensive Systems

The following defensive systems should be considered.

Notre Dame defense (Diagram 14-17).

The Notre Dame 4-4 defense gives good versatility, but unless a team has big strong defensive tackles playing on the outside shoulder of the offensive guards, their

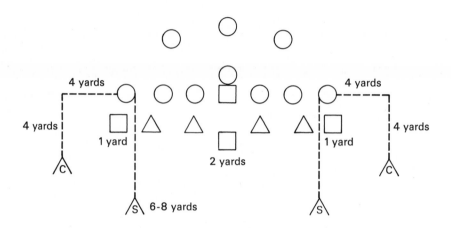

Diagram 14-18. The Pro 4-3 Defense.

"pinched-in" position is not as effective as playing a man straight up where he can move outside more effectively.

In a pinched-in position, the defensive tackles are often not big and strong enough to withstand the block of the tackle coming down, and they end up in a caved-in position. Therefore, when using the Notre Dame defense, a smaller man could play straight up so he can react to either man more effectively.

The "front four" men, the tackles and the ends, come hard all the time. The two outside linebackers will play on the inside shoulder of the tight end. The outside linebacker to a split end side can line up in varied position. The two inside linebackers play inside the legs of the defensive tackles, while the secondary will be in a three-deep alignment.

While the Notre Dame defense is in better position to trail the guard pulling

across the center and to kill the short trap, their pursuit to the outside is not as good.

Pro 4-3 (Diagram 14-18).

In the Pro 4-3, the tackles must possess quickness and durability, in addition to size and toughness. The ends should have good height and lateral movement. The linebackers should be sound thinkers with the ability to read the play. The cornerbacks and halfbacks should have height and good lateral and backward movement.

In employing the Pro 4-3, a four-point standard should be used:

1. Protection against the wide running game
2. Protection from tackle to tackle against traps, quickies, and power plays
3. Provide a defensive man in all possible passing areas

4. Apply constant pressure on the quarterback on passing situations

As many as five different stunts are used with this defense. On all plays, the Front Four "blows" across the line one yard and

pursues the football. On these stunts, the defense should try to get different movement from the linemen and linebackers. The Pro defense features a four-deep coverage allowing their men to rotate to either side.

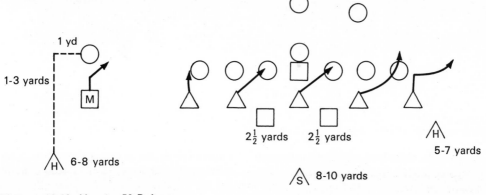

Diagram 14-19. Monster 50 Defense.

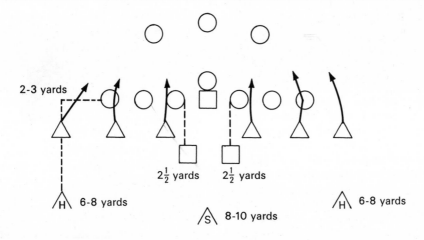

Diagram 14-20. Split-6 Defense.

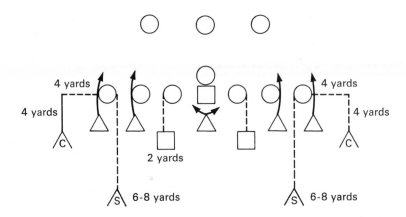

Diagram 14-21. Oklahoma 5-2 Defense.

Arkansas Monster (Diagram 14-19).

The Monster defense receives its name from the adjustment of one defensive man to the strength of the offensive alignment or to the wide side of the field. A team will line up in an unbalanced front but will slant and loop back to a balanced front.

The basic Monster 50 defense consists of two main parts, the forcing unit and the containing unit. Five main variations may be employed.

1. The odd-front monster
2. The wide tackle SIX
3. The 6-1-4
4. The 27-Front
5. The Monster Stack and 4-4 Stack

Split-6 (Diagram 14-20).

The rushmen, the four interior men, can charge through the four interior gaps in the offensive line, thereby creating a gap-8

defense with hard penetration. Or, they can play it straight and make it difficult for the blockers to get to the linebackers with a gap-8 blocking scheme. The split 6's may be divided into either the 4-4 or the true 6.

Oklahoma defense (Diagram 14-21).

With increasing emphasis on the passing game, many teams have gone more to the Oklahoma 5-2 alignment, which is also strong against the inside running game.

The 5-4 version of the Oklahoma defense is stronger against the running game. Inside linebackers in the Oklahoma set-up cannot cover the flats very well since they cannot get out fast enough. Since many teams do not use the option well, they are probably wise in using the Okie defense.

4-4 defense (Diagram 14-22).

A 4-4 alignment can be used with the linebacker and linemen units on each side,

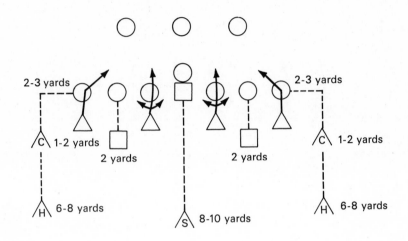

Diagram 14-22. The 4-4 Defense.

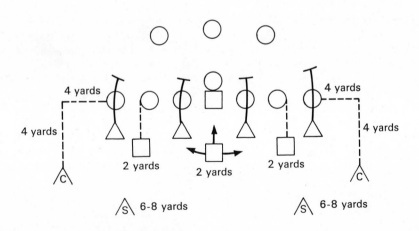

Diagram 14-23. Pro 4-5 Defense (against basic alignment).

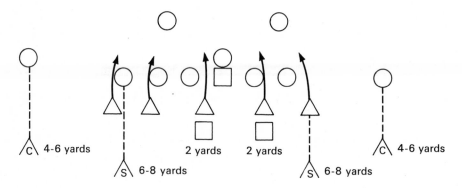

Diagram 14-24. Stack Defense (toward the offensive strength).

operating independently. It is used almost exclusively in long yardage and passing situations.

The Pro 4-5 (Diagram 14-23).

A basic defense, the 4-5-2 provides a four-man front, with five linebackers, and two safeties. The four-man pass rush can be remedied by stunting with linebackers and safeties. This defense is vulnerable to an offensive alignment which can release two receivers quickly to one side.

Group leaders in each segment will give a signal indicating the alignment and the stunt to be used. Besides the calls by the two group leaders in the line and linebacking segments, one of the backs will make a verbal call that will indicate the alignment and play of the three defensive backs, such as "Rover," "Green," and "Blue."

Pass Defense

While pass defense in the National Football League is basically all man-to-man, with some zone variations, college and high school teams generally teach their defensive secondary to play a zone defense. They want their players to cover an area instead of a man. There is a trend, however, towards an increase in man-to-man coverage.

The key to successful pass defense is simple—rush the passer. Three methods which are often used to stop a passing attack are:

1. Blitz and pressure the passer with an all-out rush
2. Delay and knock-off the intended receiver

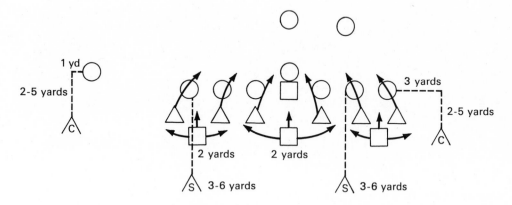

Diagram 14-25. The 6-5 Goal Line Defense.

3. Maximum coverage with a minimum rush

The pass defense of most teams is a combination of zone, man-for-man, change, or a combination of these secondary calls.

A pass defender must be taught to be tough when going for the ball. A good philosophy for him to keep in mind should be: 'Whenever the ball is in the air, it's ours."

Red Dog

The red dog, or blitz, is probably used more on the high school level, than on the college level. The blitz is not used to a great extent in college football because most of the teams do not use a drop-back pass. It is difficult for a linebacker to zero in on a quarterback if he does not know what side he is going to.

The colleges will blitz more on a half-line basis than on a full-line because of the great running ability of some quarterbacks.

Goal line defense (Diagram 14-25).

The best deep goal line defense is what everybody on the college level calls the 6-5. Behind the six men on the line are two linebackers and the outside backers.

Man-for-man coverage is commonly used whenever the goal line defense is called, or as soon as the opposition reaches the fifteen yard line.

Epilogue

As a football coach, I live by three general principles. The first is that the difference between success and failure is so small it can't be perceived by most people. This being the case, a loser is a man who is not prepared and who doesn't know he's unprepared. A winner is a man who consciously does everything he can think of to prepare himself as completely as possible. When the difference between winning and losing is imperceptible, the winner, in a word, is the man who is ready to win.

My second principle is that one must accomplish to live. The winner is the only individual who is truly alive.

The third principle is summed up in a four-letter word: work.

Taking last things first, work is simply a synonym for effort. And as I tell my players, a 100 percent effort is not enough. The world belongs to those who aim for 110 percent, and the reason for this is that almost everybody thinks he works hard. The average American pictures himself as an extremely hard worker. Sociologists and psychologists have shown, however, that most persons are really operating on less than half power. In terms of effort, they may never get over 50 percent although they think of themselves as 90 percent producers. Therefore, to get 100, you must aim for 110.

Those who think of their work goal on the level of 110 percent are persons who put leisure time into its proper perspective. To me, leisure time consists of the five or six hours each night when one is asleep. The human body was designed to

be completely regenerated on a few hours of good sound sleep. Waking hours tend to be wasted when put to leisure purposes. I don't demand, of course, that everyone in my organization work seventeen or eighteen hours a day the year around. But I have found that a man who is concerned with an eight-hour day never works that long and seldom works half that long. The same man, however, when challenged by a seventeen-hour day, will just be warmed up and driving when he hits the eighth hour. Good things don't just happen to most men. You have to make them happen. What you're after, of course, is achieving at the maximum of your ability. But no man in all of human history has ever reached his maximum if he knew ahead of time what that was.

One final point on this subject of effort: I never expect anyone to do more than I do. Long ago I learned that regardless of how little or how much a football coach works, most of those with whom he is associated will work a little less. I have known football coaches who made it a point never to work after dinner. And in each instance, their assistants made the same point. A man's work habits, are set by his boss.

My second principle is the one I feel the most deeply about: Winning is fun—and, therefore, everything I do that makes winning more likely is fun. I strongly believe that no man alive is truly alive unless he is accomplishing something. I can see no difference between a chair and the man who sits in the chair if he is not accomplishing. And I don't ask that this

man accomplish the Presidency of the United States, or peace for all time, or even the total elimination of smog in California—much as I admire those who do have such goals and strive toward them. What I'm saying is that it is irrelevant whether a man is accomplishing greatly so long as he is accomplishing. In fact, the greatest man in the world, in my opinion, is the man who can take an average job and make something of it. That guy is living, he's having fun, he's enjoying his human birthright to the fullest—and that's the guy I love.

You have to take pride in your accomplishments in order to accomplish fully. The man who manufactures an automobile but takes no pride in the finished product is a man who didn't make a very good automobile. I also feel that stick-to-it-iveness is vital in this regard. I want football players who set achievable goals, who so dedicate themselves that they can't be swerved from their accomplishments and who, when they get there, take great pride in having got there. Such players are very hard to beat even when the football, as some people say, bounces funny. I believe that nothing is impossible to those who are willing to pay the price and I believe that paying the price is in itself an enjoyable part of reaching one's goals.

One final point on this subject of living: I believe that any group of athletes who are willing to accept less than the best will end up with less than the best. If they are willing to accept a season in which they win half their games, they will win half their games, and they will emerge

half alive. If they lose all their games, and that fact does not kill them, they are already dead. Only the winner is alive.

Finally, I define winning as the science of being totally prepared. When you hold football coaching up to the X-ray, that's all it is: preparing a team to win. First, of course, the coach must himself be prepared—and that's a large order, requiring, among other things, a lifetime of thinking about it. And at the other end of the scale, on the final tactical level, the team must be prepared. My definition of preparation takes only three words—leave nothing undone—and that's what seventeen-hour workdays and 110 percent effort are all about. When your definition and your goal are both ''Leave Nothing Undone,'' it becomes obvious that no task is too big or too small; no detail is too big or too small. I think of what has to be done—not of whether it can be done. Football coaching, when reduced to what it is, consists of an unending series of problems. But this does not make it essentially different from any other worthwhile undertaking. A man without problems is dead. And in the last analysis, a problem is only a problem when you can't solve it. Every person has problems; the successful person solves his, the unsuccessful doesn't. A winner is a problem-licker; a loser is a man who is licked by his problems. And so when I talk about total preparation, I mean overcoming every problem. That is the Rams' goal—and also our delight.

One final point on the subject of preparation: life without victories is tasteless. It is possible for a loser to drive a big

car but it is not possible for him to enjoy it. The reason he can own one is that all pro football players make good salaries today, the winners and losers. I've heard that the average National Football League player draws a salary of $25,000 annually. The median is over $20,000—but I can't think of a thing this money will buy that a loser could enjoy. The best cars, the most expensive clothes and television sets, the loudest parties can only be enjoyed by men who have given their best. And they cannot give their best unless they are well prepared. It all gets back to that—and there are only two ways to judge it: did you win? or did you lose? When the ordinary athlete has the confidence that he has been completely prepared by his coaches, he becomes a good player; then the good player becomes a great player.

In conclusion, I can say that I have closely studied every coach I have known, head coach and assistant, and that I have found hardly any difference between the best of them and the worst of them. Yet some are winners and some are losers, both now and, probably, forevermore—and three things divide them all: total effort vs. not quite that much; total preparation vs. less than that; and an understanding that winning is living.

Coaching football is the greatest profession in the world and I wouldn't trade it for anything.

GEORGE ALLEN

Index